A Woman's Place

To my family, past and present,
who in so many ways have
contributed to this book.

A Woman's Place

An Oral History of Working-Class Women
1890—1940

ELIZABETH ROBERTS

Basil Blackwell

© Elizabeth Mauchline Roberts 1984

First published 1984
Basil Blackwell Publisher Limited
108 Cowley Road, Oxford OX4 1JF, England

Basil Blackwell Inc.
432 Park Avenue South, Suite 1505
New York, NY 10016, USA

British Library Cataloguing in Publication Data

Roberts, Elizabeth
    A woman's place.
    1. Women—Great Britain—History   2. Labor
    and laboring classes—Great Britain—History
    I. Title
    305.4'2'0941   HQ1597
    ISBN 0-631-13572-3

Typesetting by Pioneer, East Sussex
Printed in Great Britain by
Billings & Son Ltd, Worcester

Contents

2094)

vi

Appendices

Acknowledgements

Many people have helped to make this book possible: I owe the deepest debt of gratitude to Marion McClintock of the Centre for North-West Regional Studies at the University of Lancaster. Without her care, concern and practical help over a long period, including many discussions of the manuscript, this book would not have been written. Ivy Thexton and Sylvia Truesdale transcribed the tapes; and Helen Shaw and Judith Haxby typed the manuscript. Many colleagues offered advice and constructive criticisms, but I am particularly indebted to Michael Winstanley, John Benson and Stephen Humphries who read the manuscript and helped me to improve it. Above all my thanks are due to the respondents who provided such a wealth of information and unfailing kindness and hospitality.

I should also like to acknowledge the help of Ron Smith of the Barrow Library, Edith Tyson of Lancaster Museum, Terry Shaw of Preston Library, Winifred Clarke of the University of Lancaster Library and Audrey Linkman of Manchester Polytechnic for their help with the photographs. I am most grateful to the following people who have given permission to reproduce photographs held at Manchester Polytechnic: Mr and Mrs Derrick (photographs on pages 22, 63), Mrs Openshaw (p. 55), Mr Wayne Ashton (p. 60), Mr Francis Prendiville (p. 126), Mrs Pake (p. 130), Dr John Pickstone (p. 133), Mr R. Kirkby (p. 150).

I am particularly indebted to SSRC for their financial support between 1974—6 and 1978—81.

Introduction

This book looks at the lives of working-class women between 1890 and 1940. They were ordinary women in the sense that very few of them achieved even a small degree of public prominence, but they were truly remarkable in the extent of their real achievements.

Working-class women did not undervalue their contribution to society: as will be seen, they 'knew their place', were secure in it, and gained much satisfaction from their achievements. Women had a critical economic role to play in the management of the family budget: they fed, clothed, kept clean and housed their often large families; and they established and upheld both familial and neighbourhood mores. Despite the advances made in state education after the 1870 Education Act, the working-class mother continued to play a vital role in the education and socialisation of her children. She nursed her family and her neighbours, and operated, with others, a system of mutual support.

In the last decade several historians have come to realise our ignorance of the lives of ordinary women, and started to study them. Michelle Perrot in France writes about 'Le pouvoir des femmes [women's power]', while Joan Scott and Louise Tilly have written extensively about women's lives and achievements in their traditional sphere.[1] I hope this book will be a useful contribution to our understanding of women's roles in this country over the last century.

Although this is a book about women it is not an obviously feminist history, although I believe it to be a contribution to that literature. I began and indeed ended, my research as a feminist. Olive Banks said in *Faces of Feminism*: 'Any groups that have tried to change the position of women, or ideas about women, have been granted the title of feminist.'[2] This book may change some views on women by attempting to investigate empathetically the historical roots of some of the issues which affect women today, but that is not its prime aim.

As a feminist, in the face of the empirical evidence, I have been forced to conclude that it is not sufficient to indict the injustices of the past, nor allow one's concern for women's causes of today to obstruct the understanding of women's roles and status yesterday. Consequently, some feminists may be disturbed to find that the book does not seek to investigate patriarchy or male oppression of women. There were several reasons for not adopting that particular analysis of the evidence about the lives of women in the area of Lancashire I used as the basis for my research.[3] Ten years ago it was anticipated that there would be considerable evidence about women's oppression by men, and certainly there can be no argument about the legal, political and employment inequalities suffered by women in the public sphere. However, such a great proportion of women's lives was spent in the private sphere of home, family and neighbourhood that it was this area which became of particular interest. Much of the evidence was oral and, as the research progressed, it became evident that there was little feeling among the majority of women interviewed that they or their mothers had been particularly exploited by men, at least not by working-class men. (There was none the less a minority who *had* experienced terrible mistreatment; their evidence is examined in chapter 3. This evidence, taken alone, could well be used to construct a patriarchal interpretation of women's history, but it must be emphasised that they were a minority.) In their interviews many women indicated their awareness of the limited horizons and opportunities of their lives, but were just as likely to associate their menfolk with this lack of choice. They tended to blame the poverty which governed where they lived, the length and nature of their education, and very often the kind of jobs available to them. Those who went on to think about the roots of their poverty, and who perceived their lives in terms of exploitation, saw themselves, and their men, as being oppressed by employers, the rich, the middle classes and the bosses, who might be either male or female (but who were, of course, usually male). In other words, women who were conscious of their exploitation interpreted it in terms of class conflict. It is not without significance that when all the women in the sample studied, whether wives, mothers or daughters, are considered, only two are found to have been involved in the suffragette/suffragist movement, but eleven were active in the Labour Party (not including the two suffragettes who were also thus involved). (The nature of the sample is explained on p. 6.)

It is rare to encounter resentment among elderly working-class women towards the early feminist/suffrage movement; rather, they express indifference, with a feeling that this particular movement was not theirs and did not represent their particular needs or interests.[4] As Olive Banks wrote: 'Certainly working-class women have their own sources of discontent and by and large these have appeared to be less a result of their sex than of their class.'[5]

The patriarchal model tends to stress the negative aspects of women's lives, and thus, I believe, distorts the true picture at least in the area I studied. It would be a great pity if the power and achievements of women, such as they were, were overlooked because of the application of a rigid model.[6]

A fundamental task of social historians is to examine the processes of continuity and change. Those studying the twentieth century find it difficult not to become so involved with the obvious and fundamental changes which have occurred in almost all aspects of social life that the continuities are neglected. From the evidence obtained from interviews with nearly 160 elderly people, it is not difficult to trace changes in attitudes and standards and styles of living, but the listener is also left with a strong sense of continuity in working-class attitudes and behaviour.[7] It is obvious, too, that much of the evidence could apply to the periods both before and after 1890 and 1940; the first date was chosen because few people could speak of an earlier period, and the later date because it forms a watershed in many British lives.

The lives of working-class people (particularly men) in the earlier part of this century have been extensively written and spoken about, whether by historians, social observers and reformers, or sociologists, politicians, civil servants and clerics. It is rather less common to hear or read about how working-class people saw their own lives; they were and are less likely to keep diaries, write letters or enter items in account books than their more prosperous, educated and leisured contemporaries. In the absence of this personal documentary evidence, oral evidence is vital. Through old people's spoken testimony about their lives and those of their parents, one can attempt to reconstruct a picture of everyday life over the last century.[8]

One difficulty has proved to be finding a definition of 'working-class' which accords with the empirical evidence. Foremost among the attempts to define the concept of class are of course the works of Karl Marx and Max Weber,[9] who both believed that a person's class is determined by his or her economic standing. Marx saw the workers as the non-owners of capital who are forced to sell their labour to the capitalist in order to survive, while Weber wrote of 'property or the lack of property as the basic categories of all class situations'.[10] Certainly the mass of evidence and the perceptions of the respondents themselves would endorse the view that economic position is the basis of class. Men and women believed themselves to be working class because they worked with their hands, were employees and not employers, and, in comparison with the latter, were poor and lacked material goods: even the better-paid workers had comparatively few consumer goods and little surplus income.

Difficulties arise in reconciling the theoretical model with the empirical evidence when the Marxist view of the 'relativist' concept of class is considered. This view sees the vital element in class definition as the relationship between classes, a relationship of conflict which was the inevitable result of the exploitation of the working class by the capitalist. One of the functions of class conflict is seen to be clarification of the class structure, as working people become conscious of their own interests. It is only when individuals develop this consciousness that a true class in the full Marxist sense can be said to exist; that is, a 'class in itself' becomes a 'class for itself'.[11]

Some of the respondents (rather more men than women) had a strongly developed class consciousness and feelings of class antagonism; they usually belonged to an association whose aims were the furtherance of working-class interests. Others had little sense of class consciousness or class antagonism, although they were aware of differences in status. They could be deferential to their employers and, even if they were aware of being exploited, they displayed great reluctance to join any group in order to combat their oppressors. Furthermore, it is not unusual to find a class conscious respondent in the same family as one virtually indifferent to class conflict; in cases like this it would seem unhelpful to describe one as being working-class and the other as belonging to some other category.[12]

As a working definition, the most useful seems to be the one used by the respondents themselves, which relates their status to their manual occupations and limited economic standing. But another element must be added: the cultural ties and shared views which united working-class people.

All the respondents except one grew up in one (and sometimes more than one) denomination of the Christian Church, and the influence of the teachings of the Churches and of the Bible can be seen in many aspects of their attitudes and behaviour. Standish Meacham, in his otherwise admirable book on working-class life before the first world war, writes: 'But now, as religion lost whatever slim hold it may have had upon the urban working-class men and women awakened to the thought that redress if not vengeance might be theirs not the Lord's.'[13] But religion had not lost its hold on the urban working class in the north-west of England, and it is questionable whether it had in other areas. Robert Moore, whose work was mostly with Durham miners, writes that religion 'constituted part of a shared universe of meaning, evaluation and significances . . . they are the beliefs that are taken for granted, the statements that are presumed to be obvious. Religion is expressed in social relations, attitudes and ways of doing things, not in theological formulations.'[14] This is certainly the case, but it is important to understand that for many respondents religion also provided fundamental underpinning and comfort in what were often hard and troubled lives.

It is always difficult to equate belief and action — indeed, it is impossible to demonstrate that a specific action followed from a particular belief — but many working-class attitudes seem to have come directly from the Church's teaching. Respondents, like the Durham mining families described by Moore, were not so much interested in doctrine as in establishing an ethical pattern to their everyday lives. Women in particular were concerned with 'loving thy neighbour'; a 'good' or 'Christian' person being seen as one who cared to the best of her ability for her family and neighbours. It should be remembered that the working class were not only the recipients of charity; they were very frequently the donors.

Most respondents accepted (and indeed acted on) both the New Testament ethic of loving your neighbour and the Old Testament concept of justice, with its accompanying emphasis on the appropriateness of the punishment of sin. The inconsistency did not seem to strike them as a problem — at least none of them commented upon it.

Another universally-held belief was the work ethic. In somewhat simplistic terms, work was believed to lead to salvation, and idleness to damnation. Historians writing of the late eighteenth and early nineteenth centuries have seen Methodism as providing motivation for the new work discipline needed by manufacturers at the beginning of industrialisation. E. P. Thompson, for example, sees Methodism as contributing to the rationalisation of work through self-discipline, whereby 'the labourer must be turned into his own slave-driver.'[15] Examples of this are numerous, but by the end of the nineteenth century such men and women could be found in all the various Christian denominations. Indeed, while the theology and practices of the Churches differed, it has proved very difficult to equate particular attitudes and actions with membership of any named Church, for in practice these proved to be surprisingly similar. Of course, the importance of helping neighbours, the emphasis on justice, and the value of work were found in all classes, especially at the turn of the twentieth century. But these ideals in turn interacted with the economic determinants at the lower social levels, and together produced a distinct working-class life-style.

Working-class views were not, of course, identical; the class was not a monolithic mass. The origins of the all-powerful, universal social norm of respectability are much debated but little agreed upon. It would seem to have several roots: from the Bible, and especially the Ten Commandments, came the rejection of stealing, swearing and adultery; from the Pauline tradition came the suppression of sexuality; the by now well-established industrial discipline contributed the virtues of punctuality, obedience and rigid self-discipline; from the Methodist tradition came the maxim that 'Cleanliness is next to godliness.'

A minority of the respondents who had 'rough' backgrounds, came from families who had rejected almost all the mores of the respectable. They were relatively uncontrolled in their sexual behaviour; they drank, stole, were dirty, and fought each other and outsiders. But they, too, were still part of the working class, not only because of their economic standing but also because they shared some other fundamental beliefs — loving one's neighbour, justice, and the work ethic. And despite their everyday behaviour they were usually connected to a church. Some attended services, often in a Mission, and sent their children to Sunday school and church social activities, which were popular.[16]

There was another division within the working class, between the skilled and the unskilled, the former enjoying greater prosperity and more status. Nevertheless, they were all manual workers, being paid weekly (or in a few cases daily) and sharing the attitudes of the rest of the 'respectable' working class. (Interestingly, it is possible to detect even some skilled men and their families who would be described as 'rough'.)

The respondents who are most difficult to assign to a class or division of the working class are the shopkeepers. At one end of the spectrum were the very poor, selling a few items from their back kitchen to eke out a low income, living at subsistence level, and employing no one. They can be described as working class. At the other end are the prosperous shopkeepers, enjoying a substantial income and employing others. They were undoubtedly not working class. In between there are several gradations of status. What is clear is that becoming a shopkeeper was one way for a family to leave the working class and enter the middle class.[17]

The geographical area which was researched for this book is in central and north Lancashire, particularly the towns of Barrow, Lancaster and Preston. About 160 people, both men and women, were interviewed (biographical details of the respondents quoted in this book are given in appendix 5) in these towns, and I am confident that they are a representative sample of the working class in all three areas. They come from a wide variety of family sizes and occupations, and represent a good spread of wage levels and religious and political beliefs.[18] While it would obviously be unwise to draw conclusions from a regional study about the lives of women in other areas of Britain, I believe that because the three towns were substantially different, both economically and socially, the analysis of them could well have a wider significance. But I would not deny or underestimate the importance of local and regional differences, which show up particularly in such matters as diet.

The three towns represent a wide cross-section of English urban life in the last decade of the nineteenth century and the first decades of the twentieth. Barrow was predominantly a town of heavy industries: in 1911, 37.5 per cent of its workforce was employed by the firm of Vickers, either in the construction of ships or in heavy engineering, while another 7 per cent were iron- and steel-workers.[19] Only in Barrow was there a significant body of skilled craftsmen, although it is impossible from the Census returns to deduce exactly what percentage of the labour force they represented. Preston was a cotton town: in 1911, 45 per cent of its working population were textile workers, and although the next largest group were engaged in engineering and machine-making, these formed only 5 per cent of the workforce.[20] In the inter-war years Preston's economy benefited from a developing engineering industry, but it remained predominantly a cotton town with its associated docks, and also provided a wide range of services, for example, a general market and a cattle market. The textile industry was, however, like those of shipbuilding and heavy engineering, in decline during the inter-war period, and Barrow and Preston suffered many of the consequences of the economic depression.

Lancaster, like Barrow and Preston, had one major industry, manufacturing oil-cloth and linoleum (with associated cotton mills which provided the backing for the oil-cloth): in 1911, 30 per cent of the workforce was thus employed.[21] Lancaster attracted some new industries in the inter-war period, notably the manufacture of 'artificial' textiles, and, as the linoleum trade did not suffer a decline comparable to that of the basic industries of Barrow and Preston, Lancaster was one of the Lancashire towns least affected by the Depression. The rest of Lancaster's working population was in some form of service industry, either in retailing, as Lancaster continued its centuries-old tradition of being an important market town, or within an institution, for it had (and has) a large mental hospital, a sub-normality hospital and a prison, as well as its own local hospitals.

The towns were different not only in their commercial and industrial activities but in their physical appearance and layout. Barrow was a creation of the second half of the nineteenth century, its buildings a mixture of brick, brick rough-cast, and some occasional locally quarried sandstone. It was one of the first English industrial towns to be built to a plan, and had handsome, wide, tree-lined main streets, and rather tedious, uniform and drab secondary streets, laid down in a grid pattern. Barrow also had many distinctive blocks of sandstone tenements, built by the Furness Railway Company in the 1880s for the immigrant Scottish workers who crowded into the town. They continue to be strongly reminiscent of old Glasgow. Overall, the visitor is conscious of expanses of water, miles of beaches and a great acreage of docks. Overshadowing the central area was — and is — the huge industrial complex of Vickers, the heavy engineering and shipbuilding firm. Lancaster was very different: dominated by its medieval castle and Priory church, it was an old, established county town. At the beginning of the period its buildings were constructed almost entirely from locally quarried stone. Its central street pattern, which had evolved over many centuries, was intricate and complex, the streets themselves narrow and winding. Preston too, was originally an old town, but by 1890 little of its earlier appearance remained. The skyline had lost its windmills and was dominated by tall mill chimneys, as well as by church towers and spires; and the second half of the nineteenth century saw an enormous expansion of working-class housing, built almost exclusively in straight, red-brick rows, often with a backway separating two rows.

Those who were interviewed in the three towns grew up in a surprising range of types of dwelling. The great majority lived in terraced houses, but these varied considerably in size, number of rooms and amenities. (They are described more fully in chapter 4.)

Workers (both male and female) tried to live as close as possible to their place of work, as it was usual for working people to go home for their dinners in the middle of the day. This was rather easier in Preston and Barrow than in Lancaster where the main linoleum works was isolated across the marshes. Families also tried to live near relatives and this led, especially in Preston, to the tradition of certain small streets being almost entirely occupied by members of one extended family. After the first world war Lancaster and Preston developed new estates of council houses and all three towns acquired estates of cheap semi-detached houses. (Barrow, because of the severe depression in the town in the 1920s, built very few council houses.) A minority of the group we are looking at moved into this new housing, but the majority continued to occupy the older, terraced property (as some continue to do to the present day).

The daily lives of the women who lived in these houses was repetitious and very hard; those who worked at home tended to have a set routine for the housework which was done on a weekly rota, the hours carefully divided up between washing, ironing, cleaning, shopping and cooking, with the needs of the children fitted in around the housework. People rose early because factories, shipyards and mills, before the first world war, began work at 6.00 a.m., and consequently bed-time was early too. The round of work, however, was not entirely unrelieved: women at home found time to visit neighbours and relatives or to chat in the street. Many went to church on Sundays or to church-organised social events during the week. Even women burdened with a full-time job and a home to run usually had a little leisure time on a Saturday evening and Sunday, but, as Prestonians frequently said of mill women, for many, 'It was all bed and work, work and bed.'

The women whose lives are described in this book are almost entirely unknown outside their own family and social circle, as were their mothers before them; only a tiny minority had any connection with public life. Often, at the beginning of a series of interviews, they expressed surprise that anyone should be interested in their 'uneventful' lives. Many, however, are beginning to recognise the wider significance of these 'ordinary' lives: their achievements were formidable, as were their sufferings, in many cases. This way of life has all but disappeared today but it is hoped that this book will be a small memorial to the women who embodied it.

1

Growing Up

Working-class women did not spring into adult life ready-armed for the battle for survival. Rather, like children of all times and places, they were subjected to a variety of socialising influences which profoundly affected their role as adult women. Transmitted to them was a working-class culture, a complete design for living, and a set of rules to be learned about 'proper' behaviour.

Philippe Ariès, in his seminal book on childhood,[1] challenged the idea that childhood and youth have remained the same throughout history, and suggested that the meanings of the various stages of the life-cycle have varied over time and in different social groups. It is clear from a mass of oral evidence that even within a relatively short historical period the meaning of childhood has changed dramatically; the portrait of childhood which emerges from the late nineteenth and early twentieth centuries is in many ways in stark contrast to that which can be drawn for the late twentieth century.

Much can be said about the length of childhood. This chapter examines the lives of girls before they began their first full-time job, but childhood did not end, nor adult life begin, on that particular day. There were no recognised *rites de passage* between childhood and adulthood; many children assumed adult responsibilities at a very young age; conversely, young workers were still dominated by their parents in many aspects of their lives until, and even beyond, their own marriages — as a Preston woman remarked: 'I was fifty-six before I answered my mother back!'[2]

Ariès placed his study of childhood within a wider study of the family, a practice which has been followed by more recent historians.[3] The reason for this is clear: the family plays such a critical role in the socialisation of children. The oral evidence confirms this: throughout the period 1890—1940 the working-class family, more than any external agency, continued to play the dominant role in the development of children.

In this chapter the role of the nuclear family in particular is examined, but the working-class child usually belonged to an extended family as well. The role of this kinship group, and in particular the position of women within it, is examined in chapter 5. The educative role of the family in transmitting the mores of a social class has not been examined widely by British historians,[4] who, looking at the more recent period, have tended to concentrate on the education received by children at school after the passing of the 1870 Education Act. Undoubtedly schools had a very important role to play in the lives of working-class children, but it can be argued that the supremely important influence remained that of the family.

Helen Bosanquet, almost a lone voice at the turn of the century, in the middle of the public discussion about the provision and content of state education, stressed the unique and important educative role of the family: 'Apart from the fact that no one has ever devised an adequate substitute for a parent, the further fact remains that the family with its mingled diversity and identity of interests is the best, if not indeed, the only school for life of the citizen.'[5]

HOME LIFE

Working-class children learned the habit of obedience from a very early age. Their own wills and desires had to be subordinated to those of their parents; they were expected to do as they were told, and the overwhelming evidence from both before and after the first world war is that they did exactly that. The children were obviously not angels though, and they certainly broke their parents' rules, especially when the parents were absent. Childish 'crimes' and rule-breaking were most likely to take place in the street or back-yard away from mother's watchful eye. Much more unusual was outright, face-to-face defiance of mother or father. Some of the lapses will be described later, but working-class children appear to have followed both the implicit and explicit moral, social, and ethical guidance which they received from their parents. Such rejection as there was came in the next stage of life, when, as young adults, a minority questioned both their parents' rules and their fathers' behaviour. Virtually none criticised their mothers, and only a handful criticised the basic mores of working-class life. They were brought up by, and developed into, a conforming and conformist generation.

There appears to have been no difference between the skilled and unskilled in their attitude to the importance of obedience, although some historians and contemporary observers believed that there was.[6] Little of the philosophy of writers and poets, like Rousseau and Wordsworth, had penetrated working-class attitudes to children, even as late as the 1930s. Babies and small children were not seen as innocent beings with an undeveloped sense of morality. On the contrary, they were expected to know at a very young age the difference between right and wrong. Mrs Hudson, for example, who became a mother in the 1930s, was clear in her expectations, even if confused about whether children are naturally moral or whether they are taught to be so by their mothers.

You would get your bottom smacked when you were a little tot and that was it. I believe now, as old as I am, that our old doctor once said, somebody was on to him about the very same thing, chastising children, one woman said she saw a woman smack a baby's hands and it was only in the pram, and he said, 'That baby knew it was doing wrong. A child knows from the day it's born the difference between right and wrong and it is you that has to teach it. You can soon do it without cruelty.' I really believe that.[7]

This is perhaps a slightly extreme view, but in all families quite small children were expected either to have a clear idea of morality, or to behave on command in a moral way, without necessarily understanding the reason for their actions. It is extremely rare to hear childish misdemeanours dismissed with 'He was too young to understand', 'She didn't know it was wrong'; or 'You can't expect a baby to act differently.' And there were differences in the ways girls and boys were expected to behave. These will be examined later, but it has proved impossible to find boys being consistently treated more severely than girls, or vice versa.

How much of the obedience observed in working-class children was a result of fear of physical retribution? In *The Edwardians*, Paul Thompson argued that parents did not rely on extensive corporal punishment, as their authority was so rarely challenged.[8] Certainly there can be little doubt that this was true in some families. The range of sanctions used was, however, very varied. In some families, like Mrs Warburton's, a word was enough:

I don't think ever any of us got hit or anything like that. He just used to speak to us and that was all. I know one day, I don't know what I'd done, I was only young and m'father said, 'You're a daft lump,' and I cried my eyes out. Oh I couldn't forget that. Mother said, 'Shut up for goodness sake.' I said, 'Well do you know what he called me?' She said, 'Well that was nothing.'[9]

More usual was the occasional reinforcement of an order with a cuff, if the order was not immediately obeyed. Mrs Harrison grew up in Preston in the 1920s, a generation later than Mrs Warburton, but instant obedience was still expected:

Mother would just give us one over the ear occasionally, but it was only occasionally, she would have to be really annoyed with us, you know. Again, I probably asked for it, and I didn't do it purposely, but with always reading I never heard. She would have to tell me three or four times to do something, and I would be in this book, and then I would get a clip over the ear. But you respected them for it. My father had only to say when he was annoyed, if he was in and mother was asking us to do something, me particularly with being the youngest, and when I heard him say, 'Is your mother speaking to you?', I heard that and I would put my book away and jump up and dash round then.[10]

A third group of children were regularly hit for disobedience, by hand, cane or leather strap. Mrs Peters was one of these:

We'd a strap . . . I've got it many times on m'legs for giving cheek and answering back when I shouldn't have done. Mother didn't do it, but Father did. I would say, 'Oh well,' in such a tone and he would say, 'Now that's enough of that, and you say that again lady and you know what you'll get.' I'd say it again. 'Get up them stairs,' and you'd get it on your legs as you were going up. I used to have swellings across many a time.[11]

What were the rules, standards and customs to which working-class children had to conform? For which 'crimes' were they punished? In no family was a child allowed to be cheeky; 'answering back' with its clear implication of defiance of the parental will was instantly punished: 'I once answered my mother back and she boxed my ears for it. I didn't do it again.'[12] In many families children were not even allowed to enter spontaneously into adult conversations; again parents appear to have judged such interventions as signs of too much independence. Mealtimes were strictly controlled. Not only were table manners regulated, but conversation:

You weren't allowed to chatter. If you were spoken to directly you spoke back, but we didn't do chattering.[13]

You spoke when you were spoken to. . . . I remember we had relatives in and they were talking about something and I spoke up. I'll never forget it. Dad turned right quickly on me, 'Children should be seen and not heard.' I can see him to this day pointing at me. I know I went crimson. I thought, I'll watch my step another time. They were kind and good, but firm. You'd to toe the line.[14]

Children were allowed to play outside freely during the day, and there seem to have been few parents who restricted children from going for walks quite considerable distances from the home; but all had very strict rules about coming in at night. The time depended on the age of the child and the strictness of the family, but as young workers were usually expected in by nine o'clock, so younger children were to be at home any time after about 5.30, but usually between 7 and 8 p.m. There appears to have been considerable fear that the children would develop bad habits, like vandalism and theft (with consequent trouble from the police), after dark.

Children had to learn to be trusted with their parents' money and goods. Total honesty and accountability were expected, reflecting not only the tight and careful budgeting most working-class women had to operate, but also the respect for other people's property shown by all classes in this period. The only exceptions to this rule were members of the roughest and poorest sections of the working class, whose dire poverty forced them into theft. Examples have been found of this in the local area, and the significance of such actions are examined in depth by Stephen Humphries in 'Steal to Survive' and *Hooligans or Rebels?*[15] It was almost always boys who committed these 'crimes', the reasons including the traditions of boys and men being 'providers' for their families, of boys joining street gangs and being expected to be out of doors while girls were at home doing domestic chores. But stealing by children was not common, more usual were minor mis-appropriations of parental goods. These were punishable offences:

Mother was once baking, I was only a baby, and she gave my sister twopence to go to this old lady that grew rhubarb in the yard and would sell it at a penny a bunch. She came back with a sugar pig and a pair of celluloid glasses. . . . You can imagine . . . Mother had the pastry ready. My sister was quite a rum one for doing things. She came in with the glasses on and the sugar pig. The glasses were thrown on the fire and she, Mother, put the sugar pig in a tin. She would have a wonderful time spending twopence. She got a good hiding and was sent to bed. I don't know whatever Mother did with the pastry.[16]

Social historians studying the working class in the recent past, are almost overwhelmed at times by the total devotion and dedication shown towards the concept of respectability. It can be seen in the lives of almost all members of the working class, even in those who in the eyes of others were 'rough'. To be 'respectable' was in its original sense, to be respected, and in closely-knit communities, it was very difficult to live comfortably without the respect of one's family and neighbours. There was widespread agreement on what was *not* respectable. Swearing was not acceptable in the home (although it was tacitly understood that what men said at work in an all-male environment might be different):

Nobody swore in our house. The only word ever used in our house, and that was only when m'father was mad, 'You're flaming . . .'. I used to be at the other side of the table and I'd say 'Don't use that word.' He used to say, 'If I come across there I'll give you a smack across the face.' . . . I'd four brothers and even when they were arguing about football they never even said damn . . . I did hear our Frank swear one day, and I said 'Frank.' He just looked at me and said, 'It's working with men.'[17]

Children also learned from very early on the importance of looking clean and tidy. Hands and face had to be washed, and clothes, especially shoes and clogs, kept clean. In many families cleanliness was indeed considered next to godliness, as the juxtaposition of this quotation illustrates:

Would she say prayers with you at bedtime?
Oh yes. Now, it is the gospel truth, I never miss my morning and night prayers. I always say, 'Lord have mercy on everybody.' I say this every night of my life.
So you were all brought up to say your prayers?
We daren't miss them. My granny would say to us 'Before you come in this kitchen, get these hands washed. You don't touch a thing till them hands are washed.'[18]

Discussion or even mention of sexual matters by or to children was not only lacking in respectability; it was verging on the immoral. Decades of Victorian attitudes had produced, by the turn of the twentieth century, a generation of working-class parents who were extremely prudish. Even when they were very small, brothers and sisters were not allowed to see any part of each other's naked bodies:

I always remember m'mother used to sew for us and make us dresses and she was trying me a dress on this night and our Jim came in . . . She said, 'Stay in the passage,' and I had this dress on, and only m'arms were bare. We never saw the others undress at all.[19]

In a family with ten children, parents and grandmother in a three-bedroomed house, this would represent a considerable organisational effort on the part of the mother — bathing and washing were regimented affairs, strictly timetabled and totally segregated. This was true in all households.

Being a boy I was always separated for baths and sleeping. Louise again played mother with my sisters and saw to it that they had a good bath which was taken in front of the kitchen fire. After the bath their hair was daubed in sassafras which I believe smells, kills hair lice, or keeps them away. During this period I was sat in a corner of the room behind a clothes horse. Often you would hear the cry, 'He's peeping.' I was kept to the last. Mum got in about my turn and because girls could not bath boys, she saw to me. I think it was after my bath and just before bed that I used to get a cuddle on Mum's knee. Bathing was only a weekly affair. It was quite a job to get hot water.[20]

It is possible that parents with large numbers of adolescent children were terrified at the prospect of incest. This was certainly Robert Roberts' view: 'Here stood a hazard that faced all poor parents of large adolescent families, sleeping together perhaps with older relatives in two small bedrooms.'[21] It is extremely difficult to know how far, if at all, respondents' families worried about incest, as opposed to their obvious concern to maintain their children's modesty. Only one respondent hinted at incest, and then very obliquely. It remains a taboo subject, about which it is impossible to ask and about which no information is volunteered.

When the sleeping arrangements of families are described, it is truly surprising that the children remained so naive about sex. For example, one family of ten children had to share one bedroom, with a boys' and a girls' bed. (The parents slept in the other bedroom.) Yet despite the enforced propinquity, mothers' pregnancies went unnoticed by the children, and unmentioned by the parents:

We never knew anything about babies in those days. Mother would disappear for the day and one or two came in from outside . . . We didn't know much about it, we were sort of ignorant.[22]

Ignorance among the young about reproduction persisted throughout the period. Mrs Calvert, who was born in 1919, said:

When I got to about sixteen I used to think, babies, where do they come from? I used to think that my mother must have been cut on her stomach six times because she had six children. I thought she must have six scars on her stomach. I can't even remember seeing any women pregnant in them days. We never looked for anything like that.
    There must have been, but you didn't notice?
    That's it, we never looked for anything like that.[23]

Even innocent remarks about pregnancy were strongly disapproved of:

In fact I think I got a shock the next day when I got up and we'd got another sister. I seem to remember getting a shock.
    Did you not notice she was getting fatter?
    This is what I'm going to say. When she got up I remember saying to her, 'Oh mother you must have been poorly.' She looked at me. I said, 'Well you've gone so thin.' Well I didn't know it was the baby, I honestly didn't know. She said, 'You know far too much. Get yourself out.'[24]

The virtually total ban on the discussion of sexual matters applied to both boys and girls; both grew up equally uninformed. The absence of discussion, and the lack of shared confidences, are evident throughout the parent/child relationship.

It was, of course, impossible to ignore the subject of menstruation completely, but some mothers did manage to confine discussing it with daughters to one occasion. When their eldest daughter began her periods, she would be told the basic facts, and after that it was up to her to tell her younger sisters. By making it another taboo subject, mothers undoubtedly gave their daughters a feeling of repugnance about this natural function, as something which was shameful and to be hidden. This developed into a sense of somehow being unclean, and a belief that they were at risk in some unspecified way whenever they were 'unwell'. Mrs Stott grew up before the first world war:

I always remember when I started she said, 'Never let your brothers see this whatever you do.' She drummed it into me . . . and in those days things were a bit different to what they are today. You couldn't buy things to wash away down the toilet, they had to be washed, and she used to drum it into me, me being the only girl. No, she was most strict over anything like that. Strict over everything. She was a good mother.

Did she ever tell you about babies or just expect you to find out?

We were never told anything like that. I always remember I'd two friends and we used to go to church together and we were quite old, getting quite old, and we went to Sunday School this particular day, and when we came out of Sunday School we got on to the topic of babies, where did they come from? We knew that they came from the mother, we knew that, but we didn't know how. And I always remember, and I laugh many a time, she said, 'Well you know you've a mark down your tummy, well that's like a zip and it opens.' I've thought about that often. I thought how silly really when you think of it, innocence. We didn't know. We didn't know.[25]

Did she tell you certain things you mustn't do?

She used to say not to wash my hair and not have a bath until you have finished.[26]

Like the last respondent, Mrs Calvert grew up after the first world war (she began to menstruate in 1934). It is clear, however, that the old attitudes and taboos were as strong as they had been fifty years earlier:

Did she ever tell you the facts of life?

I found out myself. The only time I remember my mother telling me anything was when I first started my periods. I come in and when I had been to the toilet I thought, oh, what have I done? I never thought anything and I were turned fifteen. I told her that I had all colour on m'pants. All she said was, 'In my bottom drawer you will find some cloths. Put them up against you and keep warm and keep away from lads.' That's all my mother ever told me about anything.[27]

Curiously, it would seem that some of the medical profession connived with parents to reinforce negative attitudes to menstruation:[28] a Barrow woman was excused school permanently in 1901 on medical grounds because she had started menstruation when she was 12.[29] A similar story comes from Preston as late as 1921:

I was thirteen. It was a mixed class and my mother took me to Dr Rose, she was a woman doctor and I had started with my periods and she got me exempt from school before I should have been. I should have left when I was fourteen, and I wasn't so far off. She exempt me as she said it wasn't safe for me to sit with the lads and that.

The doctor said that?

Yes, and she got me exempt.[30]

The lack of understanding about personal hygiene is striking. Menstruating girls were forbidden to have baths or wash their hair. No respondent remembers using disposable sanitary towels until after the second world war, a reminder that the introduction of a new domestic product did not imply its immediate and widespread use among the working class. Sanitary towels had been patented in 1892, and a boost to their production came after the first world war when factories making bandages for the war wounded turned to the production of disposable sanitary towels instead. But they were still not used by working-class women, who at best used (and reused) pieces of old towel or sheeting which, when dirty, were left soaking in buckets of cold water well away from the enquiring eyes of men or young children (some achievement in cramped houses). Some did not even have this protection: 'The point was that when you started to menstruate you were just given a pair of navy blue knickers so that it didn't show through':[31] these were changed once a week. One elderly lady (not a respondent) remembered being told by her mother that as a young mill girl she wore no protection at all when menstruating, she simply hoped that her several layers of petticoats and skirts would both absorb the flow, and hide it from the outside world. This lack of hygiene contrasts forcibly with the great emphasis placed on cleanliness of those parts of the body seen by the outside world, notably the hands, neck and face. One can only speculate about the effects of the constant discomfort, chafing and smell experienced by menstruating women on their self-esteem. The fear of embarrassment should anyone discover their situation or find the soaking cloths must have been a constant worry. Their unquestioning acceptance of all this and their failure to attempt to ameliorate it, are both evidence of their strong sense of fatalism, and an indication of how it was fostered.

Some women resented the ignorance in which they had been brought up; others, as in so many other areas, were ambivalent:

She didn't tell you where babies came from or anything?

No. My mother wasn't a vulgar person. Still, I think it is what every girl ought to know.[32]

But the women respondents said they were very close to their mothers, and somehow the scant shared knowledge about female 'secrets' cemented this bond, which almost always proved to be of lifelong duration.

The greater part of the teaching received from parents by working-class children was of the generally negative or admonitory nature outlined here. However, in the matter of relationships with those deserving respect and help, teaching was rather more positive, and much of it was done by example. Virtually all children witnessed their mothers and neighbours helping one another in times of need, and children were usually encouraged to do the same and, what was more, not to expect any reward — although many did: 'My mother would say, "If anybody asks you to go on an errand *run*, but don't take anything for doing it."'[33] Errands were run, babies minded, and sometimes more unusual small tasks were undertaken. One little girl went every day to thread the needles of an elderly neighbour who enjoyed sewing, but whose eyesight was failing.[34] Some children felt pressured by neighbours into helping, while others only helped because of a reward (whatever their parents might have said), but they were all absorbing the strong working-class feeling of duty towards one's neighbours.

Respect was due not only to the sick, the old and the feeble, but also to the dying and the dead. While sex was unmentionable, death was not, and children learned early from their parents and neighbours about its inevitability, frequency and indeed naturalness. Between a fifth and a quarter of all respondents experienced the death of a sibling when they were children. (There were many more children who died in many of the families but whose deaths occurred before the birth of the respondent.) The same proportion experienced, before they were fifteen, the death of one or both parents. In the great majority of these cases the deaths took place at home, and the children had inevitably both to witness and to experience grief. It was unusual for children not to have seen a dead body or attended a funeral before their fourteenth birthday. They would go to neighbours and ask to see the corpses of their friends, a request rarely if ever denied: 'When we were kids we used to go and knock at the door and ask if we could go and see the bodies. They used to take us upstairs with a candle and we never used to bother.'[35] Much more traumatic was the sight of a dead sibling. Mrs Peters is describing the death and funeral of her little sister, who had died in hospital of peritonitis:

They brought her back home, and she was in the front room, the coffin was on chairs. A dreadful time. I was scared stiff. The neighbours came and the children from school as well. You didn't seem to want to deprive them of it. I only had one look and I thought well it's not my sister. She must have been in pain, torn at her little face. They'd put cotton wool in her nostrils and granny said, 'You must go in.' Fancy making you do things like that in those days, and she said, 'Now just touch her.' I remember putting my hand on her forehead and it was stone cold. I

*Funerals were important street events. This one was unusual; it was the funeral
in Preston of Private Young VC in August 1916. But despite its special
character there are many reminders of more ordinary funerals: the pulled blinds,
the neighbours' interest and the splendid hearse, carriages and horses.*

(Harris Library, Preston)

remember shuddering. I didn't ever go in again. They collected at school and we
were all dressed up in black little dresses.[36]

The custom of viewing and touching the body gradually became less common
over the period, so that it is perhaps significant that it was the grandmother
who insisted on the little girl touching the corpse, but it would be wrong to
think that the practice had entirely disappeared by 1940.

The lack of emotion some respondents displayed in recalling these events
is partly attributable to the dulling of grief through the passing of time, and
possibly also to the memory itself suppressing distressing thoughts.[37] But
perhaps it also indicates the degree to which those growing up in this period
accepted and adjusted to the frequency of death. Again, in the acceptance of
death can be found both the seeds and the nurturing of the fatalism which
was so widely felt by both working-class women and men.

The following extract is unusual in that no other respondent was asked as
a child to dispose of a dead body, but it is entirely representative of a wide
range of working-class mores: the expectation that children would assume
adult responsibilities; Rose's total ignorance about her mother's pregnancy;

but her complete understanding of what was necessary to bury the baby respectfully, with dignity, and yet with total economy (the incident took place about 1904):

Now when the baby was born we could hear . . . we used to know how fat mam was getting but we didn't know anything. Then I heard noise one night and I got up and I thought m'mamma must be bad and I went in the room and said, 'Is m'mamma bad?' Dad said, 'No, go and get yourself back into bed m'lass she'll be all right till morning.' When I got up in the morning and I went in she'd had this little baby and it was still-born. She said, 'You're not going to school today, Rose.' I said, 'Aren't I?' She said, 'No, you'll have to stay at home, I want you to do something for me.' I said, 'What's been the matter with you mamma?' She said, 'Well I've got a baby.' I said, 'Where is it?' She said, 'It's just there,' and it was on a washstand, on a pillow with a cover over it. When I looked at it it was like a little doll, very small. She said, 'I want you to go to a shop and ask for a soap box.' I said, 'A soap box mam?' She said, 'Yes.' I said, 'What's it for?' She said, 'To put that baby in.'

I brought this soap box back and I called on the road to my friend, a young girl I went with, so I told her and she went with me. She said, 'I'll come down to your house with you.' She came and we had a look at this little doll, and my friend said, 'Let's line this little box with wadding.' We lined this box with this bit of wadding and then m'mamma put this wee baby in it and the lid fastened down like the boxes do today, no nails. She said, 'There's a letter here.' . . . They didn't call them midwives then, just ladies and it used to be half a crown or five shillings to come and deliver a baby. She gave me a letter, 'Now you've got to go up to the cemetery and give this letter to the gravedigger, any gravedigger you see in.' I said, 'I can't take it wrapped up in paper,' so I went in the back and saw an old coat of m'dad's. I ripped the black lining out of this coat and we wrapped this little box in this lining and put some string round it, put it under our arms and off we went to the gravedigger. I give him this letter and he read it. He said, 'Oh yes, just take it over in the church porch love. You'll see a few parcels in that corner, just leave it there.' Me being inquisitive said, 'What are you going to do with it?' He said, 'Well we have public graves, everybody don't buy graves, they haven't the money, when the public graves get nearly full up we put one in each grave.' 'Oh that's what you do,' I said. He said, 'Yes. Tell your mammy it'll be all right,' and we turned back home.

Did it upset you at the time?

Yes, because we thought it was like a little doll. It wasn't really developed, just small.

How old would you be then?

I'd be about twelve.[38]

Working-class children did not learn only about obedience and respectable behaviour, but equally importantly they learned from a very early age that they were members of the working class and grew up with that indelible self-image. Fathers (and sometimes mothers) were absent for long hours in mills, shipyards, factories and steelworks; mothers at home rarely ceased their endless round of domestic toil. Children soon realised that just as their family belonged to the working class, so too they as individuals belonged to a working social unit, and that there was no division between the world of childhood and the adult world of work. It was, for obvious reasons, the world of domestic work which first impinged on children.

Children waiting outside a mission hall for their Sunday School outing. These outings were often the highlight of a poor child's year, as they might not have a holiday. (Manchester Studies, Manchester Polytechnic)

In some families there was little clear differentiation in the tasks done by boys and girls; for example, in families where there were no girls, the boys had to help with the full range of domestic jobs. But while boys were not necessarily exempt, in many families it is clear that girls did more domestic work than boys, and that they were much more likely to be responsible for tasks such as child-care, cooking and sewing which did undoubtedly both train and condition them for their adult roles. No respondent has ever mentioned being told as a child that 'a woman's place is in the home'; indeed, those with working mothers could see clearly that many women had lives outside the home, but the implicit lesson learned by all girls was that, fundamentally, whatever else a woman might do in her life, the ultimate

responsibility for the daily care of the home and the family lay with her, and
not with the male members of the household. While girls acted as apprentices
to their mothers, or even as their substitutes, boys were more likely to be out
of the house, doing the shopping, helping with the allotment, or accompanying
the male members of the family on an expedition, like walks, fishing trips or
food-gathering forays. Many girls simply assumed their role. It was not
discussed with their parents, and they certainly did not feel any pressure.
(Stoning was a process by which scrubbed, wet steps and flagstones were
rubbed with coloured stones rather like chalk. These special donkey-stones
were used extensively in Lancashire.)

You weren't expected, you just did it. Nobody told you to do these things. That
kitchen, that stone sink, on a Sunday you would have a big wash-up and then
afterwards Gwennie and Mabel used to stone all this sink and make it beautiful.
Then Mary and I would come along, the two younger ones, and we used to play
at public houses with the cold water and some jugs. We would make such a mess
of this sink after they had got it so nice.
Fancy stoning the sink, as they must have known it would wash off.
Yes, but it still had to be stoned.
And that was done on a Sunday, was it?
Yes, and during the week, but it was always done on a Sunday because we
always mucked it up.
What other jobs did you do besides stoning and black-leading?
The yard used to be stoned all over. I used to like stoning.[39]

Here is the commonly observed, unthinking devotion to outward, and
ephemeral, appearances, and superficial (if not basic) cleanliness. (The mother
in this family did no housework at all, which was very unusual, but not quite
unique.)
Other girls did the work expected of them but felt burdened, especially
with child-minding:

There were seven under me, Oh minding babies, I didn't only do it for my
mother, but I did it for my auntie as well.[40]

My sisters always had to look after me because I was the baby. My sisters used to
spoil me, and I remember more of my two sisters than my two brothers. The girls
were expected to look after the family and be a mother to the family and got no
peace at all.[41]

The extent of the responsibility some children were given is remarkable.[42]
Mrs Phillips in the following example was by no means a unique case. Her
mother ran a shop and loathed housework:

When the last one was born — bless him, he's dead now — I brought him up. I was eight and my father put this baby in my arms. I didn't know mother was pregnant like they do today. He said, 'It's a Belgian baby,' that was the common tale, the war was on. I went in the shop and I got a baby's bottle out and a top and I looked round the shelves and I saw Nestlé's Milk, Fit For Babies, and I mixed this milk and I fed this baby on this milk and I looked after that baby till he died. He died of cancer at fifty-three.

But you actually brought him up? Did your mother ever give you any help, did she say what you should be doing with him or did she just let you get on with it?

Oh no, she was interested, she adored her boy. She used to say, 'I don't know what I'd do without our Ann but I like my lads.' I was the mug, but I was so necessary, they couldn't do without me. I took it for granted and even now I spoil my boy, it is just a habit.

(Her 'boy' is now in his forties.) Mrs Phillips hardly seems to have had any childhood of her own:

I remember when the hooters went and that was 1918 when the war was over. I was washing new shirts that all the boys had got. They were thick twill with a blue line and everybody wore them. I couldn't get the lather on them because they were new and full of sizing. I didn't bother about the war being over, I was getting on with the washing. I was eleven then and that was what I was doing.

The cost of such a lost childhood and lost education is incalculable:

Did you ever think of going to the grammar school?

No. I had to do the work at home. They wouldn't let me sit for an exam. I don't think I would have passed anyway because I had so little time at school. I was always off when mother was ill or she was away, nursing a new baby. I got no opportunity to learn.

So you really were a kind of mother's stand-in?

I was a little old woman. I am younger for my age now than I have ever been in my life.[43]

The fact that she does not resent her lost youth, and is proud of her achievements, should not cause anyone to forget the price she paid for her training as housewife and mother. These less attractive aspects of the socialisation provided by family life force one to look with reservation on the enthusiastic polemics for this process such as that written by Helen Bosanquet in 1906.[44]

Even in their games girls tended to be conditioned into being little mothers. Not all of them had toys, but those who did always mention dolls first when asked which toys they received as Christmas presents. A few very fortunate ones also had a doll's pram:

What do you remember getting for Christmas?

Well, the first thing I remember, it was a huge doll with long auburn curls. I had ringlets then and it had huge ringlets and I can remember it standing on a box on this old huge fireplace. It was the most beautiful thing I had ever seen. Then the year before that I got a pram, a really old-fashioned pram with these shallow bodies and a huge wheel at the back and one at the front. The handlebars were up here with a white porcelain handle, really old-fashioned, and I can remember I used to polish that pram every day without fail. If I took it out, when I came back I polished it. We valued everything in those days. Of course, as I say, I was fortunate, I was the baby and I got the cream.[45]

Fragile dolls did not always survive in overcrowded homes, but there were always babies to play with: 'Of course everybody played with babies. You didn't play with dolls, you played with real babies. There were so many knocking about and you were glad to get somebody to nurse it for a bit.'[46] Through performing these tasks, whether in work or in play, girls learned the traditional patterns of child-care and discovered much about the development of children. This process had both advantages and disadvantages: when they became mothers working-class girls felt confident and relaxed in the handling of their children, unlike their middle-class counterparts who frequently had little idea of how to cope with motherhood. The latter had to resort to the advice offered in women's magazines, and appear to have worried a lot about the problems of motherhood.[47] But the middle-class woman had the advantage of being freer to innovate in the practice of child-rearing, and of not being as circumscribed by the traditional example set and advice given by her mother.

Finally, one of the most important results of girls carrying out a large amount of domestic work was that it reinforced their very close bonds with their mothers. The importance of the shared secrets about sex has already been mentioned, but possibly more important was the bond which developed out of the years of sharing domestic tasks. Very few respondents stress or even mention physical affection and tenderness within the family, but all explicitly or implicitly reveal the depth and strength of the bond between themselves and their mothers.

SCHOOL

As they grew older, children encountered authority figures other than their parents, notably policemen, clergymen and teachers. Working-class children's attitudes to them were governed by a complex range of factors: first and obviously by age (younger children were more likely to be obedient and unquestioning than were older ones). Secondly, the family's viewpoint was of

Schoolgirls at Barrow Island School, c. 1900. Note their spotless pinafores and polished boots. This area was occupied predominantly by shipyard workers. (The author attended this school after the second world war; externally little has changed since it was built in the 1870s.) (Barrow Library)

supreme importance; if their standards, attitudes, ideas and culture were reinforced by the authority figure then the children and young people would usually obey that figure. But if the family, and most importantly parents' expectations, attitudes and beliefs were in conflict with those in authority then it was very likely that the children would follow their parents' standard rather than those of the teacher, policeman or vicar.

The institution most immediately influential in a girl's life, after the home and family, was the school. All the respondents except one went to school,[48] and it was generally, but certainly not always, seen both as a reinforcement of the teaching of the home, and as a complement to it. Parents expected their children to learn the 'three Rs' — skills which they regarded as important and which some of them had been unable to acquire themselves. They also expected firmness, and a reinforcement of the habits of obedience, respectability and hard work, first learned at home. Many were not disappointed in their expectations:

It was the same with the teachers at school. You were terrified. No, not terrified, but the respect was there, you were held in awe. Everything they told us to do must be done. There was no laughing and grinning and giggling at the teachers as they do these days. But they had the respect, it was really respectful. There was no wrong-doing, you never heard of them skipping school or anything like that. It was . . . you had to be at school. We used to go to school in the morning and we had all to line up in the schoolyard and we had to stand like this. The Headmistress — in our case she was a nun — she would have each different class lined up in sections and she would go all the way along with a round wooden ruler. She always had one of these with her. You had to go like this, with your hands stretched out and your shoes had to be shining clean. Your nails and your hands had to be clean and she would go around checking and woe betide anyone that's nails weren't. You would have had a smack with this ruler, sent straight into the school cloakroom that had one little sink, they would have to scrub their nails and their hands until they were clean. Then the following day they were told they had to come back with those shoes clean. They were sticklers for cleanliness. You had to have a handkerchief and that, you had to show your handkerchief. Little things like that. But these days, they don't bother about them, do they?[49]

Some children, especially those kindly and gently reared, often found school a nightmare of harshly and sometimes unfairly administered punishments. The simple threat of corporal punishment was not felt to be a sufficient deterrent to juvenile misbehaviour. Children were frequently painfully punished for trivial offences, not only to prevent a repetition of the crime, but also as an example.

Some teachers can only be described as brutal. Several Lancaster Roman Catholic women, growing up in the 1890s, spontaneously remembered with some horror the activities of a Sister Mary Borgia, who was remembered as much for her unfairness as for her frequent beatings:

When we went to the Catholic school every Monday morning we used to take a penny and that was for school. Sister Mary Borgia used to say to me, 'Have you fetched a penny, Sarah?' 'No Sister m'grandma's hard-up.' Old lass hadn't money. 'Come out,' and there was the strap because I hadn't taken a penny.[50]

Mrs Burns as a child was very overburdened and perpetually caught between an authoritarian grandmother who expected her to do all the family's shopping before school, and an equally authoritarian teacher who always expected her to be on time. Mrs Heron too suffered at the hands of Sister Mary Borgia, and like many pupils could not expect any sympathy from her mother if stories of her punishment reached home:

I've had many a good hiding off Sister Borgia as well. I got blame many a time for what I didn't do. I was full of life.
She was very strict, was she?

Yes, to some. She had her favourites. They had in them days, some of the nuns and teachers. I've known that I've had little lumps where she's hit me with a ring.

What sort of things would she smack you for?

I don't know. I remember we were playing in the schoolyard and one of the lassies had scratched her arm and I got the blame for that and got a good hiding for that. I've known somebody to tell m'mother, 'Oh your Nellie got such a good hiding at school.' 'Ah, she'd have done summat or she wouldn't have got a hiding.'[51]

But the mores of the school were not in all cases those of the home. There were two possible areas of conflict between home and school; one was the length of time spent on schooling, the second was discipline. It is debatable whether one can describe these clashes in terms of class conflict, as is argued by Stephen Humphries,[52] because there was little *group*, still less *class* solidarity in resistance to schools; individual families made either an overt protest or a rather more covert one simply by withdrawing their children from school as soon as possible. But there can be little doubt that there was a fundamentally different attitude to education on the part of teachers and educationalists on one hand, and some parents and children on the other. In my sample there are very few indications of pupils launching counter-attacks against teachers. Mrs Nixon had heard of one sad case, although she herself was in no way involved: 'I know one teacher, Miss H. at the British School, she drowned herself. She was very mannish, masculine, and she used to be frightened to death of the scholars because they were cruel to her.'[53]

What is noticeable, however, is that while there were few examples of resistance instigated by the pupils themselves, it was not at all unknown for parents and children, acting together, to retaliate against teacher brutality. Some parents — a minority certainly — were incensed by what they regarded as the unjust, cruel treatment their children received. Once the children realised that they had their parents' backing, and that not all authority was united, then a counter-attack against the schools could be and was sometimes launched. In January 1893, the headmaster of Roose School in Barrow was fined by the magistrates for 'inflicting corporal punishment'. Both in court and in a letter to the press the teacher complained of the parents' insulting and threatening behaviour. The editorial comment revealed an ambivalent and perhaps not unfamiliar attitude: 'We are coming into an era when the old barbarities are out of date, and I for one confess that we are becoming just a little too soft and losing the wisdom which said, "Spare the rod and spoil the child."'[54] Respondents, while not remembering their parents being involved in court cases, do remember them in conflict with the school. Robert Roberts comments on the deplorable habit of teachers picking on children who, it was clear from their appearance, belonged to the poorest class: 'Some teachers publicly scolded the condition of their dirty and ill-dressed pupils, too often forgetting the poverty from which they came.'[55] This view is echoed by Mrs Nixon:

They used to show you up if you were poor. My mother once waited a week [outside the school] for a teacher, to give her a good hiding. We'd to wear all my mother's clothes and this teacher had pulled my sister and swung her round with her hair. My mother went but she never got hold of her because the schoolmaster knew and when my mother waited at one end, he let her out at the other.[56]

Mrs Hesketh's evidence is quoted in some detail, for it not only illustrates the suffering undergone by many children, but demonstrates how some parents were prepared to defend their children, and by so doing gave them the courage not only to endure the hardship, but to carry out minor acts of defiance. Mrs Hesketh was handicapped; malnutrition in childhood had stunted her growth and her legs were badly deformed by rickets. She had a very close relationship with her mother, which these incidents strengthened:

There was an incident in one class that I was in, the teacher only lived round the corner in the next street, she must have been bad-tempered that day because I was so timid, I was too frightened to be cheeky or brave. I remember something that went wrong and she was in such a bad temper that she gave me such a smack on that knuckle and it went blue, she went with such force. I was crying with the pain of it and to be true, I was making a tea-party of it, but it really hurt. When the end of the school lesson came she called me to one side and she gave me sixpence. You know what that was for? She knew my mother was only round the corner but my mother went to her just the same. She told her that if there was any hitting to be doing or clouting, as they said in them days, she said she would do it. She said, 'You tell me. I'll put them right. Don't you ever do that again.' She told her where to get off.
   You could get some really nasty lady teachers then, and I walks in and everybody's sat down and I was trembling like a leaf and she says, 'Where are you going?' I said, 'To my seat, Miss.' She said, 'I'm bothering with you no more. You go and tell the headmaster what time you've come in.' Well, that meant punishment. I thought, well fancy her, sending me for a thrashing and trusting me! So I gets down this set of stairs, comes across the corridor, genuinely looking for him, comes round to this front door and I'm going to go upstairs to these classes but when I saw this door opened, I went for it. I ran home as fast as my legs would carry me. My mum asked what was the matter with me and I told her. She said, 'You did right.' She knew it wasn't my fault. It's an interesting story because when morning came I started to think, like, what's waiting for me? Do you know, I went to that class, trembling as usual, sat in my seat and lessons went on and I was never mentioned. I was just a number. She had forgotten all

about it. I had been trembling and I couldn't sleep; I was terrified. But I got away with it, that's the main story, nobody had missed me.[57]

Did schools help to condition and train the girls specifically for their future roles of wives and mothers? It is very difficult to discover any particular differences in boys' and girls' education, except in the area of handicrafts. The home and family played an infinitely more important part in the conditioning of girls than did the school. But from the mid-nineteenth century onwards there was considerable debate, especially among social reformers, about the standard of domestic accomplishment among working-class women. These views are fully examined by Margaret Hewitt in *Wives and Mothers in Victorian Industry.* She was convinced by the volume of criticism that the level of domestic accomplishment among the working class was very low.[58] Such criticism was one of the reasons for the state insisting that girls were trained in various aspects of housewifery in schools. The new Education Code of 1876 stated that every girl must, after 31 March 1877, take domestic economy as an educational subject.[59] Plain needlework had

A group of girls enjoying a game of skipping at a Lancaster school. Judging from the pinafores this photo was taken in the years before 1914. (Lancaster Museum)

been compulsory for girls since the revised Education Code of 1862. Both codes made it clear that grants to schools would be adversely affected if these subjects were not taught. At first they were taught theoretically, but after 1882 grants were made available for the practical teaching of cookery, and after 1890 for laundry work. National debate continued about this aspect of girls' education well into the twentieth century;[60] feminists, like C. S. Bremner, complained of little girls being pressed too young into a narrow mould. On the other hand, those anxious about the state of national physical well-being (a spectre raised by the rejection rate on medical grounds of volunteers for the Boer Wars), argued for more, not less, housewifery training in schools.

It is doubtful if the respondents or their parents were aware of this debate; and it is interesting that despite the legal position, provision of housewifery courses remained very patchy until well into the twentieth century. Individual schools had their own priorities, as Miss Turner, who was born in 1912 and left school in 1926, shows:

I never went to cookery. . . . They started cookery straight after I had finished school, about twelve months after.
Did you do sewing?
She only gave us pieces of white calico, and she taught us how to do a hem, and she taught us how to join two pieces of material together. I think she called it a seam and fell, and we had to do tiny stitches. I can't remember ever making a proper garment.[61]

This girl's somewhat inadequate teaching can be contrasted with that of a near-contemporary from Preston, who was born in 1919 and left school in 1933:

We used to spend Tuesdays and Fridays sewing in the afternoon. You did all the head work in the morning and in the afternoon it was different subjects. I loved sewing and I still do to this day. I make all my own clothes today. On Mondays it was painting and I loved painting. On Wednesday we did raffia — cane work and raffia — I used to love that.
Did you ever do cooking?
That was once a week and that was at a place up in Maitland Street. We had to do different courses, one course for a period from Easter to Whitsuntide and from Christmas to Easter, we would do housewifery and they would teach us how to clean. The next one would be laundry and they would teach us how to wash and starch and ironing and all that. The next one would be just cookery alone. What we made we could buy, unless we took our own stuff, and then we would happen have to pay a penny for the gas. That was one morning every week, a Monday morning.
So you were doing a lot of lessons that weren't actually reading, writing and arithmetic?

Oh yes. They would teach you right through. The lads used to go to woodwork. I used to think that it sort of prepared us for later in life. You could wash and you could iron and you could clean your house and you could cook.

And it was useful, was it?

Every way.[62]

This respondent particularly appreciated her course because as soon as she left school she had to take charge of the family while her mother had a prolonged stay in hospital. She is, however, almost alone in her enthusiasm for her housewifery courses at school.

Some schools ran comprehensive housewifery courses much earlier than those mentioned above. The *Barrow News* in 1893 proudly announced the opening of the new laundry centre in Rawlinson Street School: 'Teaching school children all the practical details of the laundry is quite a new feature even in these days of advanced educational facilities and, so far as we are aware, the Barrow School Board deserve the credit for being the first in the provinces to open a laundry in connection with their schools.' A detailed list of the theoretical and practical lessons follows, and it includes the intriguing statement that 'the girls are allowed to take certain articles from home to wash, but these must not include bed or body linen.'[63] Mrs Hewitson (born in 1885) was a pupil at this new centre. Her oral evidence is another reminder of the different perceptions and experiences between those providing services and those receiving them:

Did you ever do any cooking at school?

Yes. I went to cookery at Rawlinson Street School. . . . But it was just so many out of the class that went. One morning you went for a lecture about your cooking and the next time you went for practical, you did it.

Do you think it was any help, or did you learn more from your mother?

It was never any help. . . . They used to sell whatever you made, and if you fancied anything you bought it. I remember bringing home scones . . . . and m'brother when he drew up his chair to sit down at the table he said, 'Where have the scones come from?' M'mother said, 'Well, May has brought them today from school.' He said, 'Oh!' And he didn't have any.

What a shame.

Well I don't know whether it was a shame or not because when I think about it, and the messy way we carried on while we were doing these things and there was only one person to look after all these kids, I bet I didn't eat any m'self.

Then we did washing and we had laundry once a week. You went to the laundry and the first thing you took was a collar of your brother's. It had to be clean when you took it, so what good was that?

And you learnt starching and ironing?

Well yes, and polishing. We had polishing irons then and after you'd ironed the collars you used to have to rub with this, it was a curved shape, and the curve at the bottom of the iron used to polish the collars. M'mother washed them when I took them home.[64]

Her view that 'It was never any help' is a common one. Many women speak of learning cooking, sewing and housewifery in general not from school, but from their mothers.

Did you ever do any cooking at school?
No, we never had no cookery. Oh yes, I'm telling a lie, the last year. Across the playground was a cookery place and it had only [just] started. We just made little cakes and soups and things like that. You could take it home with you.
Do you think you learnt more from your mother than you learnt at school?
Oh you didn't learn much at school.[65]

Mrs Sharp also shows clearly how learning at home differed from that at school. For example, she mentions making soup at school, but gives no details. On the other hand, she learned exactly how soup was made by her mother by regularly buying the ingredients for it, and then watching her mother make it:

There was ten of us, you know, and I used to go to Billy the butcher and get a penny or a twopenny marrow bone. You got a great big bone and he'd give you another one with it. I would call at Billy Macaulay the greengrocer's and I'd get about three carrots, and a couple of parsnips, a little turnip, a bit of parsley and a bit of celery for twopence. Then I'd call for a pennyworth of barley on the road up. M'mother used to have a great big iron pan and she used to make a great big pan of soup.
How long would that last you?
Just the day. There was all those kids. There wasn't room for them all to sit round the table![66]

The general dissatisfaction with school domestic science felt by the respondents was also felt by those in authority. Faced with the criticisms of the effectiveness of domestic science teaching in schools, made by the Interdepartmental Committee on Physical Deterioration,[67] the Board of Education prepared a series of reports on the subject and a new code of regulations which required more simple teaching and the avoidance of unnecessary theory.[68] These reports appear to have totally discounted the possibility of any meaningful training in domestic science taking place at home. The official view is summarised by Peter Stearns: 'Daughters had learned little before their marriage . . . . efforts from the mid-nineteenth century onwards to compensate for inadequate domestic training through education were ill-conceived and ineffective.'[69] Yet the female respondents are almost all united in their belief that it was their mothers' training (or that of a mother-substitute such as a grandmother) which was of real value to them. When their domestic skills are examined, it becomes clear that very many working-class women were skilled cooks and housewives.

The generally subordinate role played by schools in the socialisation of the working-class child, as compared with that played by the home and family, can perhaps best be illustrated in the complex relationships between the child, the family, the school, and the world of work. In the working-class family familial considerations were of much greater importance than were individualistic ones: the good and the well-being of the family came before the gratification of individual desires. The children learned early to subjugate personal ambitions to those of their parents and to care, on a daily basis, for the needs of other members of the family. When children grew older there was no real clash between the individual needs (especially academic ones) of the child and those of the family. If mother needed help, one of the girls would stay at home without question: 'We didn't go to school all the time. It was optional. She always kept one at home to mind the babies. She had to.'[70]

The respondents and their families displayed differing attitudes about the value of the education children received in school. While all were agreed on the importance of learning the basic skills of reading, writing and arithmetic, there was some divergence of opinion about the value of acquiring more advanced skills, opinions to some extent reflected in the age at which children left school. This though was a matter which was, to a very considerable degree, controlled by the statutory school-leaving age. School attendance to the age of ten was first made compulsory in 1876; this was raised to eleven in 1893, and to fourteen in 1899, but exemptions were allowed for part-time working under local bye-laws, from the age of eleven for agriculture, and from twelve under the Factory Acts provided that an adequate standard of scholastic efficiency in literacy and numeracy had been achieved, or a required number of school attendances had been recorded (e.g. Barrow and Lancaster had a Labour Examination based on skills; Preston had a Labour Certificate based on school attendances). With these provisions, total exemption was allowed at age thirteen.

In 1918 all exceptions and exemptions ended and compulsory full-time education to the age of fourteen was imposed. However, the number of pupils in all three towns who stayed at school after the age of fourteen was small. The three respondents who came from middle-class backgrounds stayed on; one boy became a bank clerk, another a local government official, and the girl stayed at home, helping with the housekeeping. Thirteen working-class children stayed on at school to the age of fifteen or more, of whom only four were girls. One was a pupil- and later a qualified primary school teacher; two became secretaries; and one went to work in the family sub-post office. The boys mostly went on to serve apprenticeships, except for two who went to university. (It is undoubtedly significant that one of these went at the very end of the 1930s, and the other in the 1940s.)

The 1921 Census returns for the county and the three towns show under 5 per cent of boys and girls at school after the age of fifteen (the exception being 8 per cent of boys in Lancaster). These figures, of course, include children from middle-class backgrounds, and so reflect (as does the sample) the small percentage of working-class children receiving post-compulsory education.[71]

Those who stayed on were not only unusual, but were also rare in generally liking school, a sentiment not shared by a large number of the early leavers. It is doubtful, however, if children's dislike of school was the chief reason for their leaving. Of much greater significance was the economic standing of the family. Financial pressures very frequently meant that a child had to leave school as soon as possible in order to contribute to the family income. The poorer the family the earlier the child was likely to be earning wages. B. S. Rowntree in his 1901 study of York makes the same point.[72] It will be seen in chapter 4 that Preston's poverty was greater than that of either Lancaster or Barrow, and this greater degree of poverty would appear to be reflected in the large number of Preston children leaving school to work either full-time or half-time before their fourteenth birthday. (Approximately half the Preston sample went to work half-time at the mill on their twelfth birthday, and another third went to work full-time in the mills at thirteen. Even in 1921 the Census recorded nearly 30 per cent of 12 to 13-year-old girls and 25 per cent of boys in full-time work in Preston.[73]

The 'half-time' children, who alternated a week of morning work and afternoon school with a week of afternoon work and morning school, gained little from their education; continuity was impossible and they were often very tired. Miss K. Baster, the headmistress of the training school at Glovers Court, Preston (a domestic science/handicraft centre), speaking at the annual conference of the Association of Teachers of Domestic Science in London in 1910, bitterly attacked the half-time system:

What wonder is it that many of the girls are half-dead with fatigue and drop asleep over their work in the afternoon. Some headmistresses have told me that they allow them to continue sleeping, as it seems almost inhuman to make them try to do brain work while they are in that condition, and any work accomplished is of a very poor quality. It is unfortunate that these textile workers who are most liable to be deprived of the benefits of sound domestic training are just the ones who need it most.[74]

It is clear that working-class Prestonians did not view the half-time system in quite the same way as its humanitarian critics. It is undoubtedly significant that none of the girls who were half-timers speaks of this exhaustion. They are much more anxious to discuss their work in the mills. The clear implication is that work in the factory, whether enjoyable or not, was what was significant to them, as was the all-important financial contribution made by them to the family. The *Preston Guardian* in 1909 carried a report of the Parliamentary Inter-Departmental Committee on Partial Exemption from School Attendance, which recommended a total abolition of the half-time scheme by June 1911. The editor commented, 'There seems to be no doubt that a large number of the working class in Lancashire are not yet prepared voluntarily to accept any raising of the age, and are averse for any legislative enactment.'[75]

The continuing working-class adherence to the Victorian work ethic meant that many parents, and indeed some children, could not accept the morality of continuing at school when one could be involved in 'real' work. It is not surprising that generations of children, brought up to work very hard physically in the home, and seeing their parents working hard, should both as children and parents regard book work as somehow wrong. As one old man remarked, 'It was *immoral* to stay at school when you could be *working*.' Another said, 'We weren't allowed a book. Didn't have a book. Daren't bring one of these little penny books home. Well, we hadn't time.'[76]

There were girls in at least two families who were so thoroughly conditioned by the work ethic that they were determined not to continue their education despite their families wishing them to do so.[77] Miss Hunter's case is interesting, but unusual. There was no financial pressure in this family, for both father and mother had full-time jobs and Miss Hunter was an only child. But she was determined in 1893 to go to work. (She is referring here to the Labour Examination. Intelligent children who did well were allowed to go to work full-time; less successful ones went half-time.)

How old were you when you went to work?
Eleven. . . . there was an examination on and I was going in for it and I said to m'dad, 'I'm going full-time.' He said, 'You're not going in the mill.' I said, 'I am.' I said, 'It was good enough for m'mother and it's good enough for me.' So he said, 'You'll go in and I don't want you to go in.' I said, 'It doesn't matter.' I said, 'I'll have a go at it,' and I never rued, I've been happy and that's all you want when you're working, isn't it, being happy. . . . I passed an examination, you could pass either for half-time or full-time and I went in for full-time and I passed and I would be eleven in October as I started in August.
So you were ten really, nearly eleven?
Nearly eleven, well I call it eleven.
What did you do when you got there?

Well I had to put cops on shuttles and change them when they were finished and look out for ends coming out.

The preference for going to work rather than school was not unusual, but such independence being displayed by a girl was uncommon. Much more usually parents decided which school a child would go to, when they would leave, and what job would follow.

I quote one respondent at length, because her evidence raises many interesting points. She mentions the unfairness of her brother being allowed to go to college (i.e. the Catholic Boys' Grammar School in Preston), while she was not allowed to go to Larkhill (the Girls' Catholic Grammar School). There was some *marginal* preference towards giving boys a grammar school education — this is shown in both the sample and the official figures — but it was unusual. The respondents have quite as many stories of boys not being able to go on to grammar school, or some other form of further education, because of family pressures as they have of girls. But there are other points of interest in Mrs Harrison's story. Her father was an active socialist and trade unionist, and a great believer in education. One of his favourite sayings was, 'Ignorance believes and education stops to think.' His beliefs, however, did not affect his daughter's career, which like so many children's was totally dominated by her mother, and by her mother's concept of what was necessary for the family budget. Mrs Harrison may have resented her mother's stand, but she accepted it. These events took place in 1930, and illustrate how long-lasting were the old values and attitudes to the competing claims of family, school, work and the individual:

That was another thing that was a sore point. I had passed my exams to go to Larkhill, but because my sister was weaving, it was thought then that girls wasn't that important to go to college and learn. He passed his and went to college and went straight to Leyland Motors office. I wanted to go to this particular confectioners that I had been going to, and the wage was 5s. a week, and she was ready to take me at fourteen. But when you went in the mill you earned a pound and mother wanted that money.

Did you give it all to her?

Oh yes. There was no question of anything else and your spending money was a shilling in the pound. I earned 30s. so I got 1s. 6d. To make a little bit I used to go three times a week at 6 o'clock, we started at quarter to eight, but I had to go three mornings and get up about half past five and walk about two miles to this mill from where we lived in Bamber Bridge to sweep the looms for my sister, her friend and my own. That meant going three particular mornings because you swept the looms whilst they were stopped and it used to be fluff, about so thick, and it was hard work. They gave me sixpence each. So mother took sixpence off my spending money and put it in the bank for me to pay for my holidays because I was getting that extra shilling. That made it two shillings then. Out of that I bought my own stockings, sixpence a pair in Woolworth's and I had to pay church money out of that and the dancing round the corner at the village hall. I started in the mill in 1930 when I was fourteen. As mother said, my sister had gone weaving and I hadn't to get any fancy ideas of working in a shop, I had to go too.

Did you ever talk to her about passing to go to Larkhill or did you keep it quiet?

I kept it quiet because they had brought a shuttle home from the weaving for me to learn how to put the cotton on and I thought, I'll never get to go. After that my father was annoyed about me keeping quiet because with him being the way he was, and I suppose he was taking up so much time with these meetings and that, he left things to Mother. She was a good mother, no doubt. The way they used to think then, you had to earn your keep, it wasn't a question of going to learn something where you didn't get a wage for four years, you had to start when you turned fourteen to earn money.[78]

Oral history continually serves to emphasise the complexity and variety of working-class experience. For every generalisation exceptions can be found, but one can also discover patterns of behaviour and attitude. The working-class girl on the point of leaving school had already learned much which would affect many aspects of her adult life. She had learned to be a child-minder and housekeeper, how to manage money and to be scrupulously honest, and the duties owed to neighbours in need. She had learned to respect authority, and to conform to a generally accepted and acceptable standard of behaviour.

The clear division between right and wrong drawn by parents, teachers and clergy tended to give both boys and girls a clear, if inflexible, moral sense. This moral certainty developed in adulthood into a self-confidence in their own personal judgement which was rarely questioned. Girls, perhaps even more than boys, grew up to accept the great importance of respectability, with its emphasis on cleanliness in body, clothing and language as well as in the home.

The working-class girl in the early twentieth century has sometimes been regarded as naive and immature. When one considers how much she had already learned, and how much responsibility she had undertaken by the time she left school, it is clear that it must be only her ignorance about sex which has given rise to this stereotype.

2
Youth, Work and Leisure

This chapter is concerned with the period between a girl's leaving school and getting married. Of course, not all girls went to work after leaving school and certainly not all married. The period, however, between the ages of about fourteen and twenty-five was distinctive for most girls, bridging as it did childhood and independent adulthood. More women worked for wages during this period than at any other time of their lives. It was also a time for enjoying leisure and of course for getting to know men and possibly finding a husband. But the girl/woman was not totally independent, and her relationship with her parents is a theme which recurs throughout the chapter.

It is worth noting first that not all young women were employed. Table 2.1 shows that approximately half the young women in Barrow were in paid employment in the years 1911 and 1921. The Barrow respondents do not explain clearly what happened to those who did not work because so few of the sample were in this category, but there are indications that these young women may have worked for a short time and then stopped, or stayed at home to help with their families, and then found a job again. Six of the respondents were not in continuous employment before they married,[1]

TABLE 2.1: Percentages of women in full-time employment
in Barrow and Preston, 1911 and 1921

| | Age groups | | | | | |
	14–19	20–24	25–34	35–44	45–54	55–65
1911						
Barrow	49.2	44.7	19.1	12.6	11.7	10.9
Preston	89.2	85.7	63.9	46.1	37.7	27.6
1921						
Barrow	50.8	47.0	19.4	14.3	12.2	12.4
Preston	86.7	84.9	61.0	43.8	32.9	26.8

The figures given are percentages of the total number of women in each age group.
Source: Census of 1911, County of Lancaster, table 23; Census of 1921, County of Lancaster, table 18.

where their families needed their domestic labour more than their wages. In all except one of the cases these were large families needing domestic help, and the respondents were among the oldest children. If these intermittent employment patterns were usual they must have affected the total numbers of young women in full-time work. Two respondents in Barrow were both the daughters of well-paid men (one a boilermaker, the other an engine driver) and never had paid jobs, although both did a little dressmaking.[2] It is likely that some craftsmen preferred to keep their daughters (as well as their wives) at home. They did not 'need' the wages, and their ability to support them indicated their own successful earning ability and status. The figures for Preston are markedly different: there, the typical young woman was in full-time paid employment, and it was very unusual for girls to stay at home before marriage, help for larger families being more likely to be given by older married sisters, aunts or grandmothers. The need for wages was much stronger in Preston.

THE STATUS OF YOUNG WORKERS IN THE FAMILY

How far did the end of schooling and the beginning of wage-earning work mark a divide between dependent childhood and independent adulthood for working-class youth? There can be no understanding of this problem without a recognition of the overwhelming importance of the young workers' wages in most working-class families, where the struggle against poverty was one of life's chief preoccupations. John Gillis, in his book *Youth and History*,[3] differentiates between the adolescent whom he describes as a middle-class phenomenon, and the man/child whom he sees as a member of the working class. He regarded poverty as the single most important factor in determining the life-cycle of a working-class young person, and certainly in the sample, until the outbreak of the second world war, the threat and reality of poverty, and the subsequent importance of young people's wages, continued to dominate working-class life.

Both parents and children recognised the value of these earnings, and consequently subtle changes in the status of the young person took place. Both boys and girls expected a better diet, for example Mrs Heron in the early 1900s:

I worked at mill half-time, I used to be going through Dalton Square b'twenty past five because a bell went. . . . I was on afternoons, the week after I believe it was, and I come home and m'mother had a herring between us. I said, 'Mother, I'm working, I should have a whole one.' She said, 'Go on, it's all right lass.' M'mother said, 'It's all right Nellie we'll enjoy it,' and we did.[4]

Mrs Heron subsequently enjoyed a whole herring.

Mrs Mulholland, from Barrow, became a drummer in the band of the local skating-rink at the age of thirteen. She earned 18s. a week at a time when her father, a labourer, was only earning 21s.: 'When I was on this job, at the skating-rink, that was my tea every day, a poached egg on toast. My mother said she was not going to kill the goose that laid the golden egg.' Obviously this woman, like many others, immensely enjoyed the feeling of being of value to her family. Her enhanced status also ensured that she was let off various household jobs. She worked in the afternoon, and three hours at night and, therefore,

My mother used to let me have it easy in a morning, and some of the neighbours said, 'Why don't you make your Carrie do this and that?' And my mother used to say, 'I'm not going to kill the goose that lays the golden eggs.'[5]

There were other concessions too. The most usual one concerned coming in at night. If, in fact, a parent was thought to be unreasonable about this, a small rebellion might well take place:

I used to go out with a girl then and we used to go to the pictures, The Palace, and it cost us 5d. It was cheaper downstairs, but we thought we were 'toffs', and we went in the side gallery. We used to go one night a week, we didn't go out other nights. You didn't go out a lot then, you know. It didn't come out until nearly eleven and do you know my father used to come to the bottom of the street to meet us. He said, 'Where have you been?' 'I've been on the corner,' I said. 'You know very well the Palace doesn't come out until a quarter to eleven.' . . . One night I said, 'Come on, we're going to diddle him.' I went along the top way. My father opened the door and said, 'Is she in?' and I said, 'I've been here ages.' I told him straight, 'I'm sick of you coming to look for us. You can see we come home.' So he never came anymore, it taught him a lesson.

Mrs Sharp, perhaps emboldened by this small triumph, went on to criticise, even if only obliquely, her parents' sexual behaviour:

My father was too easy going. I said, 'No sooner do we get one baby grown up than another one comes.' 'Oh you brazen little madam,' he said. Then on the Sunday, Dorothy was born. Yet m'mother never talked to any of us, and said that she was having a baby. I was nineteen at the time.[6]

This kind of criticism was unusual, but not unknown; the minority of respondents with fathers who bullied their mothers began to stand up to them, often successfully, in their late teens. Others went beyond criticism of certain behaviour or attitudes, and rejected the political and/or religious beliefs of their parents. Mrs Holmes, for example, was brought up as an Anglican, but as a young woman began to have serious doubts. She questioned the snobbery and hypocrisy she frequently found among her local congregation, and in old age wrote, in a short piece entitled 'How I became a socialist', about the incident which caused her finally to reject her Church and organised Christianity:

If there existed a true state of Christianity in the churches there would be neither rich nor poor in their congregations. On one occasion the vicar of Dalton preached a sermon like this. His wife's mother had just died, and his wife was worried as to what her mother's companions would be like in the world to which she had gone. He comforted his wife by telling her it was his opinion that with the social standing held in this life, they would go to the same social standing in the next world. He illustrated his point by quoting the following, 'In my father's house are many mansions.' He was of the opinion that these were mansions for the poor and mansions for the rich. He was criticised by many, but was still allowed to go on talking tripe from the pulpit. Needless to say, the mansion story was enough for me.[7]

Yet the truly independent working-class youth, whether male or female, cannot be found in any significant numbers. The wages they earned were essential, and both they and their parents realised their significance, but although realisation could and did lead to a change of status, it did not lead to the state of affairs described by Standish Meacham:

Parents were forced to acknowledge to themselves that however much their own age and experience might enable them to dominate their offspring when very young, financial reality declared their eventual reliance on the earnings of their sons and daughters, both in the short run when the elder children went to work as adolescents to help support the younger, and in the more distant future when, prematurely aged or infirm, the older generation might find itself almost totally dependent for its livelihood on its progeny. Working-class children received their share of parental love and parental discipline, but within the seldom articulated, generally unconscious framework of this generational economic calculus.[8]

The oral evidence would seem to offer a different interpretation; there is no evidence of parents feeling dependent upon, or beholden to, their offspring. Standish Meacham's interpretation overlooks the immense *moral* authority which parents continued to wield, and the great respect their children continued to show well into adult life, in most cases until the death of the parents. It was this all-prevailing moral and ethical climate which ensured that in all but the most prosperous working-class families, young people's wages were handed over intact to their parents (almost invariably to their mothers), and their financial independence voluntarily given up.

In most families (as described by Mrs Harrison in chapter 1), young people were given back a fixed percentage of their wages — a penny in the shilling, and a shilling in the pound, being most common. In a small minority of the more prosperous families, both boys and girls were allowed to board (that is, to pay a fixed amount for board and lodgings), keeping the remainder for themselves, which of course increased as their wages increased. For most, though, the financial control exerted by mothers and accepted by their children was so tight, that saving up to be married proved to be a slow and frustrating procedure.

Lack of savings partly accounts for the comparatively late age of marriage in all three towns, and also for the practice of young couples, especially in Preston, beginning married life living with relatives. In a very small number of cases (in the sample, two Preston girls and one boy),[9] respondents' treatment by their parents was such that it amounts to exploitation. In the case of the two girls this exploitation, rather than delaying their marriages, not surprisingly pushed them into very early ones:

I went to work, and she wouldn't let me go until I was fourteen. I stayed at home for twelve months. She got me to do all the housework. Anyway, I used to get 27s. 1d. in the card room. My friends used to come out with their wage-packets, and the odd penny, my friends could open that. There used to be an ice-cream shop right next door, and they would go in and get a penny ice-cream but I daren't open mine. I daren't take that penny out for love nor money. Some of the others used to give me a little bit of theirs. . . .
How much would she give you back out of your wage?
A shilling out of 27s. 1d. . . .
He [her stepfather] used to take papers round on Sunday morning. I used to go with him. . . . I used to be up at 4 o'clock and I had been up at 6 o'clock every morning in the week, go for the papers, bring them home and they sorted them all out. Then I used to walk all the way round the streets. . . . Home for 12 o'clock. They used to sit and count the money and, do you know, I never got nothing. I did that every week, I went to work seven days a week. Then I went to Sunday School in the afternoon. Sometimes some of the girls at work lived in some of those houses and as I was coming back they would only just be getting up. All their hair used to be in curling pins to go out. They used to say to me on the Monday, 'Did you go out?' I never went out like that.
So where did you meet your husband-to-be? You said you got married when you were eighteen, so you obviously met him when you were quite young.
He didn't live so far away and I met him in the park where we always went. You never had any money to go anywhere else. You went to the pictures and it was 2d. He was a near neighbour. I got married in grey, she [her mother] bought me a beautiful dress.[10]

Young people were not only financially dependent; they were morally dependent too. Most continued to live with their parents, the only exceptions being girls who went as living-in domestic servants, and young men who, having finished their apprenticeships, sought work in another town, and while young people remained at home they had to live according to their parents' rules. There were certainly more disputes in this age group (which either side might win) than between young children and their parents, but these rarely if ever resulted in the boy or girl leaving home, and certainly no respondent did so. Mrs Sharp won the argument about coming home late at night; most respondents, though, either did not argue, or fought and lost:

Go to dances? He wouldn't allow that, he'd have killed us if he thought we'd been at a dance. There was one sister much older than me, and she asked m'mother. . . . Mother let her go to this dance. . . . She'd left school, passed the Labour Exam, and she was more free than us. Mother said, 'Now, no lads.' Anyway, she went to this dance and she was out until half past ten or eleven. . . . So he took the key to bed with him. He missed her and said, 'She's not in, I'm having the key tonight,' and she slept out. We got in touch with the woman next door, and she kept her all night, but it learnt her a lesson. Mother never said anything. It was just to frighten her.[11]

Physical punishment was not unknown, even when girls were virtually grown up and the transgression a relatively minor one (although its use was limited to a small minority; only six families in the sample). Mrs Thornton is one such exception. She was out one evening with her husband-to-be and another couple, and was supposed to be in at ten o'clock:

My dad opened the door, and it wouldn't be five minutes after ten as we ran all the way home. He asked me where I had been and then he gave me a winger then. They don't know what a good hiding is today, do they? If they had got the thrashings that we had got in them days, the parents would be fetched up for cruelty. My dad gave me a winger and he knocked me one from the front door to the back of the stairs with one clout. That was only for being a few minutes late and I was on the point of getting married.[12]

Disputes about coming in at night were much more common than disputes about religion or politics. Only a tiny minority of respondents rejected their parents' views on these matters, although more were likely to drift away from their parents' Church and/or political party during their lives. Within this tiny minority there were more men than women. A larger proportion than those who rejected religion were those who discovered a deep personal faith which replaced the social duty of their childhood church-going with a philosophy of life which in some cases was to support them until death. Mrs Chadwick, from Preston, who had attended Sunday School as a child, had not had a particularly religious upbringing. As a young worker, however, she developed a passionate interest in what might be called 'fringe' religious ideas. She studied Theosophy, went to revivalist meetings, attended a local group mysteriously called Masdazan (whose female leader Mother Mollie believed in reincarnation), and also loved the Salvation Army. From all this experimentation she developed her own faith, and says simply, 'Now I have a deep faith and that sustains me.'[13]

Mrs Pearce was born a Catholic, but brought up a Protestant by foster-parents. She returned to the Catholic Church when she was about eighteen (in 1917) after going back to her own extremely poor family:

I wanted to go back in that Church. All the others at home had communion cards with lovely coloured pictures of our Lord. The pictures were beautiful. I wanted one of those you know. . . . I had been baptised a Catholic so I didn't need to go through that business. I just had to be confirmed and taken into Church. A young lady in the next street asked me to go to the Rosary with her at night. I went with her nearly every night. . . . I got so involved in it. . . . She taught me the catechism and I got so involved with that. . . . When I went to be taken in the Church for confirmation the lady that stood for me asked me what name I was taking for confirmation. I said I thought I would take Mary. . . . I liked the lovely flowers, and the candles and the statues . . . that drew me more to the Catholic Church than anything else.

As she grew older, she gradually rejected most aspects of Catholicism — 'Statues don't appeal to me as I think they are false idols' — but she has retained a deeply felt faith in the will of God.[14]

Lack of financial and moral independence was also reflected in the young people's lack of choice about the sort of work they did. As we have seen, the sort of school education received, and whether or not children stayed on after the statutory minimum leaving age depended on family circumstances, and/or parental decisions. Choice of work was also very much influenced by parental advice, example or 'string-pulling', so that once they were working they frequently found themselves either directly under a relative, or someone well known to the family. There is evidence from the 1820s about the moral control exerted by older relatives and relatives' friends[15] but the tradition was just as strong in mills, factories and shipyards in the early part of the twentieth century. Perhaps the position of both boys and girls in the period between leaving school and getting married can best be described as one of semi-independence. As with so many aspects of working-class life, financial considerations predominated, binding the young worker very firmly to his family: 'Industrialisation and urbanisation were in fact tying young workers closer to their families. . . . Poverty and insecurity bound young and old together.'[16]

EMPLOYERS AND EMPLOYEES

Historians differ in their attitude to the relationships between employers and employees in the nineteenth and early twentieth centuries. On one hand are those who perceive working relationships in terms of class consciousness and class antagonism,[17] and on the other are those who see harmony and accord in the workplace.[18] It is perhaps simplistic but true to suggest that the state of workplace relationships depended on the interplay of several variables: notably time, place and the nature of both the workforce and the type of work carried out.

Calm working relationships were found in the Preston mills right up to the second world war. There were strikes in protest against pay reductions in the Depression of the early 1930s, but these were not major confrontations. They were widespread but short-lived and ineffectual, and wages continued to fall. Employer/employee relationships were also calm in Lancaster.[19] Barrow was quite different, however. Here class antagonism can be seen within the workplace, and the labour movement was both active and effective[20] from its very beginnings in the 1860s, at first in the craft unions, then through the Trades Council, and later through political action.

It is not my province to discuss the reasons for such differences, but it is important to note that they did exist, for they provide the background to the kind of work done by women in the three towns. Taking the three together, they provide evidence of both class antagonism and hierarchical deference, paternalism and co-operation.

As far as women workers were concerned, it was the latter model which was more usual. It is difficult to find evidence of much female militancy, of open antagonism to the system, or of a consistent struggle against it. Obedience to authority was an attitude inculcated in the family which was naturally extended to employers.[21] It was unlikely that at any time in this period working-class girls entered the world of work determined to challenge the authority of their employer. The majority of women in the sample, and indeed in all three towns, never went on strike, nor became involved in organised disputes or conflicts with their employers.

But we have also seen that it was rare for a working-class child to grow up cowed and spiritless. If and when the need arose authority, whether in the guise of the teacher or father, would be challenged. Young workers, if need be, were ready to challenge their employers. Indeed, while the documentary evidence and some of the oral testimony indicate much support for the concept of 'social calm', it can also be argued that the absence of organised disputes or solid class protest by women does not *necessarily* mean that women were always deferential, respectful or submissive. Many were at times, but it is also true that most of the respondents at some time resented their employers' attitudes, their wages and their working conditions. Their methods of resistance and/or of improving their lot were, however, individualistic and usually meant either a personal dispute or departure from their job and a search for alternative employment.

Girls who worked in small workshops, retail shops, or in domestic service displayed ambivalence to their work. Sometimes they liked their employers, and even if they did not, they felt unable to criticise them openly. Girls in domestic service simply found another job, and seemed to have little difficulty in so doing; girls apprenticed in shops or workshops were more inclined to establish a 'just' scheme of things by using the firm's time, materials or machines for their own ends. More abrasive relationships between employee and employer might exist in larger organisations, without the personal bonds which existed in smaller enterprises. Workers were more likely to see themselves as exploited, and to express themselves strongly. Mrs Stott, a very gentle, mild-mannered woman, became almost apoplectic about the behaviour of her former employer, Lord Ashton, whose title she refused to acknowledge:

You know old Jimmy Williamson was an old pig, and that's speaking. He was a millionaire, but he was an old pig.[22]

Her attitude was not uncommon, and illustrates the difficulties of constructing satisfactory analyses of such terms as 'deference' and 'paternalism' when confronted with the empirical evidence. Lord Ashton was the archetypal paternalistic employer, paying his labourers wages which were higher than labouring wages in the region, bestowing upon Lancaster a hospital, Town Hall and a splendid public park, and a huge memorial, reminiscent of the Taj Mahal. Some of his workers were grateful, dutiful and deferential; others were not. They resented his lavish spending on public works, arguing that he would have done better to have increased their wages: they resented too his attempt to control his workers' political affiliations. (He sacked socialists and active trade unionists; and employed a 'spy force'.[23]) Mrs Stott's vehemence against him arose because she believed she and her husband had been exploited in his factory. But there was only one way to show their disapproval: they found jobs with other employers.

Relationships in the cotton mills were constantly strained because of the system of piecework payment, rather than a fixed wage. Here the problem lay not so much between the worker and the mill owner, or even mill manager, but between the weaver and the overlookers or tacklers, the representatives of management with whom they were in daily contact. They were blamed if

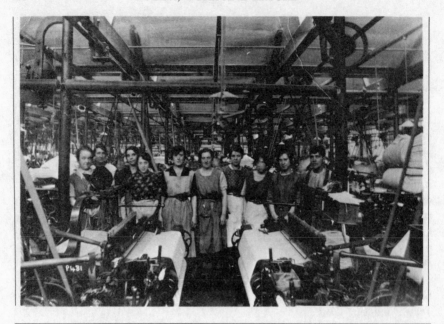

A group of weavers in the Century Mill, Preston, c. 1919.
(Harris Library, Preston)

new 'beams' did not arrive on time, or if the looms broke down, since this meant a loss of production and consequently a loss of wages. Young mill-workers would suffer at the hands of those training them, because their inexperience or inefficiency would in turn cost the skilled worker part of his wages.

Like their contemporaries in the workshops, factory girls got their own back by taking cloth for their own use. And some were bolder, directly confronting either their mistress or the overlooker. Mrs Burns worked in a Lancaster mill at the beginning of the century. She was an orphan, and had had a particularly hard childhood, growing up with various relatives in some very tough areas:

I did work hard and in them days if you'd a good Missus [an older weaver who trained young girls] you'd a good 'un but if you'd a bad one by hell you'd a bad one.

You'd the blinkin' sand roll. The sand roll is a sort of roll that is all prickly and it grips the stuff as it's coming round. I've been knocked against that roller many a time. She did it once too often and banged me against the sand roller and I picked the damn brush up what we swept the looms with and leathered her with it. She was a bad-tempered bitch.[24]

When Mrs Hill was fifteen, in the 1920s, she had a particularly bad-tempered overlooker:

He said, 'Thou has been a weaver long enough, thou should never tell a tackler what to do.' I said, 'No, they haven't the brains to take it in when you tell them.' I were nearly thumped in the eye for that, as near as I've ever been to being thumped. I said, 'It's that one, that cord top beam [part of a particular kind of loom].'. . . . He was noted for being a bad-tempered fellow and I thought, 'Well they've all cried and I'm getting nowhere, but I'm not going to cry.' So he fettled it [mended it] and he said, 'Thou hast said more to me than all my weavers put together.' I said, 'That's just the bloody trouble, they've spoiled thee.'[25]

The reason she gave for her determination to stand up to the tackler was the need for her wages at home.

However bad relationships were, it is significant how few respondents mention the strikes. Local press reports and union records show that in Preston in the Depression in the early 1930s, there were a number of strikes against the reduction of wages; but only one woman respondent talked about them. They were admittedly short-lived, and as it was common at that time to have compulsory weeks off work when there was no work to do, it would seem that periods of strikes and lockouts have become subsumed in the respondents' minds. Their basic deference, insecurity, their fear of losing respectability, but most of all their chronic poverty which drove them to work, all militated both against going on strike and remembering such an action even if they took part in it. Even Mrs Hill, the most militant woman interviewed in Preston, displayed an ambivalence towards strikes: she felt exploited, she had a burning sense of injustice about the wrongs suffered by her workmates, she collected funds for the union, and she did once strike, and yet she said,

If they got to know that you were in a union you were a bit harassed . . . you couldn't go on strike then, they just put somebody in your place. There weren't enough in the union. You had got to be able to weave good as they harassed you and if you wove bad cloth you were outside. They didn't give you any excuses.[26]

It was probably only the most militant, most politically conscious women who not only joined, but remembered with pride their part in a strike. Only Mrs Richardson was thus involved as a young worker. She started work at Barrow Jute Works when she was twelve in 1901, and left when she was seventeen to keep house for her family. Later she became politically active as a founder member of the local Communist Party.[27] It could be argued that her more abrasive attitude is a reflection of the generally abrasive labour relations existing in Barrow, especially in the pre-first world war period.

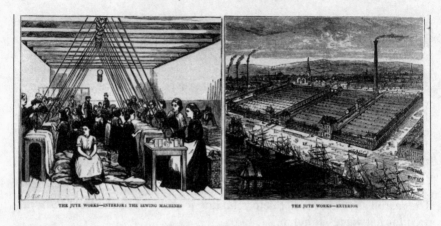

THE JUTE WORKS—INTERIOR: THE SEWING MACHINES   THE JUTE WORKS—EXTERIOR

Barrow Jute Works, the principal industrial employer of women in the town in the last quarter of the nineteenth century. There were several industrial disputes between the women and management.
(Barrow Library)

It is easier to understand the passivity of the great majority than the militancy of the minority, but the minority do have some traits in common. Almost all came from relatively prosperous backgrounds and had higher aspirations about their standard of living, and the quality of life, than their poorer contemporaries; they expected good meals, adequate clothing, and a chance to be educated. They were appalled when they realised that many of their fellow citizens did not enjoy the standards they themselves took for granted, and were determined to help produce improvements in their material standards of living. Those like Mrs Richardson who were militant at work were only able to be so if in fact they worked in an industry or for a firm where there was a tradition of militancy. This was true of the Barrow Jute Works, which had a history of strikes by its women workers. The earliest was in 1877,[28] with another in 1884, when striking women felt confident enough of their case to write about it to the local newspaper.[29] These brave activists in both industrial and political affairs are worthy of special study, but it should not be forgotten that, interesting and important as they are, they remained a tiny minority.

Non-militant attitudes to working conditions were widespread. Edward Cadbury, in his study *Women's Work and Wages* published in 1906, comments on 'the generally uncomplaining nature of factory girls', afraid of their employers, and generally accepting their working conditions.[30] Standish Meacham, after describing the good nature and high spirits of factory girls (behaviour and attitudes not always apparent in the oral evidence), went on to suggest that 'only occasionally did this general high-spirited bonhomie translate itself into an *esprit de corps* both tight enough and militant enough to produce concentrated campaigns for improved wages and working conditions.'[31]

THE WORK ETHIC

As we have seen, working-class children were brought up in the belief that not only was hard work vitally necessary for the survival of both the individual and the family, but that work had an intrinsic *moral* value. Therefore those who did not work carried the stigma of being idlers, or good-for-nothings. Children learned too, from both home and school, that it was essential to do a job to the best of one's ability.

Young adults, both male and female, had to accept and live by the financial

Girl munitions workers in the first world war. Very few respondents did this work for long, finding it hard and in some cases dangerous. Those who persevered found themselves doing highly skilled jobs and being very well paid. The jobs, opportunities and wages disappeared with the ending of the war.
(Barrow Library)

and the moral imperatives to work. But they tended to divide into two groups. On the one hand were those who took a pride in their work and in the product of their labour, and who on the whole found some enjoyment and satisfaction in it. This was especially notable in those doing skilled work, such as dressmaking, tailoring or fancy weaving. On the other hand, there was a group who disliked their working conditions, and/or their employers, and/or the type of work itself. Nevertheless, they display an obvious pride in their own endurance, their capacity for hard work, and their ability to earn money:

My sister was only saying the other day, 'Haven't we been awful!' because I have gone out cleaning. She said, 'Haven't we been daft, what have we done.' I have had to do it, I've had to go out cleaning when my kids were young. I have been a widow for twenty years. My husband was only a labourer, an outdoor labourer. So when it was raining he had to come home.[32]

Nowhere in the sample is there any evidence of the kind found by Luisa Paserini in Turin, of a refusal to do any form of work, which she argues stems from a loss of meaning in work.[33] Only one woman in the sample is recorded as giving up *all* work before a 'normal' retiring age. Deserted, and then widowed, she had spent her days as a hawker and cleaner. When her children were all in work, she not only gave up hawking, but housework too:

My mother said when I was fourteen, 'That's it, I'm not doing any more work.' She had had a hard life as she had gone out cleaning. Me and my sister used to do the work between us, the housework. I was the youngest and the boys had started work and then my sisters. I was the last so she didn't need to do as she relied on our wages altogether.[34]

All respondents when young, and many until old age, subscribed to one of the two work ideologies described; but some women, as they grew older, realised that although working was praised by all classes of society, it was not practised by everybody. Women who could afford not to work stayed at home and were 'ladies'. It thus increasingly became the ambition of socially aspiring working-class women to stay at home, sometimes before marriage but more especially afterwards, and be 'ladies of leisure'. The nearest most working-class women got to their goal was to stay at home after marriage, and not to have to earn money. But very few were freed from housework. They now display an ambivalent attitude towards work. They are proud of their own efforts as wage-earners while young, and of their housekeeping skills in marriage, but cannot understand their own daughters' wish to pursue a career *after* marriage: 'I said, "I never thought I would bring my children up to work as hard as they do. They all go out to work and I brought you all up as little ladies!" People used to think that.'[35]

YOUNG WOMEN AT WORK

Training

Before the first world war, there was a mass of literature about the problems of declining standards of living, loss of apprenticeships, and dead-end jobs.[36] The problems continued after the war, with hundreds of thousands of youths from poor homes attracted into unskilled jobs with initially high wages (as compared to those earned by an apprentice), but with no prospects.[37]

Reformers were much less concerned about the recruitment and training of girls, as the universal assumption was that a decade or so after leaving school they would marry, give up work, and raise a family,[38] a view shared by the great majority of the respondents and their families. Consequently both training and ambition in a career for girls were discounted. Mrs Peters, having started her working life as a weaver, was promoted to being a clerk at Lune Mills during the first world war. As her husband remarked: 'There were no females in the general office at Lune Mills until the war.'

You worked at Lune Mills, didn't you, in the war?
Yes, yes I was down there.
And you lost your job afterwards?
After the men came back. . . . Yes. . . .
Did you accept that, or did it bother you at the time?
No. Well I knew I was engaged to be married and . . . you see in those days as soon as you were going to be married you left a job. You knew you were going to be a housekeeper and be at home all the time. . . . That's the only thing we girls had to look forward to . . . getting married and sort of being on our own, and getting our bottom-drawer together and various things like that. Yes, that was the ambition of girls then.[39]

A few girls did, however, receive a training or served an apprenticeship after leaving school; and some achieved a white-collar job without training. In all three towns, out of a total of eighty-two female respondents, two became teachers (one as a pupil-teacher, one untrained), six clerks or secretaries (one with training), six tailoresses or dressmakers, with an appropriate apprenticeship or training, and two confectioners. Of the rest (apart from the girl who became a drummer) all did one of three jobs: they became domestic servants, shop assistants or factory workers (almost inevitably in textiles). But within each of these categories there were many variations, with differing work conditions, rates of pay, and of course status (see appendix 2).

Domestic service

Statistically, as appendix 2 illustrates, there was no decline in the overall percentage of women workers in domestic service in all three towns between 1890 and 1940. However, domestic service seems to have lost status in the eyes of some working women, and this may account for the decline in numbers of domestic servants among the respondents. Within the sample, far more mothers were living-in domestic servants in prosperous households than were their daughters. These older women appear to have had an ambivalent attitude to their work. In Barrow and Lancaster service with a wealthy, upper-class family undoubtedly gave a working woman status. Mr Fields suggested that girls who had been in service were much sought-after as brides:

It was a good thing to have the experience of being in service because a man would more readily marry a girl who was domesticated in that way than a girl who knew nothing about it.[40]

Mrs Winder remembered visits from her mother's old fellow workers, and the boost to the family's status this particular visit brought in their neighbourhood:

She was in a big house near Blackburn where they had about seven of a staff, so this would be the higher class sort of service, and they all kept their own job. I can remember . . . them coming to Aberdeen Road. The mistress allowed them to have the Rolls Royce, and the whole staff came . . . they came round for tea. Well all the kids in Moorlands got round that Rolls Royce, it wasn't safe! I mean to see a car come up there was an occasion, but to be a Rolls Royce, it was absolutely out of this world.[41]

As well as gaining status, the 'higher class' domestic servant acquired aspirations of her own: her children were to be brought up as similarly as possible to those of the family in which she had served. Particular attention was paid to table manners, or the arrangement and setting of the table. An element of social snobbery was clearly visible; rough children were to be

Elsie, a maid in service in Knutsford, 1924. Elsie was brought up in an orphanage and went straight from there into service.
(Manchester Studies, Manchester Polytechnic)

avoided, neighbours kept at a distance, and in one family, where lodgers were taken in, they had to eat at a separate table from the family. This group of women did *not* send their own daughters into domestic service: Mr Field's mother, who had been a maid for the Gladstones in 10 Downing Street, insisted that her own two daughters worked in an embroidery shop (an establishment of high social status among the working class). Mrs Winder's mother sent one daughter to be an apprentice dressmaker, and another into a high-class grocer's shop. Mrs Hewitson (whose mother segregated the lodgers) gave all her children the chance of an education at the Higher Grade School, and insisted that both her daughters were trained. Mrs Hewitson herself became a dressmaker. These are only examples, from a long list of such families.

Respondents who became domestic servants do not appear to have expected or received the status which their mothers' generation had experienced. They were more likely to change their jobs than were other girls, moving either to a different domestic post, or to a job with more status like shopwork, or more money like factory work. Only very occasionally did girls move from other jobs into domestic work before marriage; in fact, only one was discovered in the sample.[42] (The question of part-time domestic work for married women is different, and is examined in chapter 4.)

It is worth emphasising that the term 'domestic service' covered a very wide range of jobs, for there was obviously a very great difference both in social status and in actual work done between being a parlour maid in Downing Street and a part-time cleaner in a pub.

Some observers, like C. V. Butler in 1912, have suggested that country girls were more inclined to go into service than were town girls,[43] and certainly, the vast majority of respondents' mothers who were domestic servants were originally from the countryside. But in Barrow in the *later* part of the period, where there was a shortage of paid work for women, all the respondents who went into service were born and grew up in the town.

Only one respondent, Mrs Woodburn, was a living-in servant in a large house with a sizeable staff. Interestingly, like so many domestic servants in the earlier part of the period, that is the 1890s, she was a country girl living in one of the iron-mining villages near Barrow. She was recruited in Barrow by an agent, and went to work first as a kitchen maid, and later as a housemaid for a branch of the Storey family in Lancaster. The house had approximately forty rooms, and a staff of fourteen, in the charge of a German butler. At the age of thirteen, she started in the kitchen cleaning pans, and getting up at 4 a.m. to clean out the huge range before the cook got up. Indeed, the work was so hard that she became ill and had to be sent home to recover. After her return she was promoted to housemaid, and enjoyed life much more.

There were many things Mrs Woodburn remembered with pleasure — the elegance of the house, the kindness of the mistress, the new uniforms the maids were given for a family wedding:

We were all dressed in grey, lovely silver grey, shiny like alpaca, in them days, nice plain pinnies, no lace, but happen a lot of tucks round the bottom.

The food was good and plentiful. She particularly enjoyed the annual visit made by the whole household to the family's country house in North Wales:

Well everybody mucked in up there, you weren't as strict like, you could muck about and go out on the hills and sing . . . or have a cup of tea. . . .

Mrs Woodburn, who gives perhaps the most enthusiastic account of domestic service,[44] frequently mentioned her friendship and feeling of companionship with the other girls; there was none of the feeling of loneliness and isolation sometimes complained about by domestic servants in small households where they might be the only servant.

Mrs Armstrong's experiences were somewhat different. Both Lancaster and Ulverston (eight miles from Barrow) had twice-yearly hiring fairs,[45] when men and women seeking both outdoor and indoor farm work stood or walked round a certain specified area until approached and hired by a farmer seeking labourers. The hired man or woman was then contracted for a six-month period of work. They received their board and lodging for that period but no wages until the six months were over (indeed if they left before their six-month term their wages were forfeited):

We went to farm service and we used to walk from here to Ulverston, wait till eleven o'clock till they started. The old farmers used to come up King Street and say, 'Is tha for hiring lass?' I used to say, 'Aye.' He'd say, 'What's tha asking?' We used to say, 'What are you going to give us?' 'I'll give you four pound ten.' We'd say, 'No thank you.' We used to walk on a bit farther down King Street and another farmer would come up and say, 'Is tha for hiring lass?' Perhaps we'd get five pound ten off him for the six month. He used to say, 'Can you wash, can you bake, can you scrub?'[46]

Mrs Armstrong shows some of the youthful independence already noted. The family were very poor, which perhaps explains not only her father's need to 'sub' (ask for in advance) her money, but also her mother's rather token resistance to her going to the hiring fair. For Rose, earning money was rather more important than school, but the conditions she experienced are a reminder of why so many middle-class observers wanted to keep children out of work and in school until they were rather older. She went to the hiring fair in 1905:

How old were you when you first went to the Hiring Fair?

I was thirteen and I told m'mother I was going to the Hiring Fair. She said, 'You can't, you're not fourteen.' I said, 'Tell the teacher I've gone to m'grandmother's,' and she told her I'd gone to m'grandmother's. Me and m'friend, both of us.

Where did you go to, where was the farm you went to?

Longridge in Preston.

Were you homesick at all?

We used to feel it, but what was the good? Then I went to Newland Bottom Cornmill at Ulverston and m'father used to come every Sunday and it was very hard times then. It was the Durham strike that was on then and he used to come and he used to ask the old farmer if he could sub a pound off Rose's money as they hadn't anything. He used to give him a pound. Probably when Martinmas come, time to come home, I'd hardly owt to come home to.

They paid you at the end of your six months, did they?

Yes. At the end of six months. . . . Now I've to tell you this bit. One Christmas I was at Longridge and Christmas Day come and I was a bit homesick, you know, and had our Christmas Day's dinner, I washed up and all that, and she said, 'Has tha finished now?' I said, 'Yes madam,' so she said, 'Well if thou get all that paper there, you'll see a lot of paper there and there's a big needle there and a ball of string, if you go down to the paddock [that was the toilet], sit there and take the scissors and cut some paper up and thread it for the lavatory.' And I sat there on Christmas Day and I think I cried a bucketful of tears. Christmas afternoon and I was sat . . . sitting cutting bits of paper, bits of paper like that and getting this big needle, threading them and tying knots in them and tying them on these hoops, till about half past four when I went in for m'tea. Sitting there on the lavatory seat.[47]

Rose did not stay long as an ordinary domestic servant, but progressed to being first an apprentice cook, later a 'proper' cook, and finally a housekeeper. Her life as a cook, however, was even more difficult than that as a cleaning girl, for she worked fourteen hours a day, six days a week and was paid 12s. 6d. per week.

At the lowest end of the domestic service labour market, in terms of status, was the daily cleaner, usually called a charwoman if adult and married, and a day cleaning girl if young and unmarried. Mrs Wilkinson started work in 1914:

I went as a day cleaning girl for twelve months. I was fourteen on the 5th August and a friend of our Edith's came down to see if I'd take her job over as a morning girl for Mrs Postlethwaite which m'mother said, 'Take.' I was only about fourteen and six days and I took the job and it was only three-and-six a week but I only worked mornings. . . . I used to do vegetables, and the rough cleaning. There was no hoover. . . . I'd to brush the carpets, and I'd to take the stair carpet on the lawn and drag it up and down the lawn. It was hard work for a girl of fourteen, and I didn't like it. . . . But I'd to stand outside on the bay window and all those tiny little windows I'd to clean every one of them with pan shine about once a month. It was pretty hard work. Anyway I was there until I was fifteen and a half. Oh, I came home, and I'd to chop firewood of course and I'd chop m'finger. M'father used to say, 'Bring it home and I'll chop it.' I'd chopped m'finger, and m'hands were chapped with cleaning these outsides, it was frosty weather. Oh, I was generally fed up. My hands were sore and I was tired and I probably didn't like the job anymore but I always liked Miss Postlethwaite, she was always very nice.[48]

Mrs Wilkinson subsequently became a shop assistant and stayed happily with the same firm until her marriage, when her employer compelled her to stop work.

Textile workers

The vast majority of Preston girls went straight from school into weaving.[49] Those who left before they were fourteen had to have a Labour Certificate. Written on each child's Certificate was the phrase that the exemption was 'for beneficial employment only'. (It would be interesting to know what would have been regarded as *un*beneficial employment.)

More girls appear to have disliked weaving, or indeed mill work in general, than to have liked it. Most disliked it when they started; some grew to enjoy it, others never did. It is astonishing that so many stood it as long as they did: their toleration can only be explained in terms of the structure of the labour market, and the overwhelming need their families had for their wages. Both Miss Ainsworth's parents were weavers, although her mother had stopped work after the birth of her third child. Miss Ainsworth started work in 1911:

I was happy somehow. . . . I was twelve and my mother was poorly just then. . . . I can remember going on cold mornings, a little shawl pinned on my head, stood waiting on the gates opening at quarter to six. They wouldn't do that today.

What did you think of the mill when you got inside?

I needed a job. When I went full-time from 6 on a Monday morning till 12 o'clock Saturday dinner-time, I got my full money, I got six shillings a week. You can say good old days or bad old days, I don't know what you would say. I was happy somehow.

Did you like the mill?

I hated it. It was a job.

What did you hate especially?

I don't know. I used to like going to school. I always did like sums and geography. I wish I could have stopped at school, but no, I had to go to work and that was that. As time went on, it was coloured, pyjamas and nightdresses and I couldn't see the coloured work. I got many a knock from the Missus as I passed a

flaw. They weren't happy days in the mill, not to me. I had to go and I went. . . .

Was it hot in the mill?

Oh yes. You kept wiping the perspiration off, and you daren't stop, there was no stopping.[50]

Miss Ainsworth remained a weaver until she retired at sixty.

Mrs Booth received her Labour Certificate when she was thirteen in 1913 and went as her sisters had done into the mill:

And you had a medical when you went into the mill?

You did. A doctor came but you were perhaps there three or four weeks when he arrived. All I remember was him looking in your hair. I don't remember anything else. He never sounded your chest or anything like that.

So you could have been quite unhealthy, really?

I was. I was always delicate.

Do you think the mill had a bad effect on your health?

It didn't have a good effect. I did have some happy hours there. I got to like it and the work was interesting.

Were you a tenter, when you first went?

Well a learner for three weeks, then you go as a tenter and oh, what you call your Missus, she was a bad 'un. Very religious, oh she was.

Was she nasty to you?

Yes, very nasty. Oh there were a lot like that and if you just did a little thing wrong some hadn't the patience to teach you. I can understand, I don't think I would have had the patience. They would give you a push and you had to stand at the corner of your alley, as they called it. Well as you stood there you'd see another one or two stood there.

So you were learning by watching what she was doing?

Yes, and they did teach you in their way to piece ends, as they called it, but she didn't teach me a great deal, unless it didn't go in, like I think I'd been a bit of a dreamer. I liked to think a lot instead of thinking what I should have been doing. I was thinking of other things. I must have been.

What were you paid for being a tenter?

Five-and-six full-time. Oh, and you had to sweep and clean and polish your looms and oil them. I can smell all the oil and on the floor they'd sand, like gritty sand, and Saturday dinner-time you spread all this sand and you had to go early before six and get it all swept away and the floor looked white then and you had to oil all the looms. Oh, I can smell that oil. I used to dread Monday mornings.

Because you went early Monday mornings to clean up before you started?

Yes. Well, you'd clean on a Saturday, then you'd spread this sand you see, so

---

Two young weavers before the first world war. The clogs and aprons were traditional, the hat denoted aspirations to smartness (more old-fashioned weavers wore a shawl over their heads). (Manchester Studies, Manchester Polytechnic)

you had got to get that swept up before your Missus came. Oh, sometimes I was terrified. I couldn't enjoy my Saturday night for thinking about Monday mornings. But when I went to this other mill, oh, it couldn't come fast enough, the difference you see.[51]

Mrs Calvert became a weaver at fourteen, in 1933. Like many of her predecessors she hated the work. She was trained by her older sister, who had got her the job. Family needs prevented her leaving until after her second marriage:

I hated it. I used to tell my mother and she would tell me there was no other work and I would have to stick it. I said, 'I will only stick it because you have asked me to, Mother. I would rather stop at home with you.' I would like to have gone into the gold thread works but there was a list then, because I was really good at embroidering and sewing. I never got a chance there. . . . I never took to weaving at all. The noise used to get on my nerves — clatter, clatter. The times I have been hit with a picking-stick. You would just be bending down, not thinking, and it would give you a wallop. I would never go back to weaving again. I said I would scrub floors first and by God I did. I scrubbed floors before I would ever go back in the weaving shed.[52]

Not all experiences in mill work were entirely negative though. Some respondents spoke warmly of the friendships made with other workers; others remember the celebrations when a worker got married, or at Christmas. The many happy memories, nevertheless, are outweighed by the unhappy ones.

Shop workers

Not only were there clear differences in status between various aspects of retailing (working in a shop being obviously 'higher class' than selling in the street), but there was a hierarchy in the category and site of the shops, too. Privately owned shops were 'better' than chain-stores; town-centre shops had higher status than corner-shops. Mrs Windor's experiences are given in detail, because she illustrates most of the attitudes, difficulties and working conditions described by the other shopworkers. Her employer was a member of the Church which her family attended, so he knew her before she was employed. This common background may have partly accounted for his close supervision of her life, not only inside the shop, but outside as well. He had a

---

Cunningham's greengrocer's, Salford. This dates from before 1914. It could well be a parlour shop, as it is obviously an ordinary house.
(Manchester Studies, Manchester Polytechnic)

puritanical dislike of dances and would seem to have been unhappy at the thought of anyone enjoying themselves. Perhaps the reason why Mrs Windor tolerated his behaviour as long as she did was the combination of the personal link with her family, and the prestige of the shop, which kept her there for ten years, from 1924 to 1934.

Woolworth's had just come into the town before I left school, but on principle I wouldn't work in Woolworth's. I could have been getting a lot more money than I was getting in the grocer's shop, but because it was a privately owned firm it was a little bit better. It was just snobbery because later on I said, 'Let's face it, you only go for money wherever you work.' . . . I started with four shillings a week and at the month end he increased it to six. I'd only been there a month, and they increased me to six and I liked it! . . . It was seven o'clock every night, and Saturday night it was eight o'clock. . . . In the morning I went at half past eight. After a Bank Holiday when you went on a Tuesday morning instead . . . of saying 'Have you had a nice weekend?' . . . you could guarantee that on the morning after a Bank Holiday he was scrubbing the counter and the minute you walked in you felt uncomfortable and guilty. You should have come early because you'd had a day off and he sulked. He always sulked if you'd had a holiday, and he always sulked if I went anywhere that he'd think I shouldn't go. If he found I was going out with any boys . . . he found all sorts of faults. Oh he was funny. I mean, he wanted to rule your life, and you were working and getting very little for it. . . . If he knew that I was going anywhere he used to find me all sorts of jobs. . . . I was invited to the Friends' School Christmas Party, and this was considered a great honour . . . the boss knew because I'd taken my dress [to the shop] to change. . . . We were working late, we used to weigh all the currants. Nothing came ready packed. He decided after tea that we would start packing currants, and he set me off filling the top shelves, and I tried not to let him see me, but I was actually crying. The dance finished at ten o'clock, and I arrived at a quarter to ten. The shop officially closed at seven but he didn't think I should go. . . . He insisted on me wearing black stockings. I mean absolutely ridiculous . . . he bought me some, didn't reckon anything to these silk stockings. . . . M'mother said, 'Well you will have to wear them because he wants you to wear them.' . . . I used to be ashamed to go to work in these black stockings.[53]

After ten years of these conditions Mrs Windor decided to look for another job. The final straw came when her employer arbitrarily decided one Monday that she was to have a week's holiday without pay (although she had already worked the Monday), and then complained because she did not turn up for work on the Saturday!

Apprenticeships

Girls who served apprenticeships certainly learned a trade, but at a considerable cost, both financially and in terms of their health. Their earnings (if any) were likely to be considerably less than a weaver's, which may well account for only one girl in the Preston sample taking an apprenticeship. The long-term advantage was that girls gained a skill which they appear to have enjoyed using, and which enabled them to make money for themselves in later life. All six dressmakers and tailoresses augmented their family income by taking in sewing, as well as making considerable savings by making their family's clothes.

Being a confectioner was regarded as a health risk:

I wanted to be a confectioner, but the doctor put his foot down and said that I wasn't strong enough for the long time that I'd have to work.[54]

I went to serve my time as a confectioner, and I had to give it up because I wasn't strong enough. The heat. . . .[55]

Only Mrs Austin, who started work in 1921, succeeded in completing her confectionery apprenticeship:

Well, I was interested in confectionery, and m'mother knew someone that worked there and said that if I was interested I could go and try it. I did like it but it took me a while. It didn't agree with me at first, the first six months that I was there it used to make me bilious, but afterwards I settled down. . . . I got used to it and I really did enjoy it. . . . I still enjoy cooking.

He [the employer] politely told me when I started that I was the first apprentice he had paid. . . . They'd always had to work twelve months for nothing. When I'd been there twelve months I got five shillings, but he had a bad season so reduced everybody's wages, and he reduced my wages back to half a crown for another twelve months.

What hours did you work?

From six in the morning to six at night.

What time did you have off?

Only for breakfast. We got our food there. Later on he gave over giving us our food.

He charged you for it?

We could make tea when we wanted, because he wasn't always on our back.

We made cakes . . . we had a hot-plate that you used to do crumpets and muffins and scotch pancakes every morning.[56]

Hours and conditions of work for girl apprentices improved throughout the period, but can hardly be said to have changed out of all recognition. Mrs Hewitson became an apprentice dressmaker in Barrow in 1898 when she was thirteen:

I served two years with a lady who was m'Sunday school teacher. And I was so timid in those days that that was the only reason I went to work for her because I would have been afraid of anybody else.

When you went to work, what hours did you work?

From half past eight in a morning to eight o'clock at night . . . with an hour for dinner and half an hour for tea. . . . I used to go home for dinner and I'd run home for m'tea. We never had Saturday, we had Thursday afternoon. We'd all the work to finish on a Saturday to be sent out.

What would your first wage be?

Ten shillings a week. It was an average wage. In the workroom where I'd served my time we had twelve or sometimes fourteen apprentices all working for nothing, and one paid hand and she got ten shillings a week.

But you weren't paid as an apprentice?

Oh no. I served two and half years before I got my ten shillings. I've often thought about it after, when I grew up. This one was responsible for everything going out perfect for ten bob a week.

Were you paid for holidays?

We never had any holidays.

Not a fortnight in summer or anything?

Oh no. You had Bank holidays, of course.

Did you do it all by hand, or by sewing-machine?

Sewing-machine. But more was done by hand then. All the finishing work was done by hand. There was a lot of hand-work and in those days linings were all tacked in and seamed in. We'd a lot of tacking and that carry-on to do. All skirts had braid and binding in them. Sometimes we'd four times to go round a skirt — the hem and then there was a binding. You ran that on all the way round the skirt and then turned it over to hem it in. That was three times round the skirt. Then they used to be six or seven yards wide a skirt, so you'd a bit of sewing to do.

I suppose you all did a different bit, or did one person work on one dress?

No, you got different bits to do. The things that you learned when you went was to do over-casting. All seams in skirts, all seams in bodices were over-sewn and you learned to do that. You learned to tidy the workroom every morning. The youngest apprentices did that. Look after the fire. One week it was your fire week another one it was your iron week, keeping the irons hot. Then you'd learn to tack skirts out, tack them onto the lining and cut lining to match and then you learnt to put them into the belts and turn the bottoms up. It went on through stage and stage. It took two and half years to learn it all.

After that there was a very high class dressmaker and m'father got me in as an improver. . . . He used to deliver to this shop and it was a shop that had nothing in the window but a piece of material and perhaps a pair of gloves, it was a very posh shop . . . Madam had worked for Worths in Paris. She came from London and brought her milliner with her. . . . I learnt tailoring and to work with fur.

Every gown was estimated and then she made it. It was a certain price and if you wanted a little bit of something extra done you paid extra. Most dresses were silk-lined, we used to say that Mrs Thompson's dresses would stand alone. . . . They might have been fifteen or twenty guineas then. Ordinary people couldn't have gone there.

How much would the hats be?

Oh, gosh. Madam used to go to London when the Paris fashions came, and she bought pattern hats and she paid guineas for the pattern hats that nobody else could make one like it. Our girls used to make them on wire frames — they used to make them for us as well when nobody was looking![57]

Mrs Saunders became an apprentice tailoress thirty years after Mrs Hewitson, in 1928. Hours were shorter, wages were about one-third higher (wages for labourers had doubled in the same period). The practice of piecework, however, meant that there was rather more pressure on Mrs Saunders than there had been on Mrs Hewitson:

And you didn't want to go in the mill?

No, my mother didn't want me to go in the mill. So at fourteen I went to Andrew McNeill's to learn to tailor.

Were there many girls doing tailoring, or was it mostly men?

The men did the pressing and the cutting and the trimming but it was all ladies. Even the overseer was a very austere, tall, slim lady, Miss Rainford. Everyone was terrified of her, but I was the odd one out. There's always an odd one, isn't there?

Weren't you frightened of her?

Not at all. She went to the same church as I did and I thought there was a protection for me somewhere along the line. I thought I was in the Sunday School and, you know. . . . There were two apprentices at the time and we were both the same age and we started together. Mabel was terrified of her as she was a timid type and I sort of looked after her.

What did you start off doing as a tailor?

The sweeping-up, really, and tidying-up and carrying clothes over my arm down Grimshaw Street. . . . In those days we had a big Irish contingency in Preston and they wore moleskins and they were very tough, tougher than what we termed fustian, what we call cord, but the moleskins were really tough. Then I started basting the garment for try-on and I didn't get any money for, perhaps, two years.

Nothing at all?

No. Then I got six shillings and then I went on the piecework when I had been there about five years. For a button-hole in a man's vest — it was all done by hand, I was a handsewer, I didn't ever do any machining — for a button-hole in a man's vest it was three farthings, and for a button-hole in a jacket it was a penny-farthing and perhaps twopence for an overcoat button-hole. I must have done thousands of button-holes before ever I was allowed to put one in a garment. We did little pieces of cloth. We had to put canvas between to do it properly. I was always making these button-holes. There was a piece of gimp [silk or worsted twist with a wire running through it] went round it to strengthen it and we punched a hole in it. I used to bring them home and show my mother. She tackled Miss Rainford at church one Sunday and said, 'Dorothy's button-holes are beautiful. Why can't you let her put them in a garment? A little bit of encouragement would go a long way. You never encourage the girls.' Anyway, eventually, I did get to put them in. The first man's vest I punched these five button-holes and a button-hole for the watch guard and I put them in the wrong side.

How awful!

Wasn't it. One of the girls told me to put it on one side and she was a machinist and she said she would rectify it for me when Miss Rainford went for lunch. She let the lining out and chopped half an inch off all the way round and Miss Rainford never found out.

But how many could you do in an hour?

I suppose you could do a button-hole within five minutes when you were proficient.

You still wouldn't be earning very much?

The first week I went home when I went on piecework, I remember running all the way home with fifteen shillings.

You must have worked very hard for that?

I had to do. We started at 8 o'clock until half past five. We worked Saturday mornings and we never knew when we were going to finish. I had to stand there until this Miss Rainford passed everything and pulled little bits of white out. Many times it was quarter past two before we got the last load down to the shop. There was no grumbling, really, because you hadn't to grumble.[58]

As in many workshops the girls got their own back to a small extent by using the firm's machines (but their own time and materials) to make blouses for themselves and trousers for their boyfriends.

LEISURE

The young workers' life was not all work, and it is to their youth that the respondents look back with most nostalgia when discussing leisure. We have already seen that they were not free to do as they liked, but this lack of independence also carried with it a comparative lack of responsibilities; they were on the whole freer from household and family chores than they had been as children — and would later be, whether as wives or mothers, or the housekeepers and nurses of elderly relatives. Although on a very limited budget and with long working hours, they were able to enjoy a variety of leisure-time occupations — dancing, going to the cinema, country walks — as well as those social activities enjoyed in childhood and often connected with the Church.

Dancing was not only enjoyed, but taken quite seriously, many regarding it as another skill to be acquired: it was not unusual for working girls to have dancing lessons. Miss Hunter is speaking of the late 1890s:

I used to go through the week to the learners, the Phoenix Rooms, that was on Tuesday and Thursday, but you had to pay for it.

What were the dances like you went to?

They were lovely. You couldn't go without an invite — an invitation. Nearly all the shopkeepers had one and then there was the Conservative Club. . . . You used to go for about a shilling.

What kind of dances would you do?

Waltzing, polkas, lancers [a kind of quadrille]. There used to be another where you all marched round and changed partners. Oh, they used to be nice. . . . Of course m'dad wouldn't let me go to any, not any sort. I never went without asking. . . . It used to start about eight and then there was supper about ten or eleven and then they used to dance until about two. The first dance I ever went to I had a dress. Oh, it was nice, and I had a taxi.[59]

Staying up as late as this was very unusual for girls in general, and obviously a great event for Miss Hunter.

Dancing, already very popular before the first world war, became almost a mania in the 1920s, with a proliferation of dance halls, and the increasing tendency for firms, organisations, clubs and churches to hold dances in whatever premises were available. It was common for girls to go to at least

Life was not all work. Watching the Pierrots, especially before 1914, was very popular. It was also free unless one felt obliged to put something in the circulating hat. (Barrow Library)

two dances a week. However, whatever wild behaviour may or may not have occurred at the dances of the wealthy 'bright young things' in the 1920s and 1930s, working-class dances were very strictly controlled. The different denominations varied in their attitudes to dances. Some older nonconformists totally rejected them, and this led to accusations by the younger generation, both male and female, of 'Victorian hypocrisy'. As a result some transferred their allegiance to more liberal churches. None gives their Church's rejection of dances as a reason for leaving the Church altogether.

Mrs Winder was (and is) a member of the local Congregational Church (now the United Reform Church), like her employer. She had a more questioning attitude to the authority figures of her world than had a previous generation, but like her contemporaries this questioning very rarely developed into open defiance:

This was the thing, this boss of mine, I used to say to him he thought that dancing was an excuse for somebody else's husband to put his arms round you, but you know he used to go practically every Wednesday night to the theatre, and he always sat on the front row. As I got older, I suppose I was considered to be very cheeky, I used to say to him, 'Well it is not half as bad as going to the theatre sitting on the front row when they're kicking their legs up. To me that is far worse.' 'Oh, nothing of the sort.' He liked the front row because it was cooler, and that was his tale and he was sticking to it. I mean, he never took his wife. No, he never took his wife. Just went on his own and sat on the front row and that was all right.[60]

Other churches accepted the need to hold dances for the young, presumably believing that it was better for the young people to meet those of the same denomination or sect under controlled circumstances than those of a different one without authority present. There were always certain rules and restrictions made at church dances, as Mrs McLeod, growing up in the 1920s, recalls. She went to the dances at two local churches:

I can always remember that the vicar insisted that they had three or four games at least. The vicar would never dance, but he was always there. . . . They always had the Grand March to start off with, and they'd have the Grand Old Duke of York. . . . They used to get all these in in the early part of the evening and then the vicar would go home when he thought they were doing all right. Then, of course, as soon as the vicar went the games were finished, it was all dancing. . . . It was, 'Please keep the ladies on their feet in the lancers.'

(It is interesting to note that despite the new dances of the 1920s young people were still doing the lancers at this time.)

The neighbouring Church of England also had its carefully controlled dances:

They used to run a dance on a Tuesday night just for church people and the vicar would sit on the door and see that it was just church people that went. There wasn't any Tom, Dick, or Harry could get in. If he didn't like the way you were dancing he told you so. . . . I can remember one lad getting into trouble one night because he was holding a lass round her bottom, and the vicar objected to the way he was holding her.[61]

Public dances were just as strictly controlled. Mrs Mulholland's brother organised dances in Barrow both during and after the first world war:

My brother's dances, Monday, Tuesday, Thursday, Saturday afternoon and Saturday night, and that was all the time during the war. He used to run them in the Town Hall. M'brother was most strict, terrible, they had to dance so far apart. He wouldn't let them dance cheek-to-cheek. He'd separate them if they were too close, and say, 'That is enough.' And they knew.
What kind of dances did they do?
The old-fashioned ones — waltzing, lancers, quadrilles, veleta. The new dances I demonstrated were the Boston Two-Step, the Military Two-Step, and the King's Waltz. I didn't do much with the Charleston, it came along later. M'brother was a bit old-fashioned.[62]

Dances were an important meeting-place for young men and women — an assumption made by the dancers themselves, their parents, church officials, masters of ceremonies, and dance promoters alike. But the fear of uncontrolled sexual behaviour was ever-present, and explains both the tight regulations governing the dances and why working-class girls were allowed to go to them. It was preferable to meet young men in such a public and controlled environment than in a secret and potentially dangerous one. Coming home from the dances could still expose a girl to risk, and families coped with this in different ways. Some girls were brought home by a relative — an older brother or sister, or even a parent:

You would go to a dance and I had always to come home before it finished. You would come out of the dance hall which was only just round the corner from where I lived and you would see three or four or five mothers all waiting for their daughters coming out.[63]

It was also true that many girls managed to find ways of walking home with their young men unsupervised.
There were, of course, other ways for boys and girls to meet. All three towns, in common with many others, accepted 'promenading', when, at an appointed time at the weekend, groups of young men and women paraded up and down hoping to catch someone's eye.[64] 'Having no place other than the streets and public houses to carry on their acquaintance rituals, young lovers

developed the seasonal custom of promenading in large groups. On summer nights the streets of both large and small English towns were crowded with young people until 10 o'clock or so.'[65] Locally, there appears to have been no 'season' for promenading, nor do any but a very few mention courting in a public house, these on the whole being mostly for men and a small number of bolder older women.

Promenading continued until the end of the period. On the whole, it was approved of by adults because it was so public that again behaviour was strictly controlled. Both these Preston respondents are discussing promenading in the inter-war years. Mr Foster describes the 1920s, and Mrs Bridges the 1930s:

You had walks, you have the famous walk in Fishergate, what we called 'getting off'. . . . We hadn't the vocabulary that they have today you know. We had to do it in a more roundabout way. Sometimes it would take you about a month, four Saturday nights and four Sunday nights, to pluck up courage to even speak to her. . . . It would depend if she looked at you, you know. I mean if she looked at you you were quids in because you thought, well, she would like a bit of interest. But they were never long lasting, you would speak to them, you would take them out, but you couldn't afford to take them to the pictures or anything like that. You couldn't buy them chocolates. If you had a few toffees you used to share them with them.[66]

If a boy saw you, would he come up and speak to you?
  They would keep turning round and sometimes they would do a quick turn so we hadn't seen them and walk behind us. Then they would come and ask us to go on the park. Not sex, that was out and that was all private. Even in them days if you were seen with a soldier you were a soldier's Moll, and that was during the war. I didn't know what sex was until I got married.[67]

COURTING AND PRE-MARITAL PREGNANCY

Casual relationships could, of course, develop into more serious ones, and when a couple were judged to be courting the young man or woman would be taken home to meet the parents. Mrs Warburton gave this account of her courting days in the early years of this century:

When you were courting you'd still to be in at nine o'clock?
  Yes. Oh aye, if we were at the door you'd hear m'father tap the other door, nine o'clock.
  He didn't ever come out and say, 'Come in'?
  No. Then, of course, when we'd been courting two or three years, he said, 'Why don't you fetch Eddie in?' 'Oh,' I said, 'I'll ask him if he'll come in.'

Anyway, he came in and father just looked at him and said, 'Hello Eddie, how are you?' I was over the moon. I thought, oh this is it. We courted nine years.[68]

A courtship of this length was unusual, but courting for a few years was not. Not only were lengthy courtships an indication of the priority given to sustaining the family budget by working children; they were also an indication of the strict sexual self-control exercised by the great majority of young couples.

Serious courting could and did take place in the home, especially in Barrow and Lancaster where there were many more working-class homes with parlours. But even here there were strict limits and controls:

Half past seven we had to be in. And when I was courting Reg, it was half past nine. We used to go into the parlour when Reg and I were courting and about half past nine they used to give Reg a cup of tea and m'dad would get the alarm clock off the mantelpiece and wind it, he was ready for bed and that was a good hint for Reg to go. He had to go then. He used to get the clock off and wind it up. They weren't terribly strict, but perhaps I think we obeyed them better than children do nowadays.[69]

There can be little doubt that one of the reasons for the almost total reticence on the part of parents in discussing sexual matters with their children, and for their subsequent strict control of the encounters between boys and girls, was their great fear of pre-marital sex, with the risk of conception. In all families in the sample there was unanimous condemnation of sex outside marriage although the vehemence of the condemnation varied considerably.

It is clear that keeping out of 'trouble' was a much more serious preoccupation of both parents and young people than was the fear of marrying 'out' of their religion. Both Lancaster and Barrow had significant Roman Catholic minorities, while Preston had a very substantial one — some descended from the large body of Lancashire recusants, others from Irish immigrants. Derek Thompson found that in Preston: 'Religious bigotry cut down the number of possible marriage partners considerably, and if the Catholic church had more *official* sanctions against mixed marriages than the Protestant churches, everyone is agreed that the *unofficial* sanctions of the Protestant churches were just as effective, and that both Catholics and Protestants were equally bigoted.'[70] His assertions are supported by Mr Sharples, who came from a devoutly Catholic family in Preston and who married in 1943:

It was simply taken for granted that it was your duty to marry a Catholic. . . . I just knew that mother would have been desperately unhappy if I had married anyone other than a Catholic. The thought never entered my mind.[71]

Mrs Dobson, an Anglican, was married in 1930. Her fiancé was a Roman Catholic. She agreed initially to be prepared for admission to the Catholic Church.

I went as far as having instruction to turn a Catholic to save peace. They had priests in the family and they had Sisters in the family, and a Mother Superior . . . and they wanted a born Catholic. . . . They led me a life like a dog they were so bitter. . . . They wanted a born Catholic.
    Did you get married in the Catholic Church?
    No, he finished with his religion. He said he wasn't going to spoil his life. His family wanted him to marry somebody else who was a Catholic. He wouldn't do.

Her husband was killed in a road accident shortly after their marriage and his posthumous child was brought up as an Anglican. There were very few contacts with the husband's family.[72] These cases illustrate the difficulties that could arise over religion, but they are fairly rare. What is striking from the oral testimony, is the relative absence of religious bigotry; indeed, more positively, there was a considerable degree of religious tolerance, if not by the Churches, then certainly by the individual members of the working class. Undoubtedly, though, most parents preferred their children to marry within their own denomination, which explains the importance of the local Church's social activities for the young, and the majority of respondents and their parents did indeed marry within their own denomination.
    In the minority of cases, where a Catholic married a Protestant, it might have been expected that in view of the strict teaching of the Roman Catholic Church on mixed marriages, the non-Catholics would have converted to Catholicism, and this was indeed the more usual pattern in the small number of inter-faith marriages in Barrow and Lancaster. One respondent's parent from Barrow and two from Lancaster converted to Catholicism on marriage, as did one Barrovian and two Lancastrian respondents.[73] The position in Preston, with its large Catholic minority, was surprisingly different, certainly as far as the sample was concerned. With such large numbers of Roman Catholics it was to be expected that there would be statistically more chance of a non-Catholic meeting and marrying a Catholic than in the other two towns. What has proved surprising is the number of conversions out of Catholicism, rather than into it. Four Preston respondents came from mixed marriages; in three Roman Catholic women converted to Protestantism, and in the fourth the mother became a Catholic.[74] Three Catholic respondents married non-Catholics and became either Protestants or agnostics;[75] two Protestant respondents married Catholics who converted to Protestantism.[76]
    We have already seen that parents were much more preoccupied and anxious about the prevention of pre-marital sex than about their children's

religious beliefs. If, however, despite all the controls, warnings, threats, and the best efforts of parents, priests, vicars and relatives, pre-marital sex did take place and resulted in pregnancy, then both parental attitudes and those of the girl herself varied very considerably.[77] It is impossible, of course, to make any estimate of the number of couples either in the sample or known to respondents who had pre-marital sex. Not surprisingly, there is very considerable reticence on this subject. The number of cases discussed is therefore very small, too small to make possible any analysis of the responses to this family problem. All the same, changes over time, parental occupation, geographical location and religious affiliations, do not appear to account for the considerable differences in attitude.

It is possible to discern some differences between Barrow and Lancaster on the one hand, and Preston on the other. Much more emphasis has been laid in the former towns on the joint responsibility of boys and girls to follow the prescribed patterns of sexual behaviour: there was not the double standard of sexual morality placing the blame for pre-marital sex solely on the girl. Mr King, when asked if his parents minded whom he married (the question having the intention of discovering any religious bias), replied: 'My mother didn't bother who I married so long as I didn't bring any trouble home, get any girl into trouble, and that was the only thing she was bothered about.'[78] Another man remarked that the least a man could do who had made a girl pregnant, if he was unable to marry her, was to emigrate.[79] Mrs Metcalfe expressed a common view of the need for young men to 'behave' themselves. (She is also not unusual in discussing sex without once mentioning the word.) Her evidence relates to the 1930s.

I've seven brothers and there wasn't one had to be married. I mean they'd know, you know.
Your father . . . used to tell them about it, did he?
He'd have killed them. No, I mustn't say that, he must have told them and he would have mur—. You know, he would have seen there'd have been no shenanigans. There wouldn't have been no flying their kites and then changing their minds. They'd have had to marry the girl, if she'd been good enough to do that with, she'd have been good enough to marry and that would have been Dad's lot.[80]

The girls who did become pregnant before marriage reacted in very different ways. Some were overcome with grief and remorse, and so ridden with guilt that they committed suicide; others were punished by family, or friends and workmates; others again were mildly rebuked by their families and their life continued, adjustments being made to accommodate the hurried wedding, or the illegitimate child. The most relaxed attitude was found in the Cumbrian family of the mother of a Barrow respondent. It is perhaps not without significance that in the mid-nineteenth century, Cumberland and Westmorland had particularly high bastardy rates — some 80 per cent above the English average.[81] In the 1870s the girl, who had recently arrived in Barrow from rural Cumberland, found herself pregnant; she had to get married. One of her relatives remarked: 'Ah, Anna, thou hast been tasting soup before it was ready.' To which she replied, 'Yes, and I found a carrot in it.'[82] Fifty years later another Barrow girl found herself pregnant, despite the best efforts of her parents to protect her. She is an illustration of how a girl truly determined to flout the sexual mores of her day could succeed. Her younger sister (the respondent) was always sent out with her sister as chaperon, but was inevitably jettisoned when barely out of sight of the house. The older sister exerted considerable power over the younger one, who was afraid to tell her parents and believed that they would think she was telling lies, as the older girl was the mother's obvious favourite. There is an undertone of resentment in the respondent's evidence that somehow her older sister never received her due reward:

She was m'mother's favourite and she couldn't do wrong and she was the one who brought trouble to the family. She had a baby before she was married.
Did that upset your mother?
Yes. M'father never spoke to her for a long time. It did because she was m'mother's god.
Did your father ever suggest that she leave home?
No. That did happen in other families and they had the baby put out for adoption. This baby was going to stay in the family, but m'mother was heartbroken. In fact, Edith had the baby in 1919 and m'mother died in 1923 and she gradually went down and down.
Was your sister herself very upset about it?
No, I don't think so. I think she just took it quite calmly. I've never thought Edith was upset. She must have misbehaved herself so many times, I don't know.[83]

Eventually Edith got married and her husband adopted her child. And yet all was not toleration and liberality in Barrow. There were a few reported cases of pregnant girls committing suicide by drowning.[84]

Similar contrasting attitudes and behaviour are observable in Lancaster. Mrs Burns, an orphan, was living with an aunt and uncle when she became pregnant in 1910. Although she says that her aunt 'went mad', it is significant that she provided her with a wedding breakfast that was quite as lavish as the usual working-class wedding feast of the time:

I was pregnant, to be married. I hadn't missed a second period, honest I hadn't. I told our Ellen and she nearly went mad. She said, 'Oh, our Sally, if it had been anybody but you.' I said, 'Well don't carry on. I think a lot on him.' She said, 'You must do. It's not like you, but you haven't any money.' I said, 'I have. I have a few pounds.' The morning that I was married she said, 'You can walk out of here and go round to St John's Church and come back for a wedding breakfast.' She used to buy shrimps and pot them and Fanny had made nice cakes with fancy toffee on the top. Then we went to Stone Trough Farm for our honeymoon.[85]

The pregnant sister of another Lancaster woman drowned herself in the Lune.

The same extremes occur in Preston. One 'rough' family displayed a quite remarkable toleration of illegitimacy. Mr Tyrell's mother had already had an illegitimate child when she married his father, and the boy was brought up on an equal basis with his half-brothers and sisters. Mr Tyrell, too, married a girl who already had an illegitimate child. She subsequently died in childbirth, and he did his best to care for his stepson. This was not successful and the child was taken into care until Mr Tyrell's second marriage, when the boy returned home. Mr Tyrell himself later became the father of an illegitimate son. He was not ashamed of what he had done: on the contrary, he was proud of keeping up with his maintenance payments:

When you're married I know you shouldn't do it, like, but I was tempted. It was one time when there was a big do on on Moor Park. I wasn't going to marry her anyway, I didn't want to get done [i.e. for bigamy — he was married already]. . . . I never missed paying [maintenance]. . . . I used to pay so much every week . . . only about 10s. I paid it all the time.[86]

Mrs Chadwick (born in 1897) was illegitimate, but had only the happiest memories of her childhood brought up by her grandmother, her mother and an aunt, all living in the same house:

My mother was one of those good girls who never went out and she had to stay at home and look after ten children. . . . She couldn't hardly read or write. . . . She just brought me up with love. . . . My grandmother she was lovely. . . . She must have had the gift of healing without knowing it. . . . That was another love in my life . . . my auntie she was a rock to lean on. I have been blessed that way. It's never weighed upon me that I am what you would call illegitimate at all. It's what you are that counts.

And yet to arrive at such a happy outcome for the child cannot have been easy for the three women. There must have been much mutual support between them, especially when the pregnancy was first discovered:

He was married and he didn't tell her. She was thirty-six when she had me and I believe she tried to commit suicide and she would do because she was one of those good girls who would never come out.[87]

It is impossible to prove, but the investigator receives the impression that attitudes were perhaps stricter in Preston than in Barrow and Lancaster, certainly over the question of pre-marital pregnancy. In Preston there was not the same emphasis on the joint responsibility of men and women to avoid pre-marital sex. Derek Thompson observed of the inter-war period: 'even in the area of sexual morality, perhaps especially in the area of sexual morality, women came out the losers and were expected to observe a more rigid code than men.'[88] The Preston sample has several examples of the private punishment and public humiliation of the pregnant girl, and this tradition can be traced well back into the nineteenth century. Mrs Dobson received the following account of a weaver's wedding from her mother. It is not possible to date it precisely, but it must have been before the first world war, and serves as a reminder that working-class solidarity did not always mean mutual support and help:

In them days the bride and bridegroom used to walk to church to get married. Now, if the woman was pregnant, I think that was really cruel, she might not have been the willing party. It isn't always the girl's fault you know! A man's a man and he is big and strong, isn't he? They can overpower you, you know. But this here woman she worked in the same mill as my mother and this here weaver asked my mother if she was going to watch the wedding. She said that she couldn't as she had her washing to do. Anyhow, when my mother went to work on the Monday they told her what the wedding was like. They stoned the woman because she was pregnant. That was at Emmanuel Church. That was nasty-minded women!

What did the weavers think of that?

My mother said they agreed with stoning her. They thought it was a crime. My mother said it was a shame.[89]

The tradition of the Victorian patriarch killing his unmarried pregnant daughter is still discussed by older Preston residents.[90] It is difficult to asses how much truth can be deduced from these apocryphal stories, but they must surely be taken to represent a strongly held attitude to pre-marital pregnancy. In fact, in the whole sample there is only one case of a man acting the stereotypical father of a Victorian melodrama. The family were totally atypical of the sample — the girl is the only example of a daughter of a prosperous, socially aspiring family becoming pregnant before marriage. The family lived in Wigan, the respondent only moving to Preston during the first world war:

My mother, she was an only child and she had plenty of money. She married beneath her, she married a collier. . . . My grandfather was very strict and he had his own business. She had been apprenticed to Pendlebury's in Wigan as a tailoress . . . and she was just finishing when she met m'dad. . . . She had to tell him [her father] and he took her to the stable and horse-whipped her.[91]

Only one Preston respondent, Mrs Thornton, said that she was pregnant before marriage. Both she and her husband were active members of the local Church of England. To her it was not an unusual but rather a normal occurrence, the result of ignorance rather than sin:

I had to get married. I wasn't ashamed. We didn't know in them days. We knew we were doing wrong, mind you. But we didn't really know really what it was, as they do today. We didn't actually go in for this baby you know. I had been married eight months. There was no disgrace in it or anything. He was a good lad, one of the best. . . . There were six of us used to go out together, but I was a bit unlucky because they weren't any different to me. I was just one of the unlucky ones.

One of the most interesting aspects of this account is that it was recounted in front of two friends. After she left the house, the two remaining respondents gave their view of her interpretation: 'It was a *disgrace* even for Alice — and to be a Sunday School teacher!'[92]

Perhaps the most usual attitude to pre-marital sex is summed up by Mrs Harrison, which suggests that throughout the period nothing changed significantly. Her evidence relates to the 1930s, when she was living in an industrial village on Preston's outskirts. Its mores appear to have been similar to those of the urban villages within Preston's boundaries, and those of Barrow and Lancaster as well. These were villages where everybody knew everybody else, where there was tolerance and pity, but also the shame of being talked about, which could be truly terrible:

Were the girls not spoken to by the villagers? I mean, they weren't sent to Coventry at all?
No. People would talk about it and she would probably know and be ashamed. It was the shame that was the worst part. If they got married I suppose it wasn't looked on as bad, it was when they didn't get married, you know. No, they wouldn't shun her or anything, but she would know they had been talking about her. It was quite a thing.[93]

There can be no way of estimating the numbers of girls who enjoyed pre-marital sex, whilst those who became pregnant and who then married can only be calculated by an extensive examination of wedding and birth certificates for the first-born. This has not been done. The oral evidence suggests that the practice was very limited; all the cases mentioned by respondents are reported in this chapter. It is much easier to find out about illegitimacy, as this was officially recorded. The figures suggest that this was not numerically a sizeable problem, nor one which changed at all on a national scale over the whole period, ranging between 4 and 5 per cent of all live births. It is rather more difficult to explain the variations between particular years and between towns. In the fifty-year period of this investigation, Barrow's rate only twice went above 5 per cent (1930 and 1932), whereas in Lancaster there were twenty years when the rate was over 5 per cent, and in Preston twenty-seven. Neither the oral evidence nor the reports of the local Medical Officers of Health give clues, but the exceptionally high rates for Lancaster in 1918 (11.8 per cent) and 1919 (9 per cent) and Preston in the same years (9.5 and 8.3 per cent) may be explained by war fever and heightened emotions in two garrison towns. Other yearly variations remain elusive. The generally higher rates in Lancaster compared to Barrow, and Preston compared to Lancaster may be a reflection of the different population structures of the three towns (see appendix 1). It is possible to argue that if a Barrow girl found herself pregnant it was easier for her to get married, as the surplus of men over women did presumably reduce the chances of her lover being a married man. In Preston, where there was a high excess of women over men, there was more chance of a girl finding that her lover was already married. But these are only speculations, and in any case apply to very small numbers — even in the 'boom' year for illegitimate births in Lancaster in 1918, the number of girls involved was only eighty-two[94] — and the great majority of girls entered marriage almost as ignorant about sex and sexuality as when they had left school. As Rose Armstrong said in a peculiar but telling phrase: 'We were as innocent as the grave.'[95]

3

Marriage

It was universally assumed at the beginning of the twentieth century that most girls would get married within about a decade of leaving school. Not all girls got married, but the great majority did, and the assumption of the growing girl was that she would marry. In the age group 45—50 very high percentages were recorded as married, although interestingly the figures decline throughout the period: in 1891, in Preston 84.6 per cent of women were married, and 96.8 per cent in Barrow; in 1931 the figures were 80.1 and 88.6 per cent, respectively.[1] It is appropriate to examine women's experiences of marriage, because it was so central to the lives of most women and affected everything they did. The age at which women married, their expectations of marriage, attitudes to family planning, and experiences of childbirth are all important. They need to be set in the wider context of a woman's relationship with her husband. Obviously relationships between individuals varied considerably, but certain patterns concerning the distribution of power within a marriage can be discerned and described. It is easier to recognise the power than to define it. Some women were in a position of near-tyranny; others were strongly influential, and they exercised power over husband and children alike. The application of that power to the running of the household is further developed in chapter 4.

Many historians have argued that the age at which girls married depended very much on the local labour market, those areas where there was a plentiful supply of jobs producing older brides than areas where there were fewer job opportunities.[2] There were certainly lower percentages of women at work in Barrow than in Preston throughout the period (see appendix 3). However, there are no significant differences in the ages of marriage of Preston and Barrow girls despite the very different labour markets in the two towns. In 1891 women in Preston married at an average age of 25.9 years; in Barrow it was 24.7. By 1931 the two towns had almost identical figures; 25.7 years in Preston and 25.6 in Barrow.[3]

As has been mentioned, there were differences in the percentages of women married. The reason for this must be presumed to be the different ratios of men to women in Barrow and Preston (see appendix 1). Throughout the period there were substantially more men than women in Barrow, while the reverse was true in Preston, reflecting the demands of the different labour markets.

The start of what was to be for the great majority of women a lifelong state was a very low-key affair. Compared to funerals, weddings were much less grand occasions. White weddings were rare, brides choosing instead a good dress or suit which they could wear again. There was no grand reception; a few friends and family would be invited for a meal at the bride's home. Honeymoons were rarely afforded. Quite close relatives were often not present at the celebrations, an omission which would have been unthinkable at a funeral.

In Mrs William's family there was little money; her father was a labourer and a widower, and had a large number of children to support:

I got married in a blue two-piece.

Did you have many people afterwards?

No. I had nobody to make a party for me, with having no mother, and his mother made it. She only asked her own sisters and my husband and I. It was in her house.

Did you have a bridesmaid?

Don't mention that. We couldn't afford a bridesmaid. It took us all our time to have the flowers.

You didn't manage a honeymoon?

Oh no. . . . There were no honeymoons then. We were lucky if we could get married at the church as you had to pay to get married in hand.

How much would it be?

It would be £5 . . . if they went to the Registry Office it was only 7s. 6d. . . . But I had to be married in the Catholic Church as I was a real Catholic and he was too.[4]

Working-class weddings were circumscribed, as were so many aspects of life, by financial considerations. But the lack of sentiment and the absence of glamour may also reflect the very practical, unromantic view that most working-class people had of marriage. This is not to suggest that there was not much affection between husband and wife, but rather, as with the affection between parents and children, it is not often discussed and its physical expression is rarely mentioned. Mrs Saunders is one of the very few respondents to refer to physical affection within her family:

She had a great sense of humour and my father and she were a very loving couple. It is nice to have a loving family. I remember my father and mother holding hands. In fact, I was a bit jealous of my mother, I think, sometimes. I used to catch them sometimes kissing in the kitchen.[5]

By implication and by the way people lived, marriage was seen as a life-long working partnership, both husband and wife having different, clearly-defined roles, both of which were critical for the well-being of each other and of any children. The man was seen as the basic wage-earner and the woman as the household manager with prime responsibility for rearing the children. This pattern, of course, had wide variations in different households. When Mr Bowker was asked what sort of man was thought of as a 'real gentleman', as was usual with respondents, he replied not in terms of class consciousness, but in the moral and social context of family relationships. His answer is worth quoting at length because it portrays the widely held ideal of what a working-class marriage should be:

I think it was more of the moral line as to how you were as a parent, such as he's a good man is Mr X, gives his wife his pay packet and she'd perhaps give him his pocket money. He's very good to his children, works round the house and looks after his wife and very kind to you if you're ill. If he saw anyone in the street he'd do what we term today a Good Samaritan act. He'd pick you up and take you home. . . . Although he may only have a shilling in his pocket he would buy some fruit or something and share it. People were always brought up to share, and I think that was half of life. Where there was family life you were taught to share with your family and in the end you shared with your friends. Even if you had a sweetie and you were a kiddy and you got a lollipop you'd give them a suck of your own sweet. It is considered very unhygienic today, but we never bothered about that yesterday. . . . The man who was considered not good would be a man that would be drinking his pay. When he got his pay go in the pub and drink it before he went home, and when he got back home there was nothing left for the wife to look after the children. He was considered a bad sort of man, not a nice man to know. He might be nice in every way but for drink, he'd go and have his drink and that was why you often found wives meeting husbands coming out of work on a pay day. He'd either go and give it to her on the street and he'd go and have his drink or she'd coax him to go home first. A man was estimated in that light. The height of anyone's life was how they looked after their family and again, from the woman's point of view, whether she had debts, whether she run into debt or whether she'd make do and mend or do without rather than get into debt. That was the main goal of people, if they could live their life without getting into debt and meet their requirements they were all quite happy. They thought that was wonderful.[6]

SEXUAL RELATIONSHIPS AND ATTITUDES TO FAMILY SIZE

At the heart of every marriage is the personal relationship between husband and wife. It is doubtful, however, if sexual relationships in marriage were as important to couples earlier in the century as they are to our contemporaries.

Sexual intercourse was regarded as necessary for the procreation of children or as an activity indulged in by men for their own pleasure, but it was never discussed in the evidence as something which could give mutual happiness. No hint was ever made that women might have enjoyed sex.

Mr Boyle was the youngest respondent interviewed (he was born in 1926). He was conscious of the great divide separating contemporary attitudes to sexuality from those of his parents' generation. His mother had only two children. This appears to have been explained less by deliberate family planning than by the long absences from home by his father, and his mother's comparatively late age at marriage (she was thirty-eight when he was born):

She was brought up a good Roman Catholic, the purpose of marriage was the procreation of children, therefore, she would do her bit. But I don't sense there was any more to it. There was no human loving side to it. Again, one may be wrong about one's parents. As a child, one didn't know what was going on but there was very much this sense of struggle for survival and no margin for happiness in any of its different forms.[7]

Many women regarded sex as something distasteful and unpleasant; for some women the most admired men seem to have been those who 'indulged' themselves the least. Mrs Dobson was an only child, and when asked if her mother would have liked a bigger family remarked: 'No! My dad wasn't a lustful man,'[8] a remark which would seem to express a widespread, if usually unspoken, attitude to sex and sexuality in marriage. One respondent was asked by a married friend of her daughter's in the 1950s how to limit her family. 'She said that she didn't want another one. I said, "Well, you'll have to behave yourselves then." What could I tell them? I didn't know anything.'[9] This story was told to emphasise the respondent's ignorance about many aspects of sex, but it is interesting that at such a comparatively late date, sexual abstinence in marriage was equated with 'behaving yourself'.

Despite these inhibitions, working-class people in some cases did have very large numbers of children, the largest family in the sample being one of twenty-one children.[10] Although this is unusual, it is a reminder, as indeed is much of the oral evidence, of how large a proportion of women's lives was spent in child-rearing. R. M. Titmuss estimated that in 1900 a woman of twenty could expect to live another forty-six years, and would spend approximately one-third of that life in bearing and rearing children. He compared this to the average woman of twenty in 1960 who could expect to live another fifty-five years, but who would only spend 7 per cent of those years in childbearing and maternal care.[11]

TABLE 3.1: Legitimate fertility rates for women aged 15—44

| | Live births per thousand married women (five-year averages) | | |
	England and Wales	Preston	Barrow
1891—95	259.2	275.6	259.8
1896—1900	243.6	256.5	237.8
1901—05	231.2	232.8	259.4
1906—10	213.5	211.6	223.1
1911—15	190.5	182.3	212.5
1916—20	158.1	144.1	210.7
1921—25	157.3	152.3	145.4
1926—30	130.9	125.0	123.6
1931—35	117.9	113.9	111.7
1936—40	116.7	111.6	128.5

It is not possible, because of the limitations of the census returns for non-county boroughs, to calculate the Lancaster figures. Of course, it was not legal to be married at 15, but the official reports give figures for five-year age groups.

Source: These figures are calculated from data from the Medical Officers of Health *Annual Reports*, the Registrar General's *Annual Reports*, and the Census figures for 1891—1931 (inclusive).

These changes are reflected both in the legitimate fertility rates in table 3.1[12] and in the oral evidence. Married women at the turn of the century were obviously considerably more involved in childbearing and childrearing than their daughters were to be, with a consequent fundamental effect on the way they led their lives and their quality. The high fertility rates at the beginning of the century, and the steady decline in those rates until the beginning of the second world war are well-known. A clear analysis of why and how these important demographic changes took place is more difficult.[13] The whole question of family limitation is formidably complex, bedevilled as it is by inhibitions, ignorance and reticence about sex and sexuality. Respondents were profoundly and understandably ignorant about their parents' practices. Inhibitions about talking of their own experiences were reinforced by a widespread belief, quite common until the end of the period, that artificially limiting one's family was not 'respectable', and that, indeed, a woman who had only one or two children was probably practising abortion. Mrs Hudson in Preston who had, on medical advice, only one child, remarked with some bitterness: 'I was insulted like a lot that only had one. It was, "What have you been doing?" You would cry your eyes out. They wouldn't believe you that the doctor had said, no more. It was, "They know how it's done."'[14] Mrs Wilkinson of Barrow commented: 'A neighbour was very funny with us. I'd only one child, she was wicked about it. . . . She'd three children and I couldn't help that.'[15]

Too often discussions of fertility concentrate almost exclusively on contraceptive methods. It is clear, however, from the oral evidence that in some families no policy of deliberate limitation of fertility was ever adopted. Whether this resulted in large families obviously depended on the fertility of both husband and wife. Mrs Gregson's mother seems to have been almost continually pregnant: 'She said she had sixteen good and bad. You see they just didn't know what to do. The husbands just didn't prevent them.'[16] Mrs Mitchell's mother, in a later generation, had six children in eighteen years, and was forty-six-years old in 1913 when Mrs Mitchell was born:

In those days there was no birth control. They took the risk you see. If it happened, it happened. That's why they had such big families. . . . There's no need for a big family, they have a choice these days, but in those days they hadn't. If it was there, that was it.[17]

It is easy to approach the subject of family limitation with the assumption that all women, if only they had not been so ignorant and/or fatalistic, would have limited their families. But there were some women who both wanted and enjoyed a large family, like the mother of this Lancaster woman (and there is, too, an interesting implication of choice and planning in this evidence):

She loved children did my mother . . . she minded them for people while they went to work. She loved children. It was her own fault that she had the last boy. M'dad said, 'If you love kids that much you might as well have another one of your own.'[18]

In the 1920s and 1930s, despite increasing knowledge about contraception among some members of the working class, ignorance and fatalism are still easy to trace. But one response to the growing influence of the movement in favour of contraception was the strengthening of the belief that artificial contraception was either immoral or totally distasteful, but in either case not to be practised.

It is frequently asked how far the moral stance taken against contraception was a result of the Catholic Church's doctrine, especially in Preston with its large Catholic population. Neither nationally nor locally was the Catholic Church involved in the debate about contraception, until *after* the first world war. This was presumably because it was only then that the decline in the birth rate became apparent. A similar sharp drop in the birth rate in France at the end of the eighteenth century had caused the French bishops to argue for the cross-examination of parishioners in the confessional on the question of birth control.[19] The bishops in Belgium issued a pastoral on birth control in 1909, and they were in turn followed by their colleagues in France and the United States in 1919. However, in England, it was not until the Lambeth Conference of 1930, when the Anglican Church very cautiously accepted birth control, that Cardinal Bourne and the English Catholic bishops began to press Pope Pius XII for *Castii Connubii*.

These national and international statements seem curiously divorced from the reality of life in a town like Preston. The Catholic clergy there had begun preaching against contraception several years before 1930:

Can you remember when you were young the priest ever discussing in church the evils of birth control?

I can pinpoint that for you. I can remember hearing a sermon on the subject, and was vastly bewildered. I wondered what on earth it was all about . . . I must have been less than ten and that would be about 1923. I was an altar boy and later a choir boy. . . . For this series of sermons on marriage given by a celebrated Jesuit preacher called Father Radcliffe, the congregation were asked not to bring children . . . but they still had the altar boys and so I attended the first one, two or three of this series. I do well remember Mother stopped me going for the rest of the series!

Do you remember other exhortations against birth control?

It was fairly continuous from that time onwards.[20]

One woman, not a regular church-going Catholic, decided to go to confession during a Franciscan Mission to her church in the inter-war period. The friar asked her if she 'wasted her seed'. She had no idea what he meant for some time; then realised, and answered indignantly that she did not. She appears to have deeply resented the question.[21]

These two accounts are the only occasions remembered by respondents of the Catholic Church being directly involved in the question of contraception. This is not to suggest that its priests and missioners did not continually press the matter, but the oral evidence suggests that working-class people had their own views on the morality of contraception and family limitation, and these may not always have been in accordance with official Church teaching. Certainly, despite the Lambeth Conference decision, many Protestants continued to regard it as either immoral or distasteful, or both. Equally, a surprising number of Catholic couples had only one or two children, which could well indicate some form of contraception being practised (although it could equally indicate low fertility). It is very difficult to equate attitudes to birth control with membership of a particular Church, and, as the trend in the legitimate fertility rate in Preston after the first world war was reasonably in accordance with that of the national average, it would seem that the

Roman Catholic Church in Preston had neither less nor more influence on family limitation than it had elsewhere in the country.

The old, deeply felt fatalism about conception, pregnancy and childbirth was shared by women from a variety of religious backgrounds: 'Whatever was to be, was to be; it was God's will, or fate'; Mrs Morrison, a Methodist, said: 'I suppose we accepted it';[22] Mrs Booth, an Anglican, on being asked if she wanted a large family, said:

Well, I mean, we never thought of it. They just came and that was it. I mean, I was as green as grass when I got married and I don't think me husband were much . . . brighter. No, they just came.[23]

Mrs Pearce was brought up in both the Anglican and the Catholic Churches. She had six children during the 1920s and 1930s. The reaction of the hospital doctor when she went to have her last pregnancy confirmed is interesting:

There must have been tears in my eyes because I was thinking about keeping them. I loved children but it was the thought of keeping them. You want them to be as nice as others as well as feeding them. He said, 'It's no good crying now, it's too late!' I felt like saying that it wasn't the woman's fault all the time. You are married and you have got to abide by these things, you know. He [her husband] once said that if anybody had seen this squad in here, they would think that we had a wonderful time, but they don't know what I have gone through to try to avoid it, you know. We never would take anything in them days. God had sent them and they had to be there. I'm not a religious person, but that were my idea.[24]

Her evidence is virtually a summary of so many women's attitude to sex, pregnancy and children: the deep devotion to the children; the constant worry about feeding and clothing them; the admission that sex was not fun but something one tried hard to avoid; and ultimately the acceptance of whatever God sends.

Mrs Dobson, an Anglican, first heard of the cervical cap when she was nearly fifty (in the mid-1950s). She was talking to a hospital nurse and asked how prostitutes so often 'got away with it':

Then she told me what you could buy in the chemist shop, they were just like a woman's womb, made of rubber and they put that in and that man just believes . . . and then they take it out and wash it. She said, 'How dirty can they get.'
And you had never heard of that before?
Never in my life.[25]

Not only is the ignorance of the respondent interesting; so too is the disgust expressed by the nurse.

Despite these opinions which militated against either the use of artificial contraception or in some extreme cases the limitation of family size by abstinence, it is very clear from both the official statistics on birth rates, and from the local sample, that family sizes did decline dramatically during the period 1890—1940. It can be argued that working-class couples were already limiting their families by some means in the nineteenth century. If they were not, the incidence of large families would have been even greater. But it is not clear why they decided to limit their families — were the economic incentives for doing so greater than they had been before? Nor do we know what methods were used. Oral evidence does offer some interesting pointers, but it is very doubtful if conclusive evidence in this area will ever be found.

J. A. Banks has discussed the limitations of seeking a single causal factor for the decline in the birth rate, but he also tends to dismiss the adoption of a multiple-factor theory on the grounds of the difficulty of proving it.[26] This need not invalidate its relevance: indeed common sense and empirical evidence would tend to support a multiple-factor explanation, and Diana Gittins has supported this view.[27] The historian tends to look at whatever evidence is available, but in the long term would do well to retain a healthy scepticism and eschew over-simple explanations for this fundamental demographic phenomenon. Demographers have linked a falling birth rate with falling rates of infant mortality. H. J. Habakkuk has argued that while there was a high level of infant mortality there was no incentive for many parents to limit their families.[28] Given a large number of infant and child deaths, it is logical to assume that parents believed that a large number of births was necessary if a family of a desired size was to be achieved. And certainly as throughout this period in Western Europe the birth rates declined with infant mortality rates (see figure 1). It is interesting to note that when the infant mortality rate rose in Barrow, the birth rate also rose. There is an undoubted correlation, but the exact connection between falling infant mortality rates and individual decisions to limit fertility are impossible to find, and no respondent mentions it in the evidence.

There are many examples of the families conforming to a general tendency described by Habakkuk: 'At a certain stage of economic development, the disparity became evident between the existing standards of comfort and those attainable with a smaller family . . . possibilities of economic and social advancement opened up which were more accessible to members of small families.'[29] It is clear that the great majority of families with less than four children had at least one parent who could be described as 'aspiring', wanting a better education for the children, or an improved house, or more possessions. They realised that it was impossible to achieve these things

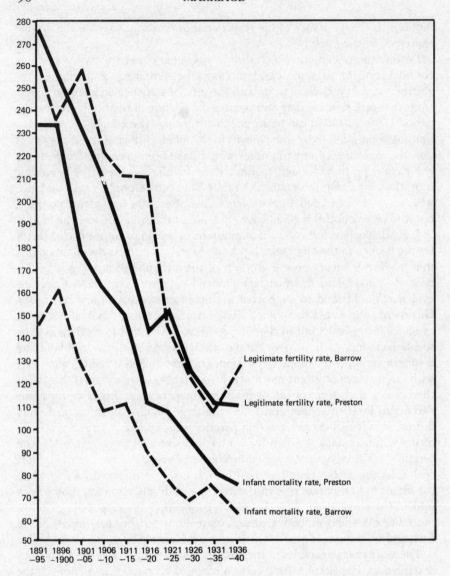

FIGURE 1: Fertility and infant mortality in Barrow and Preston, 1891–1940. Legitimate fertility rate is the number of live births per 1,000 married women aged 15–44. Infant mortality rate is the number of babies dying before their first birthday per 1,000 born.

Source: Medical Officers of Health *Annual Reports.*

unless family size was limited.[30] Mr Riley's father was a skilled woodworker, a member of the labour aristocracy, valuing education, leisure and a comfortable standard of living. It is likely that his mother, too, had views on the subject, having been a nurse and presumably knowing about contraception. There were only two children, born in 1890 and 1892:

Back to that point, you see, my mother was a nurse at the Royal Lancaster Infirmary, you see, and perhaps they talk about birth control and, well, this is it again. And I dare say, talking about m'father, he didn't want a big family owing to the economic conditions of the day. That was all we had, there was only two of us. Yes, two years between us practically.[31]

Mrs Sharp spoke disapprovingly of her own parents bringing up a family of ten children on a labourer's wage of 18s. a week: 'You cannot understand people having so many children when there was so little money to keep them. Yet my father was the easiest going man, he didn't worry whether m'mother could pay her way or not. He was too easy going.'[32] This Malthusian determination to balance one's financial resources with the number of one's children is more clearly seen among the poorer labouring families in the inter-war period than in the earlier years, presumably because their relative living standards had risen. Mrs Bibby's husband was a labourer. They had only two children and in reply to the remark: 'It's interesting how people had smaller families isn't it?', she commented 'There was no family allowance then, you know.'[33] Mrs Williams was poor, but felt herself to be much better off than both her sister and sister-in-law, who had six children each. She used to pass on to them her own children's outgrown clothes: 'I once said to my husband that if we hadn't had any children would he have been upset. He said, "Not in the least." We thought that two was quite sufficient.'[34]

In all sections of the working class men and women's perceptions of how many children they could afford, whatever their financial priorities, were changing dramatically. There was a great increase in material expectations. Mrs Phillips and her husband ran a pie shop which, from humble beginnings and with a lot of hard work, made a substantial amount of money. Her evidence relates to the end of the 1930s:

To be honest, I'm the type that would have liked a big family but my husband had other ideas because I was too valuable working. Without me, he would have been in a mess, he wasn't particular about a family as he liked a good time. My son is just like him.
So he just wanted the one really?
He didn't really want the one. I insisted. I said that I didn't get married to have no children. I would have liked a big family, but I realised that I really couldn't

afford it. . . . I stayed at home till he was three and then I sent him to a private school because the war was on and I couldn't get people to work for me. It was difficult, I used to run him in my car every morning to a private school and he wasn't three.[35]

(Few other families aspired to a car or private schools, but virtually all intended to have a higher standard of living than their parents.) Both Mrs Williams and Mrs Phillips illustrate an important factor in limiting families (dealt with extensively by Diana Gittins): the ability of husband and wife to discuss the question, for open discussion would be likely to lead to limitation.[36]

Another factor, which is rather more difficult to analyse, also affected family size. We have already noted that working-class women at the beginning of the period appear to have had a great respect for tradition and a strong sense of fatalism:

Well, my grandma had seventeen, and she lived till ninety-six. Her husband died in his fifties. My mother had six but they thought they had to, they were ignorant. The men thought they had to get drunk or they weren't men. It was a general attitude, it was tradition and people lived that sort of life. It was just the usual thing.[37]

By contrast, 'modern' men and women have been variously described as having a talent for innovation, an openness to new experiences, a belief in the values of planning one's life, a reliance on the benefits conferred by science and technology, and a certainty that the environment is open to man's control.[38] Habakkuk asserted: 'Industrialization made family size a matter of deliberate decision by promoting the application of rationality and calculation in place of custom and traditions.'[39] But the working class of Preston had been urbanised and industrialised as long (if not longer than) any comparable group of workers and yet the dawn of the twentieth century saw them, with their counterparts in Barrow and Lancaster, displaying very few of the characteristics of 'modern' men and women. By 1940, however, one can observe many of these 'modern' changes. The process, however, was markedly uneven, and the reasons for such 'modernisation' are very complex. So often an individual adopted a so-called 'modern' outlook for purely personal reasons: a quarrel with a relation or employer; the opportunity of a different job; enlistment in the army; loss of religious faith; an extended education; a chance reading of an influential book; a fortuitous encounter with someone with different ideas. A significant group of working-class women did decide quite consciously that a smaller family was better for them as individuals; their health would be improved, and their opportunity of leading a less harassed life would be greater. Quite simply, by limiting their families they believed the *quality* of their lives would be better.

From the inter-war period, especially, respondents record that they limited their families because they believed that their health would be impaired by having more children. Mrs Wood had one child, born in 1930: 'I didn't feel strong enough to have another child. I felt tired and I wouldn't like to think that I couldn't look after my own children so we never had any more.'[40] Mrs Gregson had two children at the end of the first world war:

I had two within a year and five months. My husband was a great big strong man and we didn't know anything about pills. We just thought that they were no good if you'd mentioned anything like that. I hadn't seen anything from the first child until I had the second one. They were great big babies. My son is six foot two. I just thought, oh dear I couldn't go through this again, I couldn't. Then there was no maternity home.[41]

It is significant that having made her decision, she had no more children. Doctors in general were becoming much more aware of the dangers of childbirth, and sometimes it was on their advice that couples decided to limit their family to one. Mr and Mrs Hudson had one child, and Mr Hudson said: '[the doctor] said that if I wanted to keep my wife there would have to be no more.'[42]

FAMILY LIMITATION: KNOWLEDGE AND METHODS

Once a working-class couple decided to try and restrict their family, whether for economic, medical or social reasons, they faced a problem in finding out how. It is clear from the little oral evidence which is available that neither the proliferation of various mechanical means of contraception, nor the existence of national campaigns in its favour, necessarily meant that contraceptive advice reached working-class men and women. While Richard Titmuss has described the widespread acceptance of birth control as the most important factor contributing to both the improvement in women's health and female emancipation,[43] and many historians have described and documented the national campaigns by many bodies supporting the cause, and demanding a wide distribution of information about it,[44] what is perhaps not so thoroughly discussed is the refusal by the British government to make this information available to women at large. The only concession came in the 1930s, when it was agreed that women whose health might suffer unduly from a further pregnancy might be given contraceptive advice by their own doctor. Information on family planning continued to be *un*available in maternal and infant welfare clinics or in gynaecological clinics in hospitals: 'Anxiety about the numbers of population seems to have been the main reason why government officials resisted demands for making birth control information generally available.'[45]

Where, then, did married couples find their information about contraception? Mr Riley, whose parents were successful in limiting their family to two children, attributed this to his mother's knowledge gained as a nurse at the Royal Lancaster Infirmary. There were, however, very few nurses among the sample of women in any of the towns (see appendix 2), and no other respondent mentions receiving contraceptive advice from a nurse. The medical profession as a whole appear not to have contributed in any positive way to family planning except where health was in danger; indeed, the attitude of some doctors was hostile. This was not peculiar to this geographical area: nationally, doctors very rarely gave advice, a fact corroborated by much contemporary data.[46] Remarks from two respondents about the 1920s and 1930s illustrate an attitude commonly encountered:

The doctor wouldn't help you. You daren't mention it to the doctor.

He would just tell you that that's what married life was all about.[47]

It would seem too that Dr Pilkington, the Preston Medical Officer of Health who argued against family planning in his 1902 report,[48] was wrong about people learning about family limitation from books. Books did exist and were sometimes advertised in the local press. This advertisement appeared in the *Barrow Herald* in 1895:

Married ladies who wish to enjoy health and happiness and yet keep their families within the limits of their means should read Nurse Forbes' book entitled "Prevention Better Than Cure". Post free 7*d*. from Mrs Forbes, 144 Sackville Road, Brighton, N.B. Simple reliable safe and cheap. Most flattering testimonials received daily.[49]

There is no way of knowing what was in Mrs Forbes' intriguing book, nor do we know how many local Barrovians sent for it. One who apparently had not read it was Mrs Mulholland's mother, who had sixteen children between 1878 and 1896, only three of whom survived into adulthood. When asked by her daughter why she had had so many confinements she replied: 'Ah, but we didn't know enough in those days.'[50] This woman was widely read and very intelligent; a founder of the socialist movement in Barrow; and held progressive views on many topics. She was certainly not constrained by traditional religious beliefs. Yet her ignorance about birth control seems to have been as complete as that of any other woman.

Nor was contraceptive advice and knowledge diffused from the middle classes, as suggested by J. A. and O. Banks.[51] Neither Diana Gittins nor the present author has found any evidence for the diffusion theory.[52] If it was true, one might presume that domestic servants, working as they did for middle- and upper-class families who were increasingly limiting their families, might display more knowledge about contraception than their contemporaries. This was not the case. What information was available was obtained from the peer group, work-mates, friends and relations, including husbands and neighbours, although, as will be seen later, it would be unwise to over-emphasise the importance of the textile mill as a source of contraceptive advice.

The impression gained from the oral evidence (and it must be emphasised again that this is a hypothesis which cannot be proved), is that the two most common methods of family limitation were total abstinence and coitus interruptus; this would seem to be true of the later as well as the earlier period.[53] (Coitus interruptus was not called that by those who practised it.)

You couldn't get pills. We were on the bus and Harold knew the conductor and he asked Harold if we were married. He said, 'Don't forget, always get off the bus at South Shore, don't go all the way to Blackpool.' That was how they kept their family down. It was just that the men had to be careful.
But did the men actually buy things?
No. I expect some did, French letters as they used to call them.
But you didn't hear about those?
No.[54]

(No respondent mentioned the Marie Stopes clinics or publications.) Abstinence was sometimes voluntary, sometimes as a result of one of the partners being ill, and sometimes forced on the couple by overcrowding. Sometimes it was due to successful evading tactics practised by the wife. Mrs Morrison had five children between 1924 and 1939:

We had two and then my husband was very ill with the 'flu and he was off work for a long time, eighteen or nineteen weeks, then we went nearly seven years before we had the next one. Then we had three more. I thought I had stopped. But evidently I hadn't! There was no pill! . . . . I suppose we accepted it. After he was ill, the doctor at the time said we would have to have separate beds because my husband wasn't well for a long time after. I suppose that was it. We had no sex for a while until he got better.[55]

Sleeping arrangements were particularly problematic in Preston where the typical terraced house had only two bedrooms (as opposed to the more usual three in Barrow and Lancaster). It was not thought suitable for growing boys and girls to share a room, and this decision could effectively end the sexual relationship between husband and wife:

Where did you put all the children? Did they all share a bedroom?
  At the finish, we had to separate. Especially when he came back after the war (1945). He come home and Freda was growing up. He said we would have to make some difference because they were growing up. He said that he would have to go in one room with boys and I would have to go in with the girls. So we had to move the beds. It isn't right when they are growing up and they are starting with their periods and all that.[56]

  Many wives devised their own ways of avoiding sex. This story was related by a woman's neighbour, of the 1890s:

She used to tell me about her husband who was a stonemason. . . . they went on the booze and she never got pennies for weeks on end. She said that many a night she daren't get into bed with him and sat on the window ledge until he went to sleep. The young ones of today say, 'Serve you right you had a big family,' but they hadn't a clue what went on.[57]

Infrequent sexual intercourse sometimes led to small families: 'I'm certainly not saying we tried to get any more family. We certainly didn't do anything to stop it. But we never tried very hard. One was enough for the sample we had.'[58] But others who claimed to have infrequent intercourse could still achieve a large family. One particularly outspoken woman, who became a nurse, had asked her mother if her father had been sex-mad. '"No," said her mother with truly remarkable frankness, "He didn't do it so often but when he did he made a good job of it."'[59] What is remarkable in all the respondents' evidence is the virtual absence of any reference to mechanical means of contraception.[60] Only one man, Mr Darnley, mentions using such a device, and he is a far from typical respondent. He came from an ordinary working-class home, but was always ambitious, intelligent, and determined to do well (as in fact he did). This extract comes from his autobiography, written (but not published) several years ago. He and his wife went to Blackpool for their honeymoon in the 1930s:

I realised now we were married that I would have to do something about birth control so I went along to Boots the chemist. I was surprised how busy these shops were. I stood outside for ages waiting while a male assistant was free. Then I dashed in and asked for my requirements. I was answered, I thought, in a very cultured way, 'We don't sell them.' I dashed out of the shop with my face red. I had another long wait outside another chemist's. This time I wrote my requirements on a piece of paper. The male assistant laughed and asked me what size I required. I was stunned and muttered, 'Average'. He was joking and put me at ease, 'they sold thousands.'[61]

It is likely, but impossible to prove, that some of the couples having a small number of children at any time during the period were in fact using some kind of mechanical device.

The use of contraceptives had been publicised throughout the nineteenth century. Francis Place wrote of the sponge in 1823 in *Diabolical Handbills*; three years later 10,000 copies were sold of Richard Carlile's book *Every Woman's Book on What is Love*, which recommended not only coitus interruptus but also the condom. The use of the vaginal syringe was suggested by Charles Knowlton in *Fruits of Philosophy* in 1834. By the 1840s the cervical cap was made more comfortable by the invention of vulcanised rubber.[62] It is much more difficult to estimate how widely these devices were used. Patricia Branca argues that: 'By the early 1880s advertisements reflect the fact that these methods were well-known and widely used.'[63] But her work was on middle-class women, and it would not be surprising if they differed substantially from the working class. There is very little evidence to suggest that even after the first world war contraceptive devices were widely used by the working class. Few knew about them; many could not afford them.[64]

Abortion is no longer regarded as a normal method of family limitation, although some respondents tended to talk as if they believed that contraception and abortion were more or less the same thing. The evidence about abortion comes entirely from Preston, as the interviews in Barrow and Lancaster did not include questions on it (and perhaps significantly no information was volunteered).

Abortions had been illegal since 1803. 'The exact extent of abortion before 1914 is impossible to estimate since only a small percentage of cases came to the attention of doctors, an even smaller number before the court.'[65] Sometimes there is some apparently firmer evidence. In 1936, for example, the Abortion Law Reform Association Conference reported the study made by a prominent gynaecologist in Birmingham, in which of 3,000 women questioned, 35 per cent admitted to having had an abortion.[66] Ernest Lewis Faning estimated that 10 per cent of conceptions in women married before 1910 ended in miscarriages or abortions.[67] It would seem, however, advisable to remain diffident about extending this evidence from a local to a national sphere, and equally dangerous to use national figures to make any estimates about the percentage of women who had abortions in the north-west. The evidence is simply not available.

There was no apparent consensus of opinion about abortion among the respondents. First, there was a large group who disclaimed all personal knowledge of abortions, while admitting to having heard of a relation of a woman in the fourth street away who performed or had had an abortion. This information was almost always passed on in a neutral fashion without any moral judgement. The frequency of this reaction would appear to indicate that abortions were not very common. The second group of respondents knew about abortions, often in some detail, but had rejected absolutely their use for themselves. Their motives for this were a complex mixture of fatalism, reverence for the unborn child's life, and a terror that the abortion would not work properly, and that either they or the baby would be damaged. Horror stories about the results of attempted but failed abortions abounded:

I can always remember when I came to have this one after seven years, a neighbour saying, 'You should have come to me and I would have shifted it!' It was that sort of thing. I said, 'Look, I've a long time to live, I hope, and I'm not going to ruin my inside!' I remember saying that to her. I know she had a terrible time. She is dead now. She must have moved one herself.
What did they do? Have you any idea?
Do you know what slippery elm bark is?
I do!
They pushed that up! I don't know what it did. They pushed needles up! Take washing-soda, quinine, all that sort of thing. But life isn't worth living if you are going to do that sort of thing. I don't know whether it was my mother having that baby that wasn't right and losing it. But it put a fear into me that if I did anything, it might happen to me.[68]

Mrs Dobson had also heard about slippery elm bark, from her nurse friend:

I asked her what this woman had used. She said it was like a stick and it was called slippery elm bark and it was sharpened at the end. When they got her in hospital they got it out of her, who had done it. It was like a sharp pencil at the end and they push it right up. Anyhow, she had misfired and that was how they had to take her into hospital. She said that some of them do it with syringes. I said, 'Well, by Jove, that's killing a child.' Once that has been put there, after that, they will say it's murder.[69]

There was a third group who were totally contradictory in their attitudes and who, while feeling very sorry for *some* women who procured their own or other women's abortions, condemned others. Mrs Hudson represents this group; she refused to discuss abortion at all until she had sent her husband to the kitchen to make the tea:

Did you hear any talk of abortions in those days?

Well now — *Will you pour that tea love, please?* — This was a horrifying thing when I found out. There was one woman and she was a lovely person, she had two sons and a lovely husband, she's dead and buried now. She was old enough to be my mother were Polly, she served three months' prison sentence. I'll not tell you her name. She had done something to herself to stop a baby and one of her neighbours was watching through the window and reported it. That woman didn't have another day's luck after. Polly nearly died and she was a broken woman after and yet she was a good woman. She said she had her own idea of why she did what she did but nobody else suffered for it. I had a sister-in-law, she is dead and gone now, my sister-in-law, my brother's wife, she stopped I don't know how many children. She wasn't having any children but she had one son and he's living today. My brother was a policeman, our Joe. I only got to know this after I was married myself, they have another girl Jenny, she is fifty-odd now. My brother said to his wife, 'If you don't let this baby go through I'll report you to the Chief Constable.' So she had Jenny and that was the last one. They said she had stopped, they didn't know how many. I had another sister-in-law, my eldest brother's wife, she had had eight children but she only kept three. I didn't know then because I was only a little girl but she lost three, but besides miscarriages, she had had eight altogether. I was very green, I got married and I didn't know how children were born.[70]

Lastly, there was the tiny group who admitted to abortions having been attempted either by their mothers or by themselves. They made a clear moral distinction between going to an abortionist, an action of which they disapproved, and attempting to procure their own abortion, which they regarded as a desperate but justifiable act. Mrs Hesketh's mother had nine children and a violent, suspicious husband who never believed that the children were his. She used to send her daughter for various potions from the chemist:

I remember one of them was quinine, most likely she had been worrying about her periods. . . . It must have been hell. . . . If only they had had the sense that they have now.[71]

(Quinine would be used either as a spermicide or as a drug to procure an abortion.) Mrs Dickinson, having failed to get help from her doctor, resorted to self-induced abortions. Like Mrs Hesketh's mother she does not seem to have been very successful, as she had six children:

Well, [breast feeding] was healthier and it was good for you as well. If it stopped you having another baby, it helped. It didn't stop you, but it helped. They said in those days that while you were feeding you couldn't conceive. Some did, but it did help. It was a good thing.

Would you have liked even more children?

No. I tried to stop one or two, I took my salts [Epsom salts].

And it didn't work?

No.

It didn't seem to, did it?

If you were strong. If you were weak and you hadn't had good food when you were young, it would work. There was one or two other things, hot baths and things like that. But if you were strong it would make no difference. No chance whatever. . . .

Did your friends try?

Everybody tried.

But there was no success?

No.[72]

It is possible to argue that since abortion is discussed more often by respondents than mechanical contraception, it was the former which was the more usual way of limiting families in Preston before the second world war. But this must remain hypothetical; what little oral evidence there is would in fact suggest that abstinence or coitus interruptus continued to be practised most. It is difficult to see how a historian confronted with such shadowy evidence (and it becomes even more ephemeral the further one goes back into the nineteenth century) can be as definite as Patricia Knight:

In spite of being illegal, abortion was widespread. It was probably the most prevalent form of contraception for working-class women. The evidence of such women and of their medical and other opponents shows not only that abortion was common, but that it was an accepted part of working-class life.[73]

Women's work and family limitation

To what extent, if any, was a woman's knowledge and practice of familiy limitation affected by her job and place of work?[74] Historians have long accepted that textile workers limited their families. In 1832, Dr James Blundell informed a parliamentary committee that 'Where individuals are congregated in factories I conceive that means preventative of impregnation are most likely to be generally known and practised by young persons.'[75] J. W. Innes has argued that the families of textile workers, especially those in Lancashire, were conspicuously small.[76] Diana Gittins, writing about the inter-war period, said: 'The distinguishing features of most textile towns, of course, was the unusually high proportion of married women in full-time employment. The census data clearly showed that the greater the proportion of married women working, the lower was the level of fertility in any given area.'[77] The Fertility of Marriage Census of 1911, from which many historians have drawn their data, not only argued that textile workers (men and women) had low fertility rates,[78] but also that their patterns of fertility affected those of the area in which they lived: 'The low fertility of the textile industry is very largely shared by the general population of the area in which it was carried on.'[79]

TABLE 3.2: Legitimate fertility rates in textile and non-textile areas for women aged 15—44

	Percentage of married women in full-time work in 1911 [a]	Live births per thousand married women (five-year averages)			
		1901—05	1906—10	1921—25	1926—30
Textile towns					
Blackburn	44.5	197	189	127	105
Bury	31.0	177	174	127	104
Rochdale	27.2	176	169	130	111
Bolton	15.0	227	208	152	120
Preston	35.3	233	212	152	125
Burnley	41.4	193	185	148	110
(Average)		200	189	139	112
Non-textile towns					
Barrow	4.3	259	223	145	123
St Helens	4.1	314	286	217	184
Warrington	8.2	265	264	181	158
Wigan	9.5	287	217	185	153
Bootle	5.9	262	234	223	197
(Average)		277	245	190	163
(Average for England and Wales)		231	213	157	131

[a] Widows are not included.
Source: These figures are taken from the Registrar General's *Annual Reports* 1901—10 and 1921—30, and the Census of 1911, County ot Lancashire, table 25.

These arguments present the social historian in Preston with considerable problems, because it has not been possible to prove that the existence of large numbers of textile workers resulted in Preston having low fertility rates, as compared either to those of Barrow, where there were no textile workers and very few married women in employment, or with the figures for England and

Wales as a whole. Preston's fertility rates were falling, but that was a national trend. One clue in the Fertility of Marriage report may explain Preston's fertility rates. 'The figures available show only fertility by husbands' and by wives' occupations respectively, without reference in either case to that of the other spouse.'[80] Oral evidence indicates that women weavers with a low fertility rate were frequently married to general labourers, or members of other occupational groups appearing in the 10 per cent of the most fertile men. One must presume that the fertility patterns deriving from the husband's occupational group were more important than those of the wife. Oral evidence also indicates that women weavers were likely to have smaller families than women in general because they frequently (but not always) gave up weaving when their family began to grow. It was expensive to have children looked after. In other words, a woman's job was not so likely to affect her fertility rate as her fertility rate was likely to affect her employment. Women with growing families were likely to opt for part-time work. For the sake of the children and herself there was a point, usually before the birth of a fourth child, in her interrelated careers as mother and wage-earner, when it seemed more sensible to work part-time. In Preston only one woman with more than four children continued as a full-time weaver, and then only intermittently. In Lancaster there was also only one, and she died when she was thirty-two.[81] Conversely, a woman's ability to carry out part-time work does not appear to have been affected by the number of children she had. In the Preston sample, 42 per cent of those in part-time work had more than six children; in the Lancaster sample it was also 42 per cent; and in Barrow 47 per cent.

Nothing has emerged from the oral evidence to suggest that women weavers were noticeably more informed on sexual matters than other women. Such evidence as there is reveals that even in the 1920s and 1930s there was still widespread ignorance, and that textile workers were likely to be as ignorant as other sections of the population. On the whole, the women who are willing to discuss family size are anxious to point out that neither they nor their mothers deliberately limited their families. Conversely, the women who are not anxious to discuss the matter are those with small families who might well have practised some form of contraception. These attitudes also suggest that birth control, although practised, was not regarded as a matter for pride or discussion. There is little evidence that women discussed sexual topice in the mill.

Yet the arguments of those who linked women's work in the textile industry with low fertility rates cannot be dismissed. If a study is made in Lancashire of comparable legitimate fertility rates, it is very clear that while all rates were falling, those in the towns with a high percentage of married women working in the textile mills, with the notable exception of Preston, remained lower throughout the period than those in a random sample of non-textile towns. The very considerable variations, however, both between towns within each group or between the two groups would suggest that while female occupation in textiles was obviously significant, other social and economic factors must have been important too. Otherwise how, for example, can the difference between the rates for Barrow and St Helens, or Preston and Rochdale (see table 3.2), be explained?

The childless woman

Some women would have liked to have children, but didn't. According to the Census of Population published in 1949, 8.2 per cent of women married before 1923 had no children.[82] The percentage of respondents in my sample who did not have children and who wanted them is slightly higher than this. According to one medical opinion, this may be because the childless were likely to have had easier lives, to have eaten better, and therefore been likely to live longer! The attitudes of those who were childless are interesting; regret is expressed, but none of the passionate sorrow of some of those whose children died. Many of the childless were able to explain how they had been needed as substitute parents by members of the extended family and had found fulfilment in this way. This is Mrs Bridges' and Mrs Sullivan's evidence:

Would you have liked a family?
I would have liked one, but it so happened as I didn't have one. More as I was young that I felt it. But as I have got older I have not bothered as I have had children with me, nieces and nephews.[83]

I never had any children . . . I wish I had though. I lost one, I had a miscarriage.
And you didn't have any more?
No . . . I looked after our Edna — her mother died when she was thirty-two, so I really helped to bring them up . . . there were two boys and two girls . . . They lived with their father but they always depended on me. If they wanted to do anything it would be 'go and ask your auntie'. If she say no, it stands at that! They depended on me a lot. He was only forty-six when he died. So I have had a lot of control over them. . . . They look upon me as a mother. The youngest never remembered her mother, she was only a baby-in-arms when her mother died.[84]

How were such women regarded by working-class society? Certainly, there may have been some pity for them, but none appears to have incurred the combination of envy or disapproval experienced by those who for various reasons had only one child.

PREGNANCY AND CHILDBIRTH

For many women who had children, pregnancy and confinements were and continued to be a source of both physical and psychological pain throughout the period. Some women (and men) regarded pregnancy as an embarrassment, or an unclean state. This was yet another aspect of the all-prevailing prudery about sexual matters. The *degree* to which it was experienced varied considerably from individual to individual and family to family. Mrs Grundy recounted a story from her mother-in-law which relates to the pre-first world war period:

I remember his mother telling me when she was pregnant with his brother . . . that she went to the door [of her father-in-law's house], and he said, 'Don't come in here in that condition.' Because they had a young family. She hadn't to let them see her.[85]

Sometimes older women were greatly embarrassed by becoming pregnant when they already had grown-up children. Mrs Morgan remembered her mother 'crying with shame' when her nineteen-year-old son noticed her changing shape.[86] Mrs Calvert was married in the late 1930s and had two children by her first husband, and one by her second. No one appears to have been rude to her about her pregnancies, but she was very embarrassed by them, seeing them as visible proof of sexual activity:

Although I had three good confinements and it never bothered me, I never went out when I were pregnant, not till it was over with. I used to feel ashamed, because I knew they would think what I'd been doing and I used to think it was terrible.[87]

Confinements remained, for many women, dangerous, painful and unpleasant. The dramatic fall in the infant mortality rate throughout the twentieth century was obviously of enormous significance, but it has tended to obscure the fact that the national maternal death rate actually rose until 1936, despite the training of midwives under the 1902 Midwives Act, and the great extension of hospital provision for women in childbirth after the first world war. Jane Lewis, in *The Politics of Motherhood*, examines this phenomenon at the national level.[88] It is clear that the position in Preston was similar (see table 3.3).[89]

TABLE 3.3: Maternal deaths and incidence of puerperal fever in Preston[a]

	Deaths per thousand births	Incidence of puerperal fever
1911—15	4.51	2.26
1916—20	4.08	2.47
1921—25	5.25	3.28
1925—30	6.32	14.02
1930—35	6.02	19.38
1936—40[b]	5.02	18.35

[a] per thousand births (five-year averages).
[b] There were no cases of puerperal fever in 1940. This has reduced the averages considerably.
Source: Medical Officers of Health, Annual Reports 1911—20, 1930—40.

The figures for maternal deaths were sufficiently alarming for the Preston Medical Officer of Health to comment on them throughout the 1930s. He blamed the deaths on the failure of women to seek frequent and adequate ante-natal care: 'One has to record that a large number of women come to term with very little or no assessment as to the probability of their going through labour with safety to themselves or their offspring.'[90] Certainly no respondent records regular ante-natal care; usually a woman who suspected a pregnancy went either to a doctor or midwife to have it confirmed, and then booked their services for the confinement whether at home or in hospital. But the amount of ante-natal care sought was increasing. In Preston, in 1940, out of 1,711 women giving birth, 416 mothers (24 per cent of the total) had made 1,350 attendances at ante-natal clinics (an average of 3.2 each).[91] (In 1925 the Medical Officer reported only 73 patients in the ante-natal clinics; after a publicity drive this increased to 163 patients in 1926.) Many of the respondents later resented the lack of ante-natal care. They seem simply not to have been aware of its availability when they were pregnant; obviously, much depended on the attitude of the doctor when the pregnancy was confirmed. Mrs Abbott had four pregnancies, resulting in two live births:

When I was pregnant, it was terrible. I dreaded it. The last one I had, the doctor said I must go to hospital and they wanted to terminate it, I said no, and he was stillborn, a lovely boy . . .
And what happened to the other one you lost?
That came before time. It was after my first one. . . . I had an awful time. They didn't know what to do in those days. . . . We never had any preparation beforehand like they do now. They are told what to do and they have exercises to

help them, but not us, we had to get along as best we could.

Did the doctor ever give you a check-up of any sort, or did you just book the doctor to come on such a day?

He would just examine you and say what was what, and then unless you felt ill, you would be all right.

They didn't take your blood pressure or anything like that?

Oh no.[92]

It is clear that better ante-natal care would have further decreased the infant mortality rate. It is not so clear that inadequate ante-natal care was, as the Medical Officer of Health tended to suggest, the only, or even the most important, reason for the high maternal mortality figures. Indeed in the pre- and immediate post-first world war period, when ante-natal care was virtually unknown, the maternal mortality rate was lower (see table 3.3). As the provision of care increased, so too did the incidence of puerperal fever, although it is not suggested that there was any connection between the two developments. It is impossible to assess, from the Medical Officer of Health's Reports, the reasons for the deaths of so many women, although the report for 1930 did say: 'we regret to report that two of the deaths were partly attributable to some carelessness on the part of a local midwife who was in consequence reported to the Central Midwives Board.'[93] All that one can say with some certainty is that in the inter-war period the use of more trained midwives, and the increasing use of hospitals for confinements, not only failed to reduce the maternal mortality rates, but actually coincided with their significant increase.

It is perhaps time to re-examine the role of the traditional untrained midwife. These women had virtually no formal training, although they may have been chosen and instructed by a local doctor.[94] More usually they learned their trade from an older midwife, and quite often the skill was passed down in families. Their lack of formal training did not necessarily mean they were incompetent. (They sometimes also acted as the layer-out of the dead, and generally played an important role in the neighbourhood. They will be looked at again in chapter 5.) The most usual view of the untrained midwife is 'another legacy of the nineteenth century. . . . The Mrs Gamp midwife, dirty and illiterate.'[95] But their patients or women whose mothers had been their patients were almost unanimous in their admiration for the way they performed their job. Mrs Heron's mother had eleven children, all born before 1902:

Oh, I think we managed. Martha used to come, the midwife, and they used to stop in bed a week in them days. She wasn't certified or anything but she was one of the good old midwives and it was only a few shillings for a confinement. I've heard m'mother say that she used to give her sixpence a week until she got it paid off. She was a grand old lass.[96]

(The transcript fails to convey the warmth of the respondent's voice when she discusses Martha.) Mrs Dodds commented: 'She used to have these midwives come and they were such good friends a lot of them.' As her mother had twenty-one children (all born before 1900), she presumably had a remarkable opportunity to assess the merits of her midwives.[97]

It appears that working-class women continued to prefer the old, unqualified midwives for many years after the passing of the 1902 Midwives Act.[98] In 1917, the Lancaster Medical Officer of Health reported that out of 613 babies born in that year, 184 had been delivered by one unqualified midwife.[99] A Preston doctor, a respondent, still had an unqualified woman working in his practice in the 1930s, and there was one elsewhere in the county as late as 1937. Why did they continue so long? In the earlier decades the provision of qualified midwives had been very uneven, and women did not always have a real choice.[100] But there were other reasons too: unqualified midwives were cheaper;[101] they were generally thought to be friendlier, and less 'starchy'; and they were certainly less likely to tell the woman what to do, being more likely to co-operate both with her and her female relatives. It is an example of working-class women rejecting the invasion of their homes and lives by the professional. In view of the movement of the maternal mortality figures, her confidence in the 'old ways' was perhaps not altogether misplaced.

Mary Chamberlain, in *Old Wives' Tales*, considers the possible reasons for the relative success of the 'untrained' midwives:

Home deliveries were infinitely safer than hospital deliveries, with uncomplicated deliveries there was in any case little problem, with long labours often due to poor nutrition and physical weakness . . . she was more patient in her attendance. She was also less likely to interfere; midwives did not use instruments and rarely inserted their hand inside a labouring woman, unlike many of the doctors. . . . The naturalness of her technique often meant fewer complications, and unlike some doctors she did not inspire fear.[102]

Only one respondent criticised the competence of an unqualified midwife.

At the turn of the century working-class childbirth was almost always an unprofessional event; the midwife was untrained, and the doctor was usually called only if the mother's or child's life was thought to be in danger (and not always then). There was also a fundamental belief that somehow childbirth was a female affair, and women should and could get through it on their own.

This traditional stoical attitude is expressed by Mrs Hudson, whose confinement took place in the late 1920s:

So did you have to send for the doctor?
Yes. She wanted to send for the doctor earlier but I said I would manage. She said that I wouldn't. In the end, I was living with father then, she went downstairs and told father he was going to lose both of us if I didn't let them send for the doctor. Father said, 'You send for the doctor, never mind her!' Afterwards, she asked me why I had held out on her. I told her that none of my sisters had needed a doctor, but she said that that was nothing to do with me. She said, 'Good Lord, look at her!' She was navy-blue was Evelyn when she was born. Anyhow, she didn't take any harm. They 'phoned three doctors and they were all out. She sent for Doctor Harrington and as soon as he came he just turned my head round and said, 'Oh, my God!' I was just beyond anything. I must have been too far gone to take chloroform and I had to have a proper mask on. I had to be stitched up. In them days you didn't move for ten days and I had to lie in bed. She told me that if I was going to be silly she would have to tie my feet together. She made me promise that I wouldn't move. My sister looked after me as she lived at home as well.[103]

Examples of this refusal of professional help can be found up to 1940, but a fairly rapid revolution was taking place in working-class women's attitude to childbirth. Patricia Branca has argued that throughout the nineteenth century it was middle-class women who most readily adopted new attitudes, while working-class women maintained more traditional life styles.[104] Victorian middle-class women (following the example of Queen Victoria) had long expected and accepted chloroform to relieve labour pains. This was rarely given to working-class women before the first world war, mostly because they so rarely had the doctor in attendance, and he alone could administer it. Only one respondent remembered her mother having chloroform before the first world war — and if this experience was typical, or accounts of similar occasions were common, it may help to explain working-class abstinence! The incident took place about 1909:

I must have been about nine at the time. She was very, very poorly at the time Mary was born. It was in the middle of the night, of course, and Dr Sanson got us all out of bed to shout 'Mamma', at the bedroom door. We were all shouting 'Mamma' in the middle of the night.
This was because she'd had anaesthetic?
Anaesthetic, and he couldn't get her round.[105]

Gradually, in the inter-war period, it is possible to discern women's changing attitudes to their own health and their own bodies. The fatalism, the ignorance, the shame, the stoicism, and the traditionalism are all still very apparent, but a growing number of women from all levels of the working class began to expect more professional help, whether in the form of a doctor or a qualified midwife; they began to expect analgesics, and a hospital bed 'in case something should go wrong'. Mrs Pearce belonged to the very poorest class, her husband being a casually employed outdoor labourer. At the time of her first confinement, in 1923, she was a weaver. She and her husband could not then afford a home of their own, and the confinement took place in their lodgings with the husband's mother. But even this poor family had both a doctor and a nurse, and chloroform at the confinement, and the couple decided that future confinements must take place in hospital (which they did):

They gave you chloroform at home, did they?
Yes. Well, it were a breech. They did turn me. She [her mother-in-law] said that she had never seen anything like it in her life. The nurse and doctor had both their sleeves rolled right up here. They were sweating. I was in bed about a fortnight and she looked after me while I was in bed. Because we couldn't afford to pay anybody else. After that he said it was a finisher. He said it was my work that had done a lot of that.
Was this your husband or the doctor?
My husband. He said, 'You are going away. I'm not having you messed about like that.' So after that, with the other ones, I went away. My sister was frightened to death of hospitals. I thought, if she had gone through what I did at first, then she would want to go in hospital.[106]

It was usual for couples who made this decision to do so on their own, unpressurised, at least directly, by professional medical opinion. And yet medical opinion was increasingly in favour of hospital confinements. It is difficult to assess from either the documentary or the oral evidence how these professional views became part of a more general climate of opinion, but they did. In 1938, in Preston, 863 babies were born at home (61.3 per cent), 494 (35.1 per cent) in two local hospitals, and 50 (3.5 per cent) in private nursing homes (attended by none of the women in the sample).[107]

In the sample, the Preston women gave birth to forty-three children in the inter-war period; of these thirty were born at home (69.7 per cent), and thirteen in hospital (30.2 per cent). Wherever the confinement took place, it still remained for most women a time of travail, of true labour and considerable pain. Some women felt that many of their problems stemmed from the ignorance in which they were brought up.

Mind you, after my first, that was a terrific shock. I would never like my children to be brought up in such ignorance. It was a terrific shock, it took me a long time, and I said never again, I would drown myself. And he said, 'and I'd go

with you'. You know, it was a very traumatic experience. . . . Well, my first baby
was born on a Tuesday and on the Saturday I said to my husband, 'I am bothered,'
and he said, 'What's the matter?' And I said, 'How can a baby come out?' You
know, you had a brown mark there and I thought how can a baby come out there,
how will it? I was terrified of this bursting, you know. He said, 'Well what do you
mean?' . . . He said, 'But they don't come out there.' I said, 'Where do they come
out?' and he said, 'Where it goes in.' And do you know, I nearly died. Well I was
more het up than ever. How could it? . . . and I really think I suffered more
through ignorance; you do![108]

POWER RELATIONSHIPS WITHIN MARRIAGE

The procreation and bearing of children, although central to marriage, was
only one aspect of the relationship between husbands and wives. There are
obvious difficulties in attempting to generalise about marital relationships,
but it is possible to discern some quite clear patterns. Within a marriage what
power, if any, did a woman exercise? Frederick Engels, writing in 1884, was
quite clear that women were oppressed by marriage.[109] The oral evidence
does not, however, suggest universal oppression of women within working-
class marriages; indeed, in the great majority of marriages in the sample, the
woman exerted significant power, not so much from legal rights as from
moral force. Although the source of her power was moral, it could and did
give her considerable economic control over the family. There was, for
example, no law which stated that a working-class woman should control her
family's finances, and yet in every family but one in the sample this was the
case. (In this case the father was a teetotaller, while the mother enjoyed a
drink. She may not have been a heavy drinker, but she was not given the
opportunity, as all the family's finances were dealt with by the father.)[110]
Working-class traditions were very strong; as has been seen, it was simply
assumed that all earning children gave their wages to their mother for her to
dispose of as she thought best. Similarly, 'good' husbands were expected to
hand over their wages without any deductions having been made. There
were variations in the operation of this custom. Some wives were so strict
that their husbands received no pocket money at all. One worked as a waiter
at the local pub, and was expected to rely on his tips for pocket money;
another was allowed to keep his overtime pay, but not a penny of his
wages.[111] Most men, like their children, received a set amount of pocket
money each week, as this conversation with Mrs Winder and Mr Jones
records:

[ER] It used to be mothers that sort of dominated the home?
[Mrs Winder] Oh yes, I think so and I think in those days that the man passed

over the money, much more than he does today. I mean today they sit down and talk it out and there's so much for him and so much for the house. But in those days the wages were so poor that really the man didn't get a right lot out of it. . . .

[Mr Jones] His job was to provide for the family.

[Mrs Winder] Yes, and it was handed over and the wife did the allotting where it went.

[ER] I think they perhaps gave the husband something back, didn't they?

[Mrs Winder] Yes, but, well, in some cases I don't think they got an awful lot. I mean some of these that were always drunk must have got a lot back. I think they perhaps didn't treat the wives fairly. I mean, I can remember when I was smaller when my father was at Williamsons in the warehouse office he got a shilling a week to spend, and he only smoked half an ounce of twist, and it was fourpence. And of course he never went to work on a bus or anything, he walked both ways.[112]

Mrs Winder mentions 'some of these that were always drunk'. These men certainly did not treat their wives and family fairly and certainly did not hand over their whole wages, but they rarely interfered with their wives' control of the amount which *was* handed over.

Respondents described women's position as financial controllers in very similar terms to those of respondents in Helen Bosanquet's study of working-class family life before the first world war:

[Marriage] assigns to the wife the function of manager and spender of the family income while the husband and adult children take the responsibility of providing the income. . . . She determines even the amount which the wage-earners, husbands, sons and daughters alike may reserve for their own use before handing their money to her, and both they and their husbands know that their services in the home are far more valuable than if they were themselves earning.[113]

This role of the woman was not, of course, confined either to this geographical area, or to this particular period. Scott and Tilly refer on many occasions to women, throughout Europe in the nineteenth and twentieth centuries, controlling their families' finances: 'In these families . . . everyone seems to have acknowledged the mother's managerial role.' Michelle Perrot writes of a French woman in the nineteenth century as 'le ministre des finances', and Alexander Paterson, in his study of Edwardian London, said of the working-class woman, 'Her purse or pocket is the common fund and from this she distributes the family income. They are the earner but she is the spender.'[114]

Control of the purse usually meant that it was the woman who made decisions about moving house; it was she who decided if the family could afford to buy a house, or if they could afford a higher or needed to pay a lower rent, as these conversations with Mrs Austin, Mr Pearson, Mr Matthews and Mr Shore show:

Was it your mother who wanted to move to Newsham Road or was it your father's choice; do you know?

[Mrs Austin] Oh, I think m'mother's. Oh yes, m'mother. I don't think he would object, but m'mother had all the push, definitely, hadn't she Tom? You know she took the initiative in that sort of way. Oh, she had to push m'father to get him going you know to get one. He was . . . he was a very contented man really, he could be too contented really. You know he hadn't enough push.[115]

Who decided to come here, was it your mother or dad, to this house?

[Mr Pearson] M'mother. M'father wouldn't put his name to anything. He was one of them fellows that said he didn't like anything round his neck.

A debt you mean?

A debt, yes. No, the house was never in m'father's name. When m'mother died she left the house for him to live in as long as he did but when he died it had to be divided between the children.[116]

[Mr Matthew] Our Albert Street house was about 5s. a week, but they put it up to 5s. 6d. Mother took the plunge to move, but Dad was a bit hesitant. I don't know where she got the money from to put down on the Ramsden Street home. . . . Dad wouldn't take responsibility and Mother took the responsibility and moved. . . . It was a bigger house.[117]

Was it your mother who decided to move, or your father?

[Mr Shore] Well I should think, knowing the characters of them, Mother would arrange it.

You felt she made all that sort of decision, did she?

That's right, she was the leader. There are in every couple and she was the one.[118]

Traditionally the woman had moral control of her family, again the exception being the families where the father drank a lot. Her authority extended not only over her children, but over her husband too. This was noticed and commented on by Helen Bosanquet in 1906:

Fathers are regarded by the children as plain inferior to mother in authority, in knowledge of right and wrong, and above all of 'manners'. Talk of the subjection of women, I doubt if the bare idea of father being equal to mother in rank and authority ever entered the mind of any child under sixteen. Father is generally regarded in the light of mother's eldest child and disobedience in him is far more heinous a crime, than in them.[119]

It is clear that a few men were positively afraid of their wives and many were dominated by them. Mr Logan, an ex-professional soldier, lived in Lancaster in the 1920s. He was a violent man outside the home and had several confrontations with authority, notably in the form of the Poor Law Guardians, but he said this about his marriage: 'There is something about a woman that can treat a man like hell at times. He's not afraid of anything outside; he is afraid of his wife.'[120] Mrs Charlton spoke thus of her parents:

Were your parents strict?
My mother was. She was boss, if you know what I mean. My dad was little and my mother was big. Oh yes, my mother was boss. . . . I think it was because he was deaf that she took over.
Were you the boss like your mother was?
Well I will admit it, I was. My husband always said that there was no boss in this house, but that I always got my own way. . . . He was a man of few words, shall I put it that way?[121]

And Mrs Hewitson described her mother:

She wasn't bossy, but she was the prevailing spirit in the house, you know. We knew that and we were brought up that way, if Mother said it you did it, and it wasn't a case of 'I'll ask m'dad', and he would say 'ask your mother'. And if he said anything to us m'mother never interfered, and if she said anything he never interfered, but if they didn't agree on that matter they talked about it when we weren't there, but not in front of us, never. They never fell out in front of us, never. I dare say they had their ups and downs, you know, because m'father did some things, like he liked a drink now and again which m'mother didn't agree with. And once they were going to move house. She wanted to move house, anyway, and they were living in a house belonging to a friend of his and he didn't want to move. And he said, 'Well all that upheaval,' and so on and so on, and made a thing about it and mother said, 'Well, that extra ninepence a week would shoe the children.' We went![122]

Some women used their power to change their husbands' work — sometimes with fortunate results, but sometimes unhappily. Mr Sharples said:

My mother was the more dominant personality in the family. Although, outside the family, Father was an extremely powerful personality, as I described, at home Mother generally prevailed. This even extended to my father's own career. After the war he had possibilities of advancement if he had been prepared to move to another town, and he wanted to, but Mother wouldn't hear of it. She persuaded him to stay. I rather tended to reproach her for that in a way later because, as I said to you, he was dreadfully exploited at the foundry where he worked, particularly in his later years. I think, with hindsight, it would certainly have been very much in the family's interests if he had moved.

Why wouldn't she move? Did she say?

I should think it was something inherent in her character. I don't think she had any practical or terribly logical reasons or motives.[123]

Less serious and more common were attempts to control husbands' leisure activities:

Who was the strictest in the family, your mum or your dad?

M'mother. Father had his strict way. We'd to be in at certain times. He wanted to know the reason why if we weren't. He was strict in a way, but m'mother was far more strict, far more strict.

You felt she ran the house, do you?

Yes. Oh, she did, because Father used to go to church greatly against his grain because she made him go. I never heard her swear, m'mother, never. Neither damn or nothing. And she used to go to church and she used to make m'dad go and she got him to join the Church of England Men's Society and the poor old soul must have been in agony . . . I don't know. But anyway he went to church, took us to church.[124]

Control of the husband's spare-time activities is often mentioned. Some women feared their husbands developing the habit of heavy drinking. If a man became a drunkard, or even a regular steady drinker, then the family income was threatened. The majority of men who drank did so within the limits of their pocket money, but some women thought it worthwhile to keep a check on the situation. The woman in the extract just quoted also enrolled her daughters to keep a careful eye on their father when he took them to the theatre or cinema, and questioned them closely on his behaviour. Others objected if they felt that their husbands' leisure time activities took them away from home too frequently:

Did your father ever play sports when he was young?

He used to play when they were first married. . . . All the local lads used to play football on there and my dad was one of them. He would always play on a Saturday afternoon. My mother got fed up with this here as he was always going playing football. He would wear a pair of shorts. One weekend he said to my mother, 'Where's my shorts? I can't find them and I'm going to play football.' She said, 'You're not playing football no more.' She put them on the fire. He never played football any more.[125]

Mr Matthews remembered a parental dispute over the way Sunday afternoons should be spent:

Dad, on a Sunday afternoon, beggared off for a walk with his pal, and Mother got fed up with this. . . . One Sunday afternoon she packed a bag and took us into the country and stayed there until 9 o'clock and Dad was all over the place after her, and that brought it to a head really. They went out together after that.[126]

While the wish to control the husbands' behaviour was usual, the extent to which women and men wanted to share their leisure time varied very much from marriage to marriage. It becomes more noticeable in the inter-war period, but it is clear that companionable marriage *did* exist before the first world war. A few women went to the pub with their husbands, and rather more drank with their husbands at home, although the socially more aspiring regarded this as not respectable. Each neighbourhood also had its own practices about the women's behaviour in pubs. In some men and women sat together; in others they were apart, even in different rooms; in others again women were expected for only part of the evening. Mr Maguire remembered the custom of a very poor area of Lancaster in the early 1920s:

Such as my community, the women did go out, but with hubby. Say on Friday night she'd happen to go down about nine o'clock or half past nine and have two, but she never went out same time as him. She'd go down there and have half an hour with him.

He'd be already there?

Yes. But the women round about never thought no more about it. That was in our own community. Not everyone did it, but those that didn't, didn't frown on it. They had so much tension, so much worry that every little outlet different to working in four walls all week, cooking, washing, was a godsend. It was a luxury to go and have a beer. An escape from the drudgery of the house.[127]

Others went out to the theatre, the cinema, and for walks. Virtually none went to a dance together after they were married. Some men, like Mrs Harrison's father, had great admiration and affection for their wives and often took them out, the outing being regarded as a tribute to them. This extract refers to the 1920s:

Did she ever manage a holiday?

Every year. With father being on the railway he used to get the tickets but they didn't take me. It didn't bother me, I didn't feel as though I had missed out. I used to go to an auntie. I was the youngest. My brother and sister were working. When you think about it afterwards, he used to tell us Mother had worked hard all year looking after us so she had to have a holiday without us.

Where would they go?

They would go to London, and this was quite an achievement when it was just Blackpool round here.[128]

Whether or not leisure was shared or separate did not affect the basically clear differentiation in the roles of husbands and wives in working-class marriages. When the emphasis placed on shared activities and interchangeable tasks is compared to that on independent and complementary activities, it is clear that in the great majority of marriages there was a very firm differentiation. When a man did undertake his wife's housework it was usually because of an emergency: 'When she'd been confined you'd see father with his pipe in his mouth scrubbing at the washing and looking round to see that we were doing something. He'd scrub the floor . . . until we were old enough to do it, and of course he retired from housework then.'[129] Some regularly undertook to help with the shopping, because it was heavy for the woman to carry on her own, and certain household tasks like papering and painting, and shoe-repairing, were usually regarded as 'men's work'. The majority of men believed that they proved their masculinity by never doing any domestic chore which could be construed as belonging to the sphere of women, an attitude long-recognised and frequently criticised today. But most women then shared this view; they did not necessarily appreciate a man's help except in emergencies, and seeing men doing domestic chores appears to have made them feel uncomfortable. They also felt they were more competent at most domestic chores. These three short extracts are typical of many:

He wouldn't lift a pot, wash a pot, lift a hand at nothing.[130]

Did he do anything in the house?
My father? He wasn't allowed to![131]

Oh, give him a hammer and we wouldn't have had a house. I don't think he knew the end of a nail. If my mother wanted a shelf putting up she put it up.[132]

(Men were not usually regarded as being totally incompetent, but the attitude that the house was the woman's responsibility was common.)

How and why working-class men and women adopted such segregated conjugal roles are questions examined by Elizabeth Bott, who, describing an investigation into families in the 1950s, postulates a theory which has a wider application. She argues that the degree of segregation of conjugal roles is related to the degree of interrelatedness in the total network of the family; those families which had a high degree of segregation in the role-relationship of husband and wife tending to have a close-knit network, with many of their friends, neighbours, and relatives knowing one another.[133] However, she does not suggest which was the causative factor. Both are discernible in working-class relationships in Barrow, Lancaster and Preston. If both husband and wife came from such a background, they would each have a pattern of external relationships which would provide emotional satisfaction and practical help, and each would consequently demand less of their spouse. In only one family in Lancaster was the father actively and happily involved in domestic affairs, regularly cooking the Sunday dinner, washing and caring for the children, and cleaning the house, although there was no family emergency, and no real need for him to perform these tasks. It is perhaps significant that this family had recently arrived from Cumberland and had no local relatives, and had deliberately avoided close involvement with their neighbours. In other words, they existed without a close-knit support network.[134]

There could well be another interpretation of the segregation in the role-relationship between husband and wife. It cannot be doubted that the early conditioning children of both sexes received about men's and women's roles within the home and family must have affected their later adult roles.

One of the most interesting points made by Bott was that in marriages with a considerable degree of role segregation there was not only a clear division of labour, but also a basic division of responsibilities. This is an important point, because it could be argued, in the case of the women of Barrow, Lancaster and Preston, that their responsibility for such matters as budgeting and moral standards arose simply from their husbands' lack of interest or irresponsibility, rather than from the women's dominance within the home. The extent to which men adopted this rather passive role depended on individual characteristics, but it was primarily influenced by the ways, already considered, in which women were seen as managers and men as 'providers'. If women had had these responsibilities taken away from them by their husbands then they would presumably have displayed (as did some middle-class women at that time) significantly more discontent with their lot, for without them they would have been reduced to the status of domestic servants within the marriage. When there was a conflict of opinion on domestic matters, as some of the extracts indicate, it tended to be the woman whose decision was final, because this was her sphere of responsibility.

So far, the model of marriage portrayed has been of the husband and wife playing separate, different, but equal roles. Of course, men had superior rights both legally and politically, and in the world of work. Helen Bosanquet has summarised the relative roles and status of men and women thus: 'In reference to the outside world man has power and woman "influence". Within the home woman has the active power and man "influence".'[135] Her view of the late Victorian and Edwardian marriage was markedly different from that of her contemporary feminist writers, but accords with the views of those interviewed. The undoubted power wielded by so many women must have contributed to their indifference to the suffragette movement.

At least two other patterns of marriage relationships are discernible. In the first, the roles were not separate; in the second, they were not equal. In Preston especially, where there was a large proportion of married women in full-time work, women's employment affected her relationship with her husband. In these marriages, unlike those where the wife worked part-time or not at all, the husband usually helped with the domestic chores; when both partners were earners and managers, role segregation broke down. Here, Mr Gaskell is speaking of his father before the first world war: 'He seemed to always do the Sunday dinner. . . . He would clean-up and wash-up.'[136] Mrs Williams, a ring spinner (a semi-skilled mill worker), is describing her married life in the 1920s and 1930s:

I used to get them for the night after, if it was chops and onions I used to cook them and he would be home before me and he would warm them in the frying pan. . . . I never wound a clock up in all my married life, I never made a fire and I never chopped wood and I never made a bed. He did all that whenever he had his tea and washed his hands. . . . He was very good. I would be washing up at 1 o'clock in the morning and getting up at 5 o'clock to go to work. He would look to the boy and I would look to the girl.[137]

Husbands with wives working full-time had to help in the home, because otherwise it is doubtful if their wives would have survived.[138] The Preston study reveals the difficulty of applying sociological models, like that developed by Elizabeth Bott, to all occupational groups. Husbands and wives in Preston textile families, like those in Barrow and Lancaster, also had closely knit networks of neighbours and relatives, and yet there was noticeably less segregation in their conjugal roles. Patterns of women's employment cannot be ignored in the study of role-relationships within marriage.

Despite the different roles played in housework, there is no oral evidence to support the argument that full-time working wives and mothers necessarily exerted more power and influence within their marriage than did their contemporaries with part-time or no paid work. Diana Gittins argues that 'the power relationship would depend primarily on the wife's working or not working',[139] but this was not the case in my sample. Some of the most powerful women in all three towns, who were not so much their husbands' equals but rather the dominant partner in the marriage, worked either part-time or not at all.

Is it possible to find examples of the third marriage model, that of the stereotype Victorian family with an all-powerful father dominating, sub-jugating, even terrifying his wife and children? There were indeed such marriages, a minority of the total, in the generation of the respondents' parents, but a minority which cannot be ignored, producing as it did untold physical and psychological misery. All the husbands in this group had a keen sense of what was 'manly'. This almost invariably included heavy drinking, demanding total obedience from their families, expecting and getting the best food available in the family, and spending an inordinate proportion of their wages on their own personal pleasures, whether it was clothes, jewellery or gambling. They almost inevitably had very large families, and in some cases tormented their wives even further by accusing them of having affairs with other men. Many of these men were talented and either held, or would have held, skilled supervisory jobs. (A minority only worked when they felt like it.)[140] There was another small 'patriarchal' group who, like the first, dominated their families but were not unkind, and who did not drink. But they did expect obedience and to be the head of the family. Like the majority of the first group, they often held supervisory and/or skilled jobs, and their self-confidence and habits of controlling others were obviously carried from work to home. The father of Mrs Hesketh is described in some detail because he seems to epitomise the very worst of all the husbands and fathers in the sample:

My father was a fitter by trade but he was one that wouldn't be told. He was so good at it that he would chuck it up like that. You could never reckon on him being in work but he was never without in his own pocket. But he must have kept my mother short. She was a good mother, she was lovely. . . . He would have spasms. He would turn to anything as regards work, really. I mean, you've got to be fair, but he didn't part with it. We didn't see much of him. He just come home to sort of make us [procreate us] and that was it. Mother would have to pile him up with groceries enough to last him four or five days and he would go and catch salmon. The name of the boat was the *Yarrow*, I remember that.

And did you eat the fish, or did he sell it?

Oh he sold it.

So it was all a bit of income, really?

Yes. He would take all these groceries and she would perhaps have nothing in the pantry for us. How she managed I don't know. It is a mystery to me. . . .

He always had that little wallet at the back that wasn't ours. On a Saturday night he would get ready and put his jewellery on, his gold chain and rings, and what not. He would turn with his back to Mum, like this, to count his money. He had an eye for the ladies when he were out. He used to go to what they called the Long Vaults. . . . Well, we have come a long way since then. Our mothers thought that they had to be there when the men come home, drunk or sober, to please or otherwise. . . .

Did he ever raise his hand to her, or was it just the children?

That is a story on its own, which didn't happen as we were growing up, naturally. But what neighbours have told us, it is an intimate thing, but it is true nevertheless. I have checked on it. She was having a child every year because in between where there was a three-year gap, there had been one or should have been one. What chance had she at that time with us lot. . . . He was one as got boozed on his way home from work. . . . God knows, she had enough on her plate but he has come home in a real bad state of drunkenness from all accounts and he has looked for her but she had run out of his way by fright, and she was pregnant. One of the neighbours said that many a time my mother sat on her lavatory out of the way as she was so frightened of him. Accusing all the time that it wasn't his and all that. Later on we found out that it was him that was playing the game. But poor Mum, at forty-four to die after only tasting a little bit of what life was all about.

And it was all the same pattern. Coming home from work and giving her what was left. This was a more intimate life which was told to us by my mother's friends. He used to get the blues or something when he was drunk and he was always threatening her with the axe. This is the God's truth, every time she was pregnant she daren't tell him because he would start all over again, and naturally, it were his child. She never got out and she wasn't even a drinker. She didn't know what it was to go and sit in a pub, but he accused her all the time and it led from one thing to another. It hurts me to repeat it but nevertheless it's true. When the confinement happened he stood over her with a burning lamp threatening her . . . terrifying her. He is dead, may God rest his soul![141]

The unfortunate women who were married to men like this usually behaved as Mrs Hesketh's mother did: compliant, dutiful, silent, uncomplaining. Just occasionally they fought back, but, as in all families, they had to go on being the manager. Mrs Owen's mother also suffered:

Well, you see, with my father being like this with the drink, my mother used to leave, didn't she? He used to go mad, he was a Jekyll and Hyde when he had drink, he was wild, absolutely, and he gave my mother a horrible time and, of course, I'm the youngest of eleven, you see, and the others were growing older then so she decided to just leave. You could do that then, there was always a house somewhere, there was no such thing as having to wait for a house. She left this house with the family and she left it as it stood with the furniture and the lot. Of course, this was when my sisters and brothers were all earning a bit of money, you see. She took a house and we moved lock, stock and barrel as you say. Then she went to this Jew that she had worked for and got what furniture she needed. Probably she got it on weekly payments and he didn't know where we had gone. But he found out after a bit and he came and he played hallelujah, he did. I can remember my brothers taking me out. I think then she took him back, she had three separations from him but after the third she wouldn't have him at all. . . . my father was in this house and he wanted to fight and my brother was trying to calm him down. And, you know those bannister stair rails? well he was clinging on to them and my brothers were trying to get him out and get him away and he pulled them out. He was only a little wiry man but he was so strong when he had this drink, so they sent for a policeman, a policeman would come then. But in those days a policeman couldn't go in and take him out, my brothers had to put him out on the pavement, then the policeman would take him. . . .

So your mother must have been a very tough lady to put up with all that?

Yes, she had to be. Then she was sewing all the time. After I was born he wouldn't work at all. He would say, 'I'll look after Matt.' He used to call me Matt. She used to give him, my mother used to give him, so much money a week to look after me. I can remember going to those country pubs. He'd walk, and walk me there and I can always remember him sitting me once on a windowsill outside a pub and it was high up and I couldn't get off and I was outside waiting for him coming out.

So where was your mother? Was she at home sewing?

Yes.

Did she ever try to stop him drinking, do you know?

One thing that she would not go with him. Even in later life, when we had all grown up, she would always let him go on his own and I think, really, if she had gone with him it might have been better, he might not have got so much to drink.[142]

Some women (although none in the sample), sought the protection of the courts. Although no systematic investigation has been made of police records, random searches show that, from the beginning of the period, women were not only taking drunken, brutal husbands to court; they were also winning their cases. The following case was reported in the *Lancaster Guardian* in 1890 and is typical of many:

Timothy Cragg a joiner of Brittania Street was charged with assault on his wife Sarah Ann Cragg. The complainant who appeared in the box with a black eye and several bruises on her face said that about 6 o'clock on Sunday morning the defendant struck her on the face and gave her a black eye. He then knocked her off a chair onto the floor. Threw the chair and table over her and jumped on her bowels. Finally he did something worse than that but she could not tell the bench what it was. He also abused her on Saturday night. The complainant who was very hysterical said that all she wanted was a separation. She did not ask for money from him as she would support herself and her children. There were 4 children aged 8 to 13. She had been married 15 years and 'had nothing but black flesh ever since'. The neighbours said that he was brutal. He was sentenced to 3 months hard labour. The wife was granted a judicial separation and 10/- a week maintenance.[143]

THE EFFECT OF SOCIAL CHANGE

The incidence of brutality, drunkenness, neglect and overbearing behaviour in husbands appears to have been much less in the respondents' generation compared to that of their parents. There are many reasons for this, but undoubtedly the most important for the transformation in working-class social life was brought about by the decline in drinking.[144] There was widespread revulsion against the social evils resulting from excessive drinking, gained from childhood experiences both in the home and in the temperance organisations. While not being a generation of total abstainers, the respondents — or more exactly the male respondents and the husbands of female respondents — drank conspicuously less than their fathers' generation did.

Some of this restraint was forced upon them by government policy. In 1915, alarmed by the adverse effect on the war effort of munition workers spending a substantial part of the increase in their wages on drink, the government, in the Defence of The Realm Acts, established a Central Control Board to take charge of licensing in those areas where it was judged that extensive drinking was impeding the war effort.[145] These areas (which included Barrow, which had a special mention in the Report of Bad Time-Keeping) were extended until, by 1917, 38 million out of a population of 41 million were subjected to the Board's regulations. The sale of alcohol was limited to two and a half hours in the middle of the day, and three hours in the evening. At the same time the potency of beer was reduced, and the tax on spirits increased (four- to five-fold between 1914 and 1920). These measures combined to have a dramatic effect on local drinking habits, as the conviction rates and the oral evidence reveal. In 1914 the average national weekly convictions for drunkenness were 3,388; by the end of 1918 this had fallen to 444.[146]

The restrictions on licensing hours, with some modifications, continued after the war, as did the increased taxes and the reduced potency of the beer. The relative importance of these measures as opposed to the working-class revulsion against drinking cannot be assessed, but the latter should not be underestimated.

The decrease in working-class drinking both coincided with, and was partially caused by, two other radical changes in working-class social life. First, throughout this period, but especially during and after the war, it became more and more socially acceptable for 'respectable' women to go into pubs with their husbands. The unconventional and the 'rough' had always been seen in bars, but respectable women in many areas would not have dreamed of entering such a place. It is possible that by refusing to accompany her husband she lost an opportunity to control his drinking, as Mrs Owen suggested about her own mother. Mrs Chadwick had the same idea:

Did you mind your husband not helping about the house?
I just took it for granted that he wouldn't because, honestly, very early in my marriage I realised what a drastic mistake I had made. He was a lovely man when we were courting, manners, because he had a very good upbringing but he soon

went off the rails after he was married. I mean in drinking.

Oh, dear, that is a shame! Did you go with him or did he go out on his own?

Oh, I never went with him because there was nothing for me in pubs. I didn't like it. He had got the wrong type, he should have got a raw brash type that would go and have a drink with him and perhaps knock sense into him. But I'm not that type. It's no good. I don't thrive on bother. I like to be happy.[147]

Her description of the kind of wife who would have suited her husband could have applied in several other cases in the sample for the previous generation. In her own generation she is one of only two respondents who had trouble with a drunken husband. The other was Mrs Pearce whose husband, having suffered greatly in the war, came home determined that his home should be his own truly private domain, without intrusions from either neighbours or even relatives. While he sought solace in the pub, his wife was expected to preside in lonely isolation over home and family. She offered little resistance, knowing she was likely to be battered if she did. She was aware, however, that this way of life was looked upon with increasing disfavour by her friends and family:

He asked why I had went to Molly's. I told him that I had nobody to talk to and that I daren't have any friends. I told him that I just got fed up as I just had a child to talk to all day. I said to him, 'Do you know, anybody that has a dog, they take it for walks. Dogs are better-off than me. I never get taken out.' He didn't know what to say. . . . My sister used to get vexed. She had only had three children and when I was expecting again it was worse than having a mother as she used to shout at me. She said, 'He doesn't care a thing about you and I think it's awful.'[148]

The other great change came with the arrival of the cinema, which became established in all towns in the four or five years before the first world war, and which did not have the disreputable reputation of either the pub or the music hall. Indeed, many parents were happy for their children to go to the cinema on their own. Moreover, the cinema was considerably cheaper than the theatre. Adults could buy a seat in the cinema for 3d., children could go in for 1d., whereas theatre seats tended to start at 6d. (and could cost as much as 3s. in the dress circle).[149] The chairman of the London branch of the Cinematograph Exhibitors' Association said in 1917, 'The cheapness of this form of amusement has created what is really a new type of audience. Over half the visitors to the picture theatres occupy seats to the value of 3d. or less. . . . The picture house is emphatically the poor man's theatre.'[150]

By the 1920s a new working-class social habit was developing, that of the family going together to the cinema on a Saturday night:

It [social life] was very much divided until about Saturday, and then you might get groups of families queuing for the pictures. . . . You could see the whole family queuing, and that was the first house. Afterwards he'd slip into the local boozer, and she would carry on with fish and chips and take the kids home . . . even when there was unemployment I've seen queues for the local picture house.

I suppose it was a way of escapism, a way of getting away from it all?

No. It's only modern people that talk about escapism. . . . It was just somewhere to go . . . it's because it was the thing to do, a habit.[151]

Many women welcomed this new habit, not only because they too enjoyed it, but because they saw that the cinema tended to keep their men out of the pub.

Although the increased sharing of leisure, and the pattern of husbands and wives sharing domestic work in families where the wife had full-time employment, presaged the more usual companionate marriages evident after the second world war, it must be emphasised that separate roles were the norm throughout the period. The way power was distributed within those marriages depended on a complex variety of factors, including individual personalities, drinking habits, and the nature of the employment of both partners, but in the majority of working-class marriages it would appear to be misleading and inaccurate to see the wife as downtrodden, bullied and dependent. She was much more likely to be respected and highly regarded, financial and household manager, and the arbiter of familial and indeed neighbourhood standards.

4

Women as Housewives and Managers

Woman's dual role as family financial manager and moral guide cannot be underestimated. She acted within tight financial and social constraints. However good her managerial abilities, she was necessarily restricted by the family's income; she was further restricted in her choice of action by the mores of her family, her kinship group, and her neighbourhood. She was, of course, limited by her actual physical environment, her home; finally, she would generally be hampered by frequent and prolonged childbearing.

WORKING-CLASS HOMES

Working-class women had learned when young that their place was in the home: they might work outside it for greater or lesser periods; they could leave it freely for social or charitable excursions; their husbands and children might well help in its care and maintenance; but it was accepted by all that the ultimate responsibility for the home was theirs, as was seen in chapter 3.

It would seem appropriate to begin this chapter with Mrs Mitchell's memories of her home in the 1920s. It is typical of many descriptions of homes, both before and after that date; and it illustrates the relation between continuity and change mentioned earlier. It is a reminder that very few working-class homes had any mechanical aids to alleviate the burden of housework before 1940:

Now, it was a really old fireplace, all black iron and steel. There was what we called a little two-bar in front, like a small table and it used to hook on, there was a kettle there with water, they were always brewing up. Now on the side here there was a lid and you just lifted the lid and that was a kind of cavity. That was always full of water and the heat from the fire always kept it hot and boiling. They used to use that for washing-up or when they were having a bath. Then the other side there was an oven and they used to bake the bread in there.
How did your mother do her washing?

Washing day. Apart from the mangle, the other equipment used for washing are the dollytub in the background and the bucket and bowl. (Manchester Studies, Manchester Polytechnic)

Well, in the back kitchen, not the living-room, where all the cooking and everything was, in the corner there . . . the boiler fit in there and it was rounded at the front and at the bottom, it was an earth floor, flagged floor. Now just higher up this was made of brick, in the middle there was a little metal door which you opened, and there was a grid inside and you used to take the coal off the living-room fire and put it in there first thing Monday morning to get that fire going. And you pushed it in this boiler, close the little metal door, and then you had to fill this boiler from the cold water tap at the sink. We used to have what we called a lading can, a tin one, a huge cup with a big handle and filled it at the tap, pour it in this boiler till this big iron boiler inside was full of water, and then you waited till that got hot, then they put all the clothes in after they were steeped in water all night. They were put in and they were all boiled in there. They would boil for so long, and then it all came out and there was two big wooden tubs, like there beer barrels, and they would come out of this boiler and they would go in this butt of water to rinse. Then they would have a good rinse and be taken out of there, put through an old-fashioned wooden wringer. It was solid, you had to drag them out, you couldn't move them, made of solid iron with huge wooden rollers. This was the children's stuff, turning this big wheel while mother put the washing through, then it was taken from there. Now in this other tub, it was cold water and a dolly blue dipped in it to make it blue, a little blue bag with a little wooden top. Then she'd get a dish where she would mix some Reckitt's starch, and she would mix it up, and it was all poured into this big tub, all mixed up, and all these clothes were put back into there. That was to put the final stiffness, the starch and the blue to whiten them. Then they were taken out and they were put back through these rollers, the old mangles, they were called then, and as they came through there, they were all folded neatly and all put outside to dry. Outside we had a flagged yard and there was rows and rows of rope from one end to the other, and all these clothes used to be blowing, it was lovely. After that they had all this fire to clean out and scrape, the flagged floors, they were swimming in water. I used to detest Mondays, going home from school.

She must have been up early.

Well, they did get up early because this fire had to be made, it took so long to do it and, of course, if we had gone to school, if she was late, then they had to do it themselves. Turn it with one hand and guide the clothes through with the other. That was the washing. Well, there was all the ironing. Now in those days, we had Nottingham lace curtains, they were full-length, beautiful lace, and the ends were scalloped. Almost everyone had these. Now all those had to be washed by hand, and then they were all starched and we used to have to get hold, the children, mother would work one end and the children at the other, and we pulled them like this, draw them together and pull and that was to straighten them and then all that had to be ironed and it was who could have the nicest curtains. They were really houseproud, you know. They used to vie with each other, who could have the nicest curtains. Of course, some didn't bother, they did any old rag up. But I remember coming home and thinking Mummy's put up clean curtains, they used to look so lovely.

Did she donkey stone her doorstep?

Yes. I still use it. There was no carpet or anything on the stairs. They were wooden, and the table tops were wood with polished legs, but it was who could have the whitest table top. The stairs were scrubbed every day, they shone snow-white, the wood spotless. The table tops were white. Now after this washing-day, all this lovely soapy water, they used to do all their heavy cleaning with it. The floors would be washed. . . . Then there was the toilets outside in the yard. They had a long board across with a hole in the middle, and that had to be scrubbed snow white. They used to pride themselves, they were really clean.

Did you ever whitewash the yard?

Oh, everybody whitewashed. My yard was beautiful.

What did she have on the floor apart from flags? Did she have any peg rugs?

Yes, as the children got bigger, and they left school at fourteen and went to work, and a little bit more money came in, they used to get linos, no carpet, cheap lino which it was then and they used to go on the market and get a remnant and it would cover the centre. Oh, I've made peg rugs, dozens of them. Any old coats, they were kept specially . . . our jobs were to cut the pieces of cloth and we used to peg these rugs at the hearth.

When do you first remember getting a stair carpet?

Oh, I think it was about when I started work. . . . Then at one wall we had a sofa. It curled up like an 'S' at one end, but the other end was smooth, like a divan, with four legs, and if you had horsehair stuffing inside you were wealthy, and that was mahogany. That was on one side of the wall, and then there was these two chairs and there was always a sewing-machine, they always had a sewing-machine because they made a lot of clothes. Always an old-fashioned Singer sewing-machine with wrought iron frames. Upstairs, of course, there was just the iron bedstead with the brass knobs on, which are fashionable today. In the beginning I can just recall we had no electricity, and we had a gas jet in the living-room. It was shaped like a letter 'L', coming from the wall. A very narrow pipe, and it just went up at the end and you turned the tap and put a match to it. Now that was the light that we had in the living-room. Now a lot of people didn't even have that, they had a candle or a little old paraffin lamp, but we had this gas jet because my father was a fitter. He made it, you see. That was the light that we had. Then from that I remember, we improved and we got a mantle put on it. Father fixed a hook and put a white mantle and had a glass shade over it. Now that gave a better light with this gas mantle. It was like a butterfly's wing. You had to be very careful with it. They used to be only 2*d*. like. Now that lasted until electricity came, but even then it was who could have the nicest glass shade. People used to take a pride in things.[1]

All the respondents grew up in small terraced houses, although some eventually moved to semi-detached houses, either council-built or, in the case of the materially successful minority, to a new 1930s 'semi', of which they became the proud owners. There were some noticeable differences in the terraced houses both between towns and between areas within a town.

It is difficult to say who lived in the best or the worst housing. Barrow, being a new town, certainly had the highest percentage of newly built houses, all with an indoor water supply and an outside flush lavatory. Lancaster had some noticeable variation in its working-class housing. The small number of very old houses in central Lancaster were probably the worst in the whole survey, with one up and one down and an outside stand tap and lavatory. Some of Preston's oldest houses still had earth closets in 1900 (these had been cleared in Lancaster by this date), but the great majority had an indoor tap and an outside flush lavatory.

In the provision of amenities, and in the number of houses with three bedrooms, Barrow would appear to have the 'best' housing, but it was the most overcrowded of all three towns having, in 1901, 5.6 persons per dwelling compared to 5.4 for Lancaster and 4.7 for Preston.[2] Preston did not have Barrow's problems of overcrowding but did (judging from the evidence) have more problems with bugs and fleas.

Most terraced houses in Barrow and Lancaster had three bedrooms, with two rooms downstairs, and a tiny scullery at the back. In this room all the washing was done: pots, hands and faces in the brown slopstone sink, the major washing in a variety of tubs and bowls, and the boiler (usually coal-fired). Cooking was done in the kitchen, in the early period on a coal range, but increasingly on a gas stove (which was usually fitted in the scullery). The family also lived in the kitchen, and the front room (the parlour) was kept for very special occasions. Parlours were virtually never used as an extra bedroom, even in very overcrowded houses, and there was in the sample only one recorded attempt of a husband attempting (and failing) to make a more rational use of this infrequently used room. The father was a skilled cabinet-maker, as was his son:

It was class to have a parlour . . . but my dad made some nice furniture and he made all our furniture. . . . We had it as a parlour, and then we altered it . . . we made it into a workshop. She went mad about that, and that had to come out. One day she'd pulled it out [removed the equipment] when we were all at work.
What did she use the parlour for?
You lived in the kitchen and then you went in the parlour for your best room. . . . It was dusted and kept nice and never sat on. It was just used on special occasions . . . [for] visitors, weddings, funerals, birthdays, happen on a Sunday.[3]

Some Preston houses also had this downstairs layout, but there were many others which had a dining/kitchen with a range at the front of the house, and a large washing/kitchen at the back; and Preston houses usually had only two bedrooms, compared to Barrow and Lancaster's three.

These tiny houses, most of which are still standing, are by modern

There are few pictures of the inside of working-class homes. It is perhaps significant that the dominant features in this photograph are the fireplace and mantelpiece. (Manchester Studies, Manchester Polytechnic)

standards very small for families of even four people, and for those who brought up ten children life must have been extremely uncomfortable. Children very rarely had a bed to themselves, and sharing with at least one other sibling was quite usual. Mrs Allen, born in 1872, recalled that all ten children in her family slept in one room (in two beds), while the third bedroom was kept for storing the dirty washing![4] Mrs Wilkinson described her childhood with eight siblings and two parents in a three-bedroomed terraced house:

Well Jim and Edward slept in a double bed in that small room . . . with there being so many girls we had the front bedroom with two double beds in it, and a very big cot more like a hospital bed, five of us slept in that room and my parents' room took the double bed and the child's cot.[5]

Mr Logan brought up his own family in very poor circumstances in the inter-war period. Two parents and six children shared a small two-bedroomed house: 'There were boys at one end and girls at the other end in a double bed.'[6] In many families there was so little spare room round the dining-room table that children were forced to stand for their meals, only graduating to a chair when they became wage-earners.

The overcrowding meant that as much time as possible was spent outside; children played in the streets, men went to the pub, women (and men) sat on chairs by their front doors in good weather and chatted to neighbours. Overcrowding also meant that their houses quickly got dirty, and conscientious women (and those who cared for their reputation) fought an unceasing battle to keep them clean. Windows were washed at least once a week, doorsteps were donkey-stoned, as indeed were the flagstones immediately in front of the house in some cases. Flagged and linoleum-covered floors were scrubbed (the former might be sanded (sprinkled with sand) as an alternative, and the latter would also be polished). It was very rare for working-class homes to have a carpet square, but most had several peg rugs of the sort mentioned by Mrs Mitchell, made from old clothes and a sack by members of the family during the winter. Only the more aspiring and more prosperous had a stair carpet. Peg rugs were hung on the line and beaten with a carpet beater, or alternatively shaken. All houses were heated by a coal fire, and many used the fireside range for cooking too. This not only involved the frequent lifting in of buckets of coal, and out of buckets of ashes, but also tended to create dust which settled on the furniture. Great pride was taken in the ornaments, which were frequently made of brass, displayed on the mantelpiece. These required regular polishing, as did the fire irons. The range itself was blackleaded every week, and the steel fender rubbed over with emery paper.

Great efforts too had to be made to keep the family's clothes clean. Houses built before 1914 had no hot water supply; some had a boiler by the fire, which had to be filled and emptied by hand. Almost all houses had a copper or boiler lit by a fire or gas; and the washing was done in the way described above by Mrs Mitchell. The time and energy needed for washing, and the immense time it took to iron it all, using a flat or box iron, probably explains why both underclothes and top clothes were changed only once a week.

Life was particularly difficult in the earlier part of the century for the declining minority of women who had no water in the house, and had to rely on an outside tap which was frequently shared. Most evidence of this has been found in Lancaster, coming from respondents who lived in the very old properties in the town centre: 'It used to freeze up in the winter. I don't know how mother managed.'[7] 'You had to do your washing-up in a dish on the table where you had your meals from. Of course your kettle was an old iron kettle you filled from the water tap in the yard and put on the fireplace.'[8] Sometimes these communal taps were unhealthy places: 'They swilled their buckets out at a tap when they took their urine round in a morning.'[9]

Personal washing was also difficult. Before the first world war very few working-class homes had a bath. Mr Vernon remarked: 'Anyone working-class that had a bath or a bathroom was a king amongst men.'[10] A very small minority both aspired to and gained one. Mrs Matthews' parents bought a

A few houses had no water supply even in the 1920s. This Lancaster woman undoubtedly shared this outside tap with other homes. (Notice too the woman in the background scrubbing her flagstones.)
(University Library, University of Lancaster)

new terraced house in about 1902: 'It didn't have a bathroom so my dad put one in and I think there was only us and next door, my dad's brother, who had one.'[11] In the inter-war period baths became rather more common. Enterprising tenants found places to put one even without a bathroom: 'It would be about 1925, we rented a house two up and two down, but it was rather a big kitchen and it had a fire boiler, and we had it taken out, and a bath put in, and a table over the top of it.'[12]

Those lucky enough to rent one of the new council houses in the 1920s or to buy one of the new 1930s semi-detached houses, had the luxury of a proper bathroom and a proper hot water system: 'It had a bathroom that was another luxury . . . and what my mother particularly enjoyed was hot water from the boiler, just open the tap and that was it. Smashing.'[13] But however much the luxury of a bathroom was appreciated, its benefits remained the preserve of a fortunate minority. The majority continued to make do with a weekly wash in a portable tin or zinc bath filled and emptied by hand. This performance was so time-consuming and laborious that a few respondents could not remember having had a bath while they were children at all: 'We never had a bath. I never knew one with m'grandma. If you washed your body, you washed it in a bowl.'[14] The poor could not be blamed for the grossly inadequate provision of baths and bathrooms in their small rented houses;

nor could they be blamed for the inadequacy of the outside lavatories. In a small minority of families even the lavatory was shared: 'When I lived up Edward Street . . . there were four lavatories and twelve houses. Everybody had a key and sometimes you'd open the door and somebody would be sat in.'[15] Not only is it clear that these arrangements did little for human dignity, they must also have provided a considerable health hazard, with the constant risk of cross-infection. Medical Officers of Health had realised by the last quarter of the nineteenth century that the old dry-earth closets were very unhealthy, and they began what they themselves saw as a crusade against them. Such closets had disappeared from Lancaster by 1900,[16] and Preston by 1910.[17] (They had never existed in Barrow except in a very small number of rural properties.) Only the very oldest respondents remember them:

The other houses were two up and two down, and they each had their own little midden and dry closet, and the night soil men would go round the back with a barrow, dig the stuff out, and put it in the barrow, take it back down the lobby

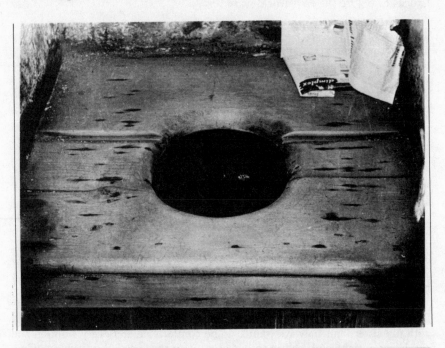

One of the old dry closets. Women spent a lot of effort in scrubbing the boards. The walls were whitewashed once a year with lime provided free by the local council. The privies were usually emptied once a week by the night-soil men.
(Manchester Studies, Manchester Polytechnic)

and tip it in the street. Then later on, when they had finished all the rows, a cart would come and they'd scoop it up and throw it in the cart, then put down some disinfectant powder. The conditions by modern standards were really awful.[18]

Long after Preston adopted a system of keeping household rubbish in dustbins with lids, Barrow and Lancaster retained their open middens, which were a haven for flies. Standards of personal hygiene were low. Even after the second world war it was quite usual to board a bus in this area and be repelled by the overpowering smell of unwashed human bodies and/or dirty clothes.

A minority of houses suffered from the visible and troublesome manifestations of low standards of cleanliness. Respondents report fleas, bed bugs and cockroaches, especially in very old properties. More reports of these infestations come from Preston than from Barrow and Lancaster, probably because Preston had a larger stock of older housing, but possibly also because so many Preston women were in full-time work and therefore had less time for thorough cleaning. Mrs Hutchinson lived in a very old house in central Lancaster before the first world war:

There were bugs on Bulk [in the area], every house nearly had bugs in. My mother tried her best . . . my mother spoiled beds without end, because she used to take them down and get them down and get these bugs out. They got into the woodwork. They had all sorts of powder, but they did it more with creosote. They reckoned green paint got rid of them better than anything. All the bedrooms were painted green, walls, woodwork, everything.[19]

Mrs Pearce lived in an old house in Preston until after the second world war, when her family finally got a new council house:

We used to have a lot of vermin of all descriptions. They brought out some DDT at one time. I nearly killed myself with this DDT.

That was the first time that you were without them when you moved after the [second world] war?

Yes. You could tell how bad it was because they didn't take our furniture direct, they took it somewhere to be disinfected or something. When the fellow came he told us to put our mattresses at the front of the fire because they must have sprayed them with something. . . .

We had fleas as well. I don't know which is worse, to tell the truth, because fleas bite you and leave a mark. People used to take notice. I know I used to sleep with my sister, and I always wanted to be comfortable and every so often she would come right up here [up to her neck] with the sheets. I would say, 'Give over. Get it down. You don't want them on your neck and everybody looking at you at work.'

When we lived in Brunswick Street the kiddies' beds were single beds with wire things and the wire was going. This chap could mend them and I told my husband to ask him to mend this one. I said I would take it downstairs to the yard to clean it. I had this boiling water down and I had a cloth with paraffin and I did up every spring and I did give it a good clean. The day after, I let the smell go away from the paraffin, and I said, 'Do you mind doing this bed for me?' We fetched the bed back and paid for it and the fellow said, 'Do you know, that's the first bed I have ever mended with no bugs in it.' I thought, he didn't know what I did before it went. I didn't want to be talked about. There was another woman down the road and she was a bit queer, and she used to put her bedding out the window to shake it. This other woman used to shout, 'Take them in, we have enough bugs of our own.'[20]

How successful was the working-class woman in her struggle against household dirt? According to her own standards and those of her neighbours, on the whole very successful. The woman's first preoccupation tended to be with outward show — windows shone, framed by immaculate starched white curtains; front doorsteps were unblemished with human footprints. One Lancaster woman used to say: 'Keep the front doorstep clean. There's more passes by than comes inside.'[21] The interiors gleamed and sparkled in the fire and gas light. Girls frequently appeared at school in elaborately frilled, spotless white pinafores, and everyone's shoes and boots shone like mirrors. And yet it is very doubtful whether all these houses or their occupants were as clean as they appeared to be. The sanitary inadequacies all militated strongly against the housewives' best efforts, and were of course beyond her powers of remedy.[22]

FAMILY INCOME

Women's abilities as financial managers were obviously affected by the levels of family income.[23] Men's real wages are of fundamental importance in assessing working-class standards of living, and, of course, real wages varied from industry to industry, from town to town, and for an individual from week to week. Before the first world war no labourer in the area earned as much as £1 1s. 8d., which Seebohm Rowntree estimated as the poverty line (that is, the minimum amount essential for a family of four to five persons to be provided with the basic necessities of life) in 1901.[24] Labourers who usually earned anything between 17s. and £1 0s. 3d. were therefore very poor. Their position improved after the first world war, when the average labouring wage reached about £2. (This was above the poverty line set by Bowley and Hogg,[25] but below the new one suggested by Rowntree of £2 13s.)[26] Skilled men were better paid than labourers, earning about twice as much before the first world war and about 50 per cent more in the inter-war period. Even they could not, of course, be regarded as prosperous, affected as they were by piecework rates, bonus schemes and above all unemployment.

Cotton workers were particularly badly paid; their rates were low, and wages depended entirely on what they produced and were therefore irregular. In 1931 the Board of Trade gave the average textile wage as £1 14s. 6d., the only workers receiving a lower wage being those in the linen, dressmaking, tailoring and laundry industries.[27]

Unemployment was a serious problem in the inter-war years, especially in Barrow where 49 per cent of the insured workers were unemployed in 1922, and in Preston, where 27 per cent were unemployed in 1931.[28] Undoubtedly, the families who had to rely on poor relief and unemployment pay were placed substantially below the poverty line. For example, in 1921 an unemployed man received 22s. for himself, his wife and two children, each additional child receiving 1s. a week. By 1938 this benefit had risen to 33s. for a family of four, with 3s. per additional child.[29]

The low wage levels and low real wages raise the crucial question of how working-class wives, especially those whose husbands were either unskilled or unemployed, managed on such incomes. How did they feed, clothe and house their families, given such an inadequate financial basis?

In the majority of families in the sample, incomes were augmented by the earnings of the women themselves. There was, however, the sharpest difference between those women who worked on a part-time, casual basis, and those who worked full-time outside the home. Part-time work may or may not have been enumerated in the Census returns, but it seems likely that, because of its very casual, frequently temporary, and indeed rather ephemeral nature, neither the women nor the enumerators felt that it was important enough to be noted. There is certainly a very big discrepancy in all three towns between the number of married women enumerated as working full-time in the Census (see table 4.2), and the large number of women in the sample who worked at some point in their lives on a casual, part-time basis — about 40 per cent in Preston and Lancaster, and 50 per cent in Barrow. Apart from this very rough calculation, it is impossible to estimate the number of hours these women worked, or how much they earned, or for how many years they worked. However, it is clear from the oral evidence that their contribution to the family budget was frequently critical.

Women in all three towns shared a common attitude to wage-earning work; it was not in itself a good thing, but was undertaken because the family income was perceived to be inadequate without their contribution. (It could well have been seen as inadequate even when the family was above the poverty line, but the further family incomes rose above a minimum level, the less likelihood there was of the woman earning money on her own account.) Often there was a specific aim, such as buying a house or educating the children.

These women's aims and ambitions were family-centred and thus very limited in employment or business terms. Hardly any of the female 'penny capitalists', that is, those who chose to provide goods and services on their own account rather than be employed by someone else, developed into running businesses full-time, although there were a few notable exceptions in the sample.[30] It would seem that if their enterprise became very successful, it was usually taken over by the men of the family, who appear to have been more concerned with earning money for its own sake, than for definite and finite ends.

The ideal of many working-class women was that which had been increasingly adopted by middle-class women throughout the nineteenth century.[31] This was the 'beau idyll', romantically expressed in the writings of John Ruskin and Coventry Patmore, who saw the home as a sanctuary, a haven of spirituality presided over by an angel wife, a place of refuge and shelter from the struggles of the world of work outside with which the woman would have no contact, thus keeping herself and the home unpolluted. Herbert Spencer suggested that the dependence of women might be used as a measure of social progress; while even earlier Auguste Comte, the French sociologist, argued that in the highest type of civilisation women would be protected from any kind of productive work outside the home.

Of course, for economic reasons it was often not possible in practice for working-class women to pursue this idyll, but it still remained as a goal. The importance of mothers staying at home to care for their families was stressed by a constant stream of advice and exhortation from Medical Officers of Health, Health Visitors, and other 'experts'. Working-class married women displayed an ambivalence towards their wage-earning work. Those who worked were proud of their skill, their efforts, and their contributions to the family budget. But they rarely had any ambition to go on earning wages all their lives, and regarded it as a matter of social progress and of status to be able to give up wage-earning work. Their emancipation lay, in their estimation, in the move *away* from work and into the home. It is impossible to find either from documentary or oral evidence any signs of a trend (clearly observable in more recent decades) of women staying at home to raise their children, and then returning to work in early middle age. Table 4.1 shows clearly this trend in Preston of women in full-time work moving away from work and into the home.

Part-time work was regarded as preferable to full-time work, and wage-earning work in the home was preferable to outside work because it meant less disruption to home routines. Because it was generally (and rightly) presumed that a woman only worked if there was an inadequate family income, many skilled men did not like their wives to be seen earning money — it reflected badly on their own status as the breadwinner. There is no evidence to suggest that women questioned this point of view.

Mrs Sloan was too young to know why her mother did not work outside the home (she was only eight when her mother died). Her comments, however, sum up some of the reasons given by several respondents from the more socially-aspiring ranks of the working class as to why married women should not go out to work:

Did she work after she was married?
I couldn't say. No, I couldn't say. I wouldn't think so 'cause — let me see, mam was married — I have it in a book, she was married at High Street Chapel 1897. I was born 1898 and my sister was born 1901, so she'd have enough with two children, wouldn't she? Yes, and there wasn't much work really. Then tradesmen were very proud of being able to keep their wives you see. M'father was nicely brought up and I think he wouldn't want her to go to work. I can't remember mother ever working.[32]

TABLE 4.1: Variations by age in the number of women in full-time employment, Preston, 1921

	Age groups							
	14—19	20—24	25—34	35—44	45—54	55—59	60—64	65—70
Percentage in full-time work	86.7	84.9	61.0	43.8	32.9	28.7	24.4	20.3

Source: Census of 1921, County of Lancaster, table 18

The point that 'there wasn't much work' in Lancaster is interesting; full-time work was only easily available in Preston, but part-time work seems to have been available in all three towns for those who wanted it.

Similar attitudes to women's employment have been described for a much wider area by Joan Scott, Louise Tilly and Miriam Cohen. Writing of nineteenth-century Europe, they state, 'Throughout the period, British women tended to give up work outside the home when they married, although many worked at home, or moved in and out of the labour force when necessary. This demonstrates that women married or single were motivated to work by economic necessity, and not by a drive for liberation.'[33] In *Women, Work and Family*, Scott and Tilly say of the Edwardian working-class woman: 'The continuing pressure on these women to earn money was a sign of need in their households. It is no wonder then that working-class culture adopted the image of the married woman at home as the sign of the health, stability, and prosperity of a household.'[34] It is clear from the oral evidence that in the early twentieth century, many working-class women shared this domestic ideology. It is, of course, debatable whether or not this had always been a working-class ideal or whether it was one which had been adopted from the middle class.

The biographical details of the respondents show the range of work done by working-class women in the period studied here. The least popular jobs were those which involved going out to work and being tied by another woman's timetable, but several women did go out cleaning or doing someone else's washing and ironing. They were not particularly proud of this. In the 1920s, Mrs Morrison went out cleaning three mornings a week (9 a.m. to 2 p.m.), and for that received 2s. 6d. a day.[35] Although this seems a very small amount, it compared not unfavourably with the wages of full-time working women once their necessary and heavy expenses had been deducted. Women who went to clean for other women frequently received some payment in kind, such as food or clothing for their children. Other women went out as unqualified but often highly skilled nurses of women in childbirth, or of the sick and dying.

There were more unusual jobs away from the home: one woman went out as a painter and decorator, asking 2s. per room.[36] Quite the most unusual part-time job, and perhaps the most successful, was the one done by Mr Pearson's mother, who with a friend speculated, successfully and legally, at the local auctions. It is interesting that once her ambition was realised (to help each of her six children to buy their own homes) she gave up her enterprise:

M'father was only a labourer at the steelworks and at that period they were in and out, in and out, and there was one period that she used to go to the saleroom and bid on things, and then . . . anything she thought going cheap she'd buy it, leave it there, go the following week and let it go up again and she'd bid it and make a bob or two that way. . . . and do you know she couldn't write her own name but she could reckon up money and that. Funny.
She must have been a very clever woman.
Well she knew a bargain, and she used to knock about, had a good friend as well, worked between them like, but she was good. You only had to think of anything [needed] in our house. You'd be talking here, and it was here the next day.[37]

Rather more women worked at home than went out to part-time jobs. Apart from conforming more to the ideal of the woman's place being in the home, home work did have other very practical advantages: the control to a large extent of her own timetable, the opportunity to devote time and attention to her children when necessary, to fit in the cooking, and perhaps most important not to be at the beck-and-call of an employer. This did not mean that her life was easy. Life was particularly hard for the washerwoman who took in large quantities of other people's dirty washing.

On the outskirts of Lancaster lies the hamlet of Golgotha (once the site of the gallows). The houses there are very old, probably early eighteenth-century. A group of washerwomen living in Golgotha had plied their trade for several successive generations. Their husbands apparently carried on their own trades. Mrs Stott, born in 1896, was the youngest child of one of the Golgotha washerwomen, and her father was a gravedigger:

We weren't very well-off, you know. We were poor people, and my mother worked hard and took washing in for all the big bugs. She used to wash Saturday, Monday, Tuesday and Wednesday and the other two days she'd be ironing. She used to wash for all these important people, these gentry. We had, and it's there yet, a field opposite next to the farm and it used to have so many lines. Oh, she was a marvellous woman, was my mother, but she wouldn't do anything on a Sunday. She wouldn't even let you put a button on on a Sunday. She was such a stickler for things, for church, though she could neither read nor write. . . .

You shared a toilet with about five different houses and you shared the wash-house too. There was no water inside the house or anything like that. You even hadn't a sink, it was all in the wash-house.

I suppose you'd come to an agreement with the neighbours when they were using the wash house?

Yes. One would use it and then another would use it. The washing that they used to do wasn't ordinary washing you know it used to need goffering [ironing in pin tucks. A special iron was used]. Oh, I can see my mother goffering now.

These were maids' hats and things?

Yes. The caps and aprons and such like, the gowns. The caps had to be goffered and down the sides of the apron all goffered.

Did she have to starch them as well?

Yes. My mother used to make her starch and she used to have a bowl, a beautiful Wedgwood bowl, a brown Wedgwood. . . . You've heard of Billy Mitchell, the brewer. Well, my mother washed for him and they lived at Belle Vue and we used to take our washing there, and as soon as we knocked on the door there was a parrot there and it used to shout, 'Annie, there's Sally. Annie there's Sally', and we always got a bottle of lemonade. Oh, it was a prize in those days to get anything like that. . . . I always remember my brother and I going, and when we came out she used to pay Mother for doing it, we had Mother's money, you see, perhaps about fifteen pence for doing a load of washing . . . 1s. 3d. for doing a load of washing. Oh, they got very poor pay, you know.

Did your mother charge per article, or so much a load?

She charged so much an article. Well in some cases . . . I took washing in myself when I was young and I used to get two shillings for doing all the bloomin' family wash, sheets and everything.[38]

Some women took in dressmaking or alterations. Only one did outwork for a commercial enterprise, and that was Mrs Owen's mother in Preston, who made bed tickings.

It is very difficult, even from oral evidence, to estimate how many families made money from taking in lodgers. Many families had relatives living with them (see chapter 5). Some of these were looked after for no financial return; others undoubtedly paid their way; and this kind of lodger was much more usual than taking in strangers. The reason was the smallness of the houses in which the overwhelming majority of respondents lived. Sharing a room or a bed with a relative was acceptable, indeed usual, but such familiarity with strangers was not. Usually landladies were widows with no family living at home.

In only two families were non-related lodgers somehow squeezed in. The grandmother of Mrs Burns had been left with her dead daughter's five children to bring up, and her husband was only a labourer. Ways had to be found to supplement a very meagre family income, and so lodgers were taken in. There were three small bedrooms, and seven members of the family already living there. Mrs Burns remembered that the lodgers were in fact a small German Band (a source of great joy in working-class streets), consisting of two brothers and one sister. Their presence obviously strained the family's accommodation to the utmost:

I've just forgot where the devil they slept. Our bedroom went over the house and the back kitchen. It was a big room and would hold two full-sized beds and then you could put a mattress in the corner.[39]

Another way of making money at home was baby- or child-minding for mothers who worked full-time. Two mothers in the sample were minders in Lancaster, but many more did this in Preston. There were no set rates, the amounts quoted ranging from 3s. to 10s. per week.[40] This was not all clear profit because the child had to be fed, but a woman minding only a few children could earn as much as a weaver in full-time work.

The other kind of part-time wage-earning was in small-scale trading. Only one mother traded in the street (she was a hawker who travelled in the country areas selling ribbons, pins etc.). More usual were the women who sold certain foods and drinks from either their front parlour or back kitchen: pies, cooked hams, lemonade, ginger beer, and so on. Many women who would not buy such convenience foods as fish and chips or commercially produced pies often patronised these small part-time traders, sometimes as a charitable gesture, or a sign of sisterly solidarity (depending on their own point of view). Sometimes these small part-time shops developed into proper 'house shops', selling a wide range of goods. Others disappeared as and when the financial need which created them disappeared. In Barrow, Mrs Morris's mother opened a parlour shop to make enough money to send all her children to the Higher Grade School. In Lancaster, Mr Maguire's mother made and sold pies after being deserted by her husband and before her eldest son earned enough to support the family. Mrs Bridges' mother made cakes when her father was ill (usually she was a winder at the mill, winding thread onto cops or bobbins):

My dad was ill once over and he had to go to Buxton for these baths and she couldn't work because my grandma was ill as well. She opened a little shop, and she started making meat and potato pies, and some teacakes to keep the home going. I told her after that if we had kept it up we would have had a shop. It was hard work. . . . She had to do that shop because they were both ill. She couldn't leave her mother. The neighbours were very good as they used to patronise her, and they would come for pies and that. She only did it to get the money.

Mrs Bridges added that her family, who were fiercely proud, would not go to the Guardians for Poor Relief.[41]

It is clear that these women held an idea of an ideal family income, usually one which would adequately clothe, feed and house the family, and leave a small surplus for entertainment, or savings. Once the ideal level was reached, it was more important to have less work than to have more money. Material expectations were very low compared to those of the present day, a fact which many respondents mentioned. But the lack of material ambition should not lead one to underestimate the importance of women's part-time wages. In many families they successfully raised the family income from below to above the poverty line, and they solved many financial crises. In poor families their contribution was critical.

Mrs Manning, born in 1914, grew up in one of the poorest streets in Lancaster. Her own mother took in washing, and she was able to remember the money-earning activities of many of her neighbours in the 1920s:

Mrs A. had this lodging house, and then Mrs H. had the pub. Mrs H. used to brew pop and sell it. Next door to us Mrs P., she used to make apple pies and jam pies, and charge a penny a piece. She used to roast potatoes and make a living like that. There was a shop just a bit lower down . . . Mrs R., a halfpenny of milk, a halfpenny biscuit, and a halfpenny packet of cocoa. We used to often go in for cocoa and have it for school. . . . There was Mrs H. she used to cut up firewood and sell it in bundles, 3d. or 6d. a bundle.[42]

The Census returns, which only give figures for the full-time employment of married women for the years 1901 and 1911, indicate the very varied levels of female employment in the three towns (see table 4.2). Lancaster was quite near the national average of 13 per cent, while Barrow was well below and Preston substantially above. The official figures are reflected in the samples, as can be seen in the biographical details of respondents.

TABLE 4.2: Percentages of married women and widows in full-time employment, 1901 and 1911

	Barrow	Lancaster	Preston
1901	5.8	10.2	30.5
1911	6.9	11.0	35.0

Source: Census of 1901, County of Lancaster, table 35a; Census of 1911, County of Lancaster, table 25.

The great majority of married women who worked in Preston were employed in the textile industry, usually as weavers, but also as winders, carders, intermediate tenters and ring spinners. The reasons for their working can be found in both the long-established structure of Preston's industries and its wage rates, which tended to be lower for unskilled men than those of Barrow and Lancaster,[43] and were often not enough to keep families above the poverty line. Women's reasons for choosing full-time work are fairly obvious: they needed full-time wages. In Preston there was constant demand from the mills for thousands of women and adolescent workers, which enabled such large numbers of women to use their labour to supplement the family income. However, meeting the demands of the labour market is, of course, not the reason given by these women and their mothers for working; they claim it was sheer financial necessity.

The lives these women led were stressful and demanding in the extreme. One of the commonest expressions heard in Preston is 'It was bed and work all the time.' Housework had somehow to be fitted in before work, after work, and at the weekends, involving the whole family in a ceaseless round of toil. Mr Terry's father was a labourer, and his mother a weaver:

Oh yes, she could bake bread. I used to get the job of thumping it.
When did she do her baking?
At night.
What energy!
You had to. You couldn't do anything else. She used to get up at 5.45 in the morning to have a drink of tea and take a sandwich. You prepared at night for the following morning. It was always a question of you washed yourself, you looked at the buttons, and there was a row if you wanted a button at the last minute. You cleaned your clogs, you put them there and you went to bed. Then everything was ready for morning; they all did the same. Then off to work. They had a break for breakfast and then off for lunch. It was a question of living near

the mill to come home for dinner. Dinner was only a snack for most people with a preparation for tea.

You had a cooked tea in the evening, did you?

More or less every day. Then again, you wouldn't get home before 6 o'clock, all depending on how far you lived.

So it was very hard work all the time?

It was bed and work all the time in those days. The 'good old days'.[44]

Mrs Harrison's mother was also a weaver while her husband was a poorly paid railwayman. (When he was promoted and became an engine driver she stopped work.)

How did your mother manage the housework when she was out such a lot?

It was done in the evening. . . . they didn't have gas in the kitchen, so they had to do the washing with the great big mangle with two candles on top. That was starting at 6 o'clock and baking and washing.

What about doing the housework?

There had to be so much done each night. It was at weekends mostly when everything was bottomed [done thoroughly]. It was hard work, it was all bed and work so they were content to sit when it got dark. . . . washing up and cooking and things like that during the week, tidying and dusting, but Saturday and Sunday was the main days for a good clean-up.[45]

Some of the effects of women working, notably on their relationships with their husbands and the burden of housework on growing children, have already been noted in chapter 3. The youngest children, who were 'minded' by other women — what was the effect on them? Sometimes the minder would be a relative, sometimes a neighbour. There is absolutely no evidence that the child-minders did not do their job well, according to the standards of the time. In the days of large, extended families children who were minded by aunts or grandmothers were brought up and cared for in more or less the same way their mothers would have brought them up. Neighbours who acted as minders appear to have been genuinely fond of their young charges, and in any case knew that if they got a reputation for being a bad minder, then their occupation would be at an end. It must be again emphasised that 'getting a bad name' was an awful fate in a working-class neighbourhood:

May be somebody would look after two or three. It had to be a reliable person. You often came to the point where it would be 'Oh, not her kind of thing', and this was bush telegraph in the mill, you know. The deaf-and-dumb language was fantastic.

And the lady that looked after your brother and sister and you was all right, was she?

Oh, yes. They were neighbours, you see. Because they had to be good otherwise you were across the road, and you got a bad name if you were a bad minder.[46]

These patterns of child-care appear to have been neglected by the Medical Officers of Health for Preston. However, in 1930 the Health Visitors reported on thirty-five children, aged 0−2, not cared for by their mothers. Eighteen were minded at home by relatives; thirteen were cared for in the homes of relatives; only five were cared for by strangers. The Health Visitor reported that all the children were well looked after, and in good surroundings.[47] Only one respondent, Mrs Pearce, expressed dissatisfaction about her own child's minder. On one occasion she failed to take her to the doctor, and on another was thought not to have changed her nappy often enough.[48] A more serious problem was the psychological one; the children do not appear to have been upset at being left, but some mothers hated having to leave them.

Mrs Hey remembered being taken to minders so her mother could go to the mill:

When I lived at Euston Street my mother worked at a mill and they called it Fishers in Spa Road. She used to carry me in a blanket to be nursed out to these people and they were called the Fowlers. . . . I thought the world of these people.

You can remember them, can you?

Oh yes. It was a silly thing for a mother to not stop at home and mind her own baby for, happen, a couple of years. You get attached to these people, especially when they have a grown-up son and daughter, and they made such a fuss of me.

How young were you then, when she took you there?

A baby in arms.

So, would she feed you with a bottle then?

She had a bottle and pobs [pieces of bread steeped in hot milk, and spoon-fed] and things like that. My dad was a spinner at Horrockses and when he married he had 16s. 10d. of a wage and my mother was a four-loom weaver at Fishers. A four-loom weaver in them days had about 24s. off four looms.[49]

The small girl's attachment to her minders is echoed by many other respondents. Her remark that 'it was a silly thing for a mother to not stop at home' could be interpreted as acceptance of the prevailing views of various authorities and the general domestic ideology. But the remark, taken in context, could also indicate regret that her mother missed both a vital stage of her child's development, and a lot of affection which was given instead to the minder. 'Silly', as used in northern dialect, means 'pathetic, deserving of pity, poor'. A few years after this, Mrs Hey's father became a mule minder earning £2 a week, the family moved to a much better house in a more respectable area, and her mother immediately stopped work. They felt they had much higher status and were much more prosperous than their near relations. And yet if one calculates their family wage (i.e. including the mother's) before and after the father's promotion (when the mother's wage ceased) it is consistently about £2. How, then, can their increase in prosperity be explained? It is only comprehensible in terms of the very considerable expenses incurred by working mothers, and their inability to make economies other women could make. Baby- and child-minders were always paid, the amount varying quite considerably, and convenience foods were more expensive than home-made dinners. Also, of course, a weaver's wage was likely to be highly irregular. But the impact on their view of their situation must also be explained in terms of social expectations and the relief to the household of the woman having time to devote to household matters.

Mr and Mrs Gaskell's experience dates from the early 1930s, and indicates that in some cases a woman would have been better off doing part-time work, than full-time. Curiously, relatives minding a child for two or three mornings a week never charged, and, of course, there was no need for bought dinners:

When the wife and I worked, we lived in Harrington Street and her sister lived next door-but-one to us. We paid her for minding our oldest child, David, and he would be about two, and Ella went out to work. We paid 10s. a week for him being minded. Now, there were times in the cotton trade when it were funny, if you had four looms and one loom stopped, you didn't get paid. You only got paid on what you produced. I know it happened one week, the wage was 18s. and she had to pay her sister 10s. so she had worked all week for 8s. She went to her mother's for her dinner and paid her and I went to my father's and paid there. So we could be actually out of pocket sometimes. Provided they were in full work, there was very little gain by going out to work.

Can you remember how much you would pay for your dinners?

I think it was about 6d. a day.[50]

In that particular week Mrs Gaskell had a clear profit of 3s., about the wage for one morning's cleaning. Thus although many women worked full-time because they felt they had to, they did not always succeed in substantially improving their family's financial position.

It is reasonably clear that the presence of large numbers of women in the mills tended to depress textile wage rates. E. H. Hunt commented on this with reference to both the cotton and the woollen textile industries:

The female weavers who worked with men for identical rates were among the highest paid women workers in Britain, whereas male weavers were badly paid compared with [other] men. If the women gained from doing work that was not unequivocably women's work the men . . . clearly lost something by competing in an occupation where pay was affected by the prevailing level of women's wages.[51]

The Preston Weavers, Winders, and Warpers Association, although it had a large membership, was remarkably unmilitant about wage rates, confining its attention to the fixing of prices for the production of various types of cloth or yarn.[52] Many women belonged to the union, but most appear to have been concerned only with their wages and their domestic affairs; they simply paid their small subscription as a kind of insurance against the day when they might find themselves in dispute with the management. Apart from the fact that this lack of militancy may have helped keep textile wages at a depressed level, it seems probable that the existence of a large number of textile working wives had an effect on labouring rates in general in the area. This was certainly the view expressed by the Pilgrim Trust for the inter-war period. Writing especially of Blackburn, but obviously with reference to other textile towns, their report stated: 'Wages have always been fixed in Blackburn on the assumption that several members of the family will be working', and 'the wages of most of the Lancashire cotton towns assume the double earnings of man and wife. The husband's wage alone would reduce many families into poverty and it is consequently necessary for the wife to earn all the time.'[53] The evidence from before the first world war would appear to support this argument. The Board of Trade Inquiry gave wage indices for the major industrial towns in Lancashire (see appendix 4) from which it can be seen that the average labourer's wages in the three towns, where more than 30 per cent of the married women were in work, were lower both for the average for the whole of Lancashire and Cheshire, and for the towns where less than 20 per cent of married women were in full-time work.

While it is impossible to prove an exact correlation between a high percentage of employed married women and general low wage rates, it is evident that they did not produce high rates, at least in Lancashire. The exigencies of the labour market in Preston meant that many married women had to work because of their husbands' low wage rates; ironically, and of course unwittingly, their labour may well have helped maintain those low rates.

The wages of full-time working women, as with the earnings of part-time workers, made a marginal, but significant, difference to their families' budgets. But the evidence suggests that the improvement to the family budget was nothing like as substantial as the earnings of an apparently full second wage would indicate because of the costs incurred. Perhaps more importantly, the nutritional standards of the family suffered, as did the health not only of the women, but of their husbands too. No one will ever know how many deaths in Preston, whatever was given as the official cause, were caused by exhaustion: 'The women, they worked and worked. They had their babies and worked like idiots. They died, they were old at forty.'[54]

BALANCING THE BUDGET

Not all women were able to earn money and not all, of course, needed to. Many, however, had to develop alternative strategies to augment their incomes in order to balance their budgets.

It is impossible to know how many working-class women sought some form of credit loan. The amount of indebtedness cannot be quantified, as so many records of failed businesses have disappeared, but it can only be presumed to have been substantial. The most acceptable form of borrowing, in social terms, was that of patronising the 'Scotchman' (a door-to-door salesman who sold £1 worth of goods for 21s., to be paid for over twenty-one weeks), a procedure which appears to have carried little or no social stigma. Other forms of borrowing were something to be ashamed of, and only the very poorest families were driven to seek credit from ordinary shopkeepers. Women themselves or their children asked for credit; men virtually never did this, partly, presumably, because it was the woman's responsibility to make ends meet, but also perhaps because of the reflection on a man's character which inability to provide for his family meant. Women who sent their children presumably hoped that their very childishness would be more successful in moving the shopkeeper to pity than their own maturity. Mr Maguire grew up in one of the poorest streets in Lancaster, and his father deserted the family when he was a small child. His evidence relates as much to the neighbourhood as to his own family:

It was known as tick. In fact some shops had a clock with no hands on — no tick here. But most shops did [give] credit. I'd go in there and another word they'd use was 'on the strap' — 'Are you going to strap it?'. . . . When you got paid on a Friday you went and paid it off, or some of it off. In most cases it was never-ending. It was never paid off. The shopkeeper never got his money . . . you either owed the milkman, the coalman, the doctor, or you were in arrears with the rent. There were a lot of arrears in them days.[55]

Mr Gaskell referred disparagingly to the little corner shops in Preston which played an essential part in the lives of married women textile workers. Coming home late and tired, they had to rely on shops which were near, and had no time to search out the cheaper places. Moreover, with their low and irregular incomes, they had to use the credit facilities offered by these little shops: 'A lot of them had shop books . . . they called them Belly Bibles, these little corner shops they were gold mines because their prices were sky-high.'[56]

The undoubted poverty which drove so many to seek credit should not necessarily lead to such a condemnation of the credit-giving shopkeeper, and indeed their shops were not all 'gold mines'. Mr Morton, as a young man in Barrow in the early 1920s, when the town was suffering from a very bad economic slump, acted as a traveller for his grandfather's business:

I used to go round all the small shops . . . they had what they called tick, quite a number [of customers] were conscientious and paid, but when the bad times came they wouldn't settle a week's bill. . . . As soon as the shopkeeper started pressing them they simply took their ready money somewhere else so the shopkeeper lost both the ready money and the tick. . . . A friend of mine had a little business . . . a parlour-window business . . . she told me once she was too worried to count out how much money she had out. . . . She knew it was over £650, and so thought that it was in the region of £1,000.[57]

It is not surprising that many little shops failed.

A tiny minority of women quite deliberately set out to defraud the shopkeeper. Mrs Winder worked in a grocer's shop:

Anyway, a woman came in that I knew and her husband had been in a burning accident at Storeys . . . and I knew he was improving. She'd come in and ordered off another assistant for a funeral tea. Her husband had died. I said, 'Her husband hasn't died . . . she'll not pay.' Do you know she didn't, and they'd a right old party and all this stuff laid on.[58]

A less socially acceptable way for women to balance their budgets was to seek a loan from a pawnbroker, giving some household or personal item as collateral. Feelings against using the services of a pawnbroker could be very strong even in very poor families. Mr Gordon's father was unemployed for a long time after the first world war, but the family managed: 'They were necessary, although my mother was very bigoted against them. She'd starve rather than go to the pawn shop.'[59] It may have been the prevalence of these attitudes, or it may have been the availability and indeed success of other financial strategies, but going to the pawnshop does not appear to have been a usual feature of working-class financial management in the area; rather, it was used as a last resort. Mrs Nixon grew up in a poor household, and was the mother of a poor family in the inter-war period; her family was too large for her husband's low wages:

I took my wedding ring three times. It was a good one . . . each time I took it I was caught with babies. My mother was a servant [a charwoman]. I used to go and

A Manchester Pawnbroker's. Although this pawnbroker advertises for jewellery, furniture and pianos, the most commonly pawned goods were clothing, bedding and small household articles. With the arrival of alternative forms of credit in the inter-war years (e.g. credit catalogues) and generally rising standards of living, the pawnbroker's trade declined.
(Manchester Studies, Manchester Polytechnic)

see her every Saturday night. I used to be down to a few coppers and I used to think, 'I'll ask m'mother to lend me two shillings. I'll get some washing on Monday and take it back.' But I never had any need to ask her, she always popped it into my hand. She used to say, 'Where is it and how much is it? Eh m'lass you shouldn't.' I can always remember asking 12s. 6d. . . . It used to cost me 14s. to get it back and I daren't ask any more because I couldn't afford to get it out.[60]

None of the respondents remembers using moneylenders. Money was sometimes borrowed from relatives, or more rarely from neighbours, but borrowing from moneylenders and paying interest on the loan is not recorded. Nor is there evidence of any significant reliance on crime to make ends meet. Living off the land, which is discussed below, sometimes included poaching, and the concept was also sometimes extended to include the removal of goods from the place of work, both of which were illegal. But there is no oral evidence of theft from family or neighbours.

Some working-class women only balanced their budgets by the most stringent economies: men, women and children were under a constant pressure not to waste anything. Most women had their own favoured economies: one family did not use any lighting in the front bedroom, relying instead on a gas lamp just outside the window; one woman unfolded every tea packet, not only to extract the last tea leaf, but also to use the packet (twisted up) as a fire lighter. Old flour bags were used as pillow cases and towels; old sacks and old coats were used to make peg rugs. Old clothes were very frequently made up into patchwork quilts; some women converted bacon or orange boxes into furniture; one used a banana box as a baby's cradle. One woman used to buy half a dozen eggs, or some other item, and raffle them with her neighbours; old shoes were converted into clogs by the dozen; tailors' samples were begged and made into woollen patchwork blankets; brown paper was put between blankets to provide extra warmth in the winter. Other women never peeled carrots or potatoes in case they lost some food in the discarded peel. Children went picking on railway banks for pieces of coal; others collected lumps which fell off carts in the street. Not only did these endless economies save money, however small the amount, but the practising of them seems to have given many women the satisfaction of having managed well:

When mother was getting on in her seventies . . . sister said to her, 'Why don't you go and buy this? If you go and you leave a few hundred pounds, somebody else will spend it quickly.' Mother said, 'Well if they enjoy spending it as much as I've enjoyed saving it, it will be all right.' She got pleasure out of thinking she had saved fourpence on a meal.[61]

In really bad times very poor families had to rely on soup kitchens and charities which gave clothing, bedding and Christmas gifts for children.[62]

Diet

The most substantial part of the working-class family income was spent on food. It was the woman's task to buy and cook this food, and her choices and abilities obviously affected the overall balancing of the budget and, of course, her family's health.

Working-class women have been heavily criticised for their lack of ability as household managers, and most especially for their lack of cooking skills. In the selection of food, they have either been criticised for choosing a limited, unbalanced diet, or one which was nutritious but uneconomical, because it relied heavily on animal protein. Rowntree regretted that the working class did not select a diet which was both economical and nutritious, but recognised that 'the adoption of such a diet would require considerable changes in established customs and many prejudices would have to be uprooted.'[63] In

1904, the Report of the Inter-Departmental Committee on Physical Deterioration stated that 'a diet of bread and butter for breakfast, potatoes and herrings for dinner, and bread and butter for tea, enlivened by some cheap cuts of meat on Sunday and purchases from the fried fish shop during the week, when funds permitted, was the normal working-class diet.' The Report also stated that the poor could have obtained a better diet in terms of calories and nutrients if less had been spent on animal protein: 'It is no doubt the case that with greater knowledge the poor might live more cheaply than they do.'[64] Derek Oddy has said: 'We know little about the status of foods in the nineteenth century, but there is a suggestion that certain prejudices against fruit, vegetables, and milk were retained until the beginnings of the twentieth century.'[65]

These criticisms are criticisms of the working-class woman, for she, as controller of the family's budget and shopping, created and sustained both her family's preferences and prejudices in their tastes in food. Criticisms of her abilities as a cook have been even more direct. Eunice Schofield states bluntly, 'Many housewives did not know how to cook, and they generally speaking had no training in the art of cooking.'[66] Margaret Hewitt has quoted Victorian eye-witnesses to prove that the standards of cooking and house-keeping in general were very poor.[67] Robert Roberts, writing of Salford at the turn of the century, says, 'In the poorest household through a lack of knowledge and utensils little cooking of any kind went on except for the grilling on a fork before the kitchen fire of bits of bacon and fish. Many never cooked vegetables, not even potatoes.'[68]

Oral evidence suggests that there must have been considerable regional and indeed local variations. For example, it was very rare for any local family to have herrings for dinner, although it was quite usual to have bread and butter for breakfast. The great majority of women did know how to cook, having learned from an older generation; while prejudices against certain foods were far less common than the ability to afford them (especially out-of-season fruits). In no family in the sample, even those living in very old sub-standard housing in Preston and Lancaster, were there no cooking facilities — all had access to a fireside range, and in no family were *no* vegetables eaten.

There were variations within the area (and these will be examined further), but these would appear to be not so striking as the differences between this and other areas. Work done by D. E. Allen on commercial surveys of consumer expenditure in the decade 1955—65 revealed many regional variations in food consumption which he believed had existed for centuries.[69] In this region there were two types of basic diet: one which was customary for textile workers especially, but which to some extent affected the population of Preston as a whole, and which can be called the 'textile diet'; and one found in Barrow and Lancaster, and in some non-textile families in Preston, which could be described as a traditional North Lancashire diet. Oral evidence also indicates the difficulties of constructing a price index, as no significant correlation has been established between the lists of commodities whose prices were quoted in the local press, and the actual patterns of consumption of the working classes.

The working classes were poor and they also worked hard physically; consequently, for both economic and nutritional reasons they consumed large amounts of carbohydrates. All the Victorian surveys show that bread and potatoes were the staple foods of working-class diets. Oddy's analysis of the available data gives the per capita consumption of bread as 6.7 lb per week, and that of potatoes as 1.6 lb per week.[70] It is impossible to give an aggregated picture of the per capita consumption of bread and potatoes from oral evidence, although some respondents do remember clearly how much bread was made and/or bought per week in their families. Their anecdotal evidence reveals that in poor families the average consumption of bread per week was not substantially different from the national average as estimated by Oddy. Bread was very much the basis of the diet in all three towns, and particularly in Barrow and Lancaster it continued to be made at home until well into the inter-war period. Large poor families consumed more bread per capita than did smaller and more prosperous ones, but in all families the major part of the meals of breakfast and tea was bread.

Mrs Sharp, from Barrow, whose very poor family consisted of three adults and ten children, remembers them eating eight or nine 2 lb loaves every day.[71] Mr Matthews also came from a very poor family of two parents and twelve children. He said:

She made everything. She was a wonderful woman and on Thursday she used to do about two stone of flour and another half-stone on a Sunday and another half-stone on Tuesday to take to the bakehouse.[72]

As a stone of flour makes about two stones of bread, this particular family of fourteen was consuming about 6 lb of bread each per week. Mrs Heron, a Lancaster respondent, was the eldest of nine children:

I used to knead a stone of bread twice a week. Knead it before I went to school. I can see her now. 'Do it again, Nellie,' and then she'd lift it up and sprinkle flour in and she'd turn it over. Lovely bread, oven bottom buns, lovely, and a little bit of butter on.[73]

This family was consuming about 5 lb of bread each per week.

The position in Preston was different. Home baking disappeared earlier in

Preston than it did in Barrow and Lancaster, and one of the poorest and biggest families (that of Mr Tyrell), with two parents and thirteen children, had to buy about sixty loaves a week. (It is presumed these were 2 lb loaves, which gives a weekly per capita consumption of about 8 lb. This could well be accurate as he talks of eating half a loaf per meal if he was allowed to.) The oral historian receives the impression that rather more bread was eaten in Preston than in Barrow and Lancaster, but this is, of course, only an impression. One reason for the possibly higher per capita bread consumption there might have been the rather wider range of carbohydrate foods in working-class diets in Barrow and Lancaster. Much more porridge was eaten in these two towns, the nutritional value of which was enthusiastically canvassed by both Rowntree and the Barrow Schools' Medical Officer.[74] The habit of putting treacle on top gave people a valuable source of iron. Large amounts of suet were eaten, either as dumplings in stews and soups, or as suet pudding. This sometimes followed the savoury course at dinnertime, or could be a teatime dish on its own. (Prestonians rarely speak of eating puddings except after Sunday dinner.) There were, of course, ordinary pastry puddings too.

We had a pudding nearly every day, mainly suet puddings with stewed apples in the middle or sometimes spotted dick with currants, and plums and rhubarb, whichever fruit was cheap at the time, blackberries and red currants when they were ready in the garden. We had them all in a pastry casing. Then she'd make jam roly-poly, apple roly-poly, and plum roly-poly, with custard and milk pudding. Sometimes we'd have them for tea instead of meat or eggs. When we came home, Mother had made a roly-poly pudding for our tea because she had no money, and evidently she had suet and flour in, so she used that and made a good solid sort of tea without being expensive.[75]

This respondent mentions milk puddings, which appear to have been eaten much more in Barrow and Lancaster than in Preston. These used yet another range of carbohydrates: rice and pasta, which were virtually never eaten as savouries. Finally many, indeed the majority, of working-class women in Barrow and Lancaster were enthusiastic bakers, not just of bread, but of all kinds of scones and cakes. Exactly what they made depended more on family tradition than economic circumstances. Mrs Sharp, bringing up four children in the inter-war period, existed on an income of 30s. a week, which placed the family well below the poverty line; but she still managed to bake for them:

I used to bake on a Thursday and Sunday. . . . I used to make little rock buns, and apple pies, and jam pies, and a fruit loaf. On a Thursday, I used to bake a Madeira cake, and some little cakes for the kiddies, and some scones and a bit of bread. . . .[76]

In all three towns the great majority of men worked near their homes and the children, similarly, attended nearby schools, so that there was little difficulty in returning home at midday for the main meal. (In the minority of cases where this was impossible, the main meal was in the early evening, with a bread-based snack eaten at midday.) There were some noticeable differences in what was eaten as the main meal. In Barrow and Lancaster, housewives did not rely on expensive animal protein (except on Sunday when the family usually had a joint). They were not, however, vegetarians, except occasionally, when forced to be by dire economic necessity: a meal was generally not seen as a main meal unless it contained some animal protein, but instead of buying expensive cuts, women relied on breast of lamb, belly of pork, stewing beef, and all kinds of bones and offal. They appear to have produced some very appetising meals out of apparently unpromising ingredients.

Mrs Stott's family were very poor; her father was a gravedigger, and her mother a washerwoman, and there were nine children:

Making the meals — when you think of the smells there used to be. I never smell anything good now. You don't. My mother, every Saturday our dinner was pluck [pig/sheep heart and/or lung], . . . stewed pluck with sage and onions. Oh, the smell of it give you a meal. You see, they'd turn their nose up at it now.
What did you have with it?
Potatoes and vegetables.
What else would she do for you that perhaps you wouldn't have now?
Rabbit pie, and things like that. Rabbits used to be about a shilling a couple. We used to buy them by the couple, and we used to have rabbit pie and potato pie, sheep's head broth, things like that. You know you never hear of them things now when you think of it.[77]

Even in Preston, where there was not such a strong tradition of 'making something out of nothing', this kind of cookery continued in some families well into the inter-war period. Mrs Calvert was born in 1919 and remembered her mother's recipe for stuffed heart:

She used to boil it and boil it. Then she used to have me chopping bread up very fine, fine as I could, and then rubbing it like breadcrumbs. There was no such thing as dried sage then. You had to rub it and rub it, and take all the stems off, and mix it all together and chop your onions fine. There were holes [in the heart] where all the valves go in and we used to have to stuff it all down there, and then she used to put it in a big roasting tin with a lid on, and push it in the oven for about an hour. After that it were cut up fine for sandwiches and that.[78]

Sometimes, particularly in Barrow and Lancaster, the protein source was free. For this, however, the woman had to rely on the activities of either the men in her immediate family, or on her neighbourhood, for it was they who went treading for cockles or flukes in the sands off Barrow or Morecambe, or who went fishing, or more rarely poaching rabbits. After childhood, women never pursued what were thought of as the traditionally male occupations of hunting and fishing:

> Did you ever have rabbit?
> Oh yes, I've had a lot of rabbit, m'father used to go rabbiting.
> How did he catch them?
> He had a ferret. And then mother used to clean them, skin them and stuff inside it, get a needle and cotton and sew it all up and put it in the cooker.[79]

I used to go fishing at Heysham, but you'd to do a lot of waiting, and Dad was a bit impatient so somebody said, 'Tell you what, go down to Conder Green and fish the tide in, tread them.' I said, 'Right-o.' Well, of course, the first time I went in when it got four foot I fell back in the water. The next time I went I pulled as many flukes out, I pulled sixty flukes out in as many minutes.

> Did you sell them or eat them all?
> Give them away.[80]

'Living off the land'. These are 'cocklers' working in Morecambe Bay. The horse and cart suggest that they might have been more professional than some of the other shellfish gatherers. (Barrow Library)

Flukes were one of the few fried meals which Barrovians and Lancastrians had, for usually their protein was not of a quality which could be dealt with in any other fashion than by long, slow cooking. The extent and importance of fishing in Barrow and Lancaster cannot be quantified, but it should not be underestimated, as it is clear from oral evidence that it provided a significant element in working-class diets.

As well as cheap protein, Barrow and Lancastrian women served an extensive range of vegetables to their families. Rowntree had argued (and he was later supported by Oddy)[81] that there was a basic prejudice against vegetables among the working class of York, where there are few references to vegetables in the menus given, and only six recorded instances of a family eating soup. It was possibly, as Rowntree argued, because soups and broths took a long time and some skill to make. Barrovians and Lancastrians, on the other hand, regarded vegetables as a cheap, nutritious, enjoyable and essential part of their diet, as indeed they were, providing iron, vitamins and protein: 'I think in my own mind that vegetables is as good as if you've a lot of meat';[82] 'It was a good thing really, the vegetables, and I think that made us because we're all big boned.'[83] A wide variety was eaten: potatoes, turnips, carrots, parsnips, leeks, onions, beans, peas (dried, or fresh in season), lettuce, cucumber, tomatoes, celery, watercress, cabbage, mushrooms, beetroot, cauliflower and lentils. They were usually combined with the available protein to make a variety of soups, broths, stews and other casseroled dishes:

There was always soups and stuff made from vegetables and leftovers.
   What kind of soups would your mother make?
   It could vary. Sheep's head broth. . . . I might have a go and get a few bones and half a sheep's head . . . that went in and a few vegetables chopped into it and that was it, a meal.[84]

Occasionally vegetables were eaten alone when economies demanded it, cooked in various ways. The most common was potatoes, carrots and turnips mashed together with butter. Dishes could, however, be more elaborate:

My mother's vegetarian hot-pot. It was a layer of potatoes, a layer of tapioca, a layer of carrots, and there was split peas, another layer of potatoes, onion, and tapioca, and seasoning. It was cooked in the fireside oven and it was lovely.[85]

In the summer salads (with or without cold meat) were very popular, but were eaten with bread and butter for tea, presumably not being thought substantial enough to be offered as the main meal of the day: 'She [a neighbour] used to come up for tea and when salads was out used to open the door and shout, 'Are you there?', and she'd bring me a great big plate of salad in. Did I enjoy it!'[86]

One of the more obvious (but not the sole) explanations for the marked inclusion of vegetables and seasonal, home-grown fruit in the diets of Barrovians and Lancastrians was their widespread availability and consequent cheapness. We do not know how many families in the two towns had allotments (where a minority might also keep pigs and hens). But in the sample, one-third of Barrow families, and a half of those in Lancaster, had plots, and, significantly, a substantial proportion were held by poor labouring families, who were most in need of the extra food they provided, and of the income earned from selling surplus products. The produce of these allotments, often situated in between the houses in the poorest areas, improved the diets not only of the families of the allotment holders, but also those of the entire surrounding neighbourhood. The majority of respondents remember either being given surplus products or buying them at very low prices. (And it would seem doubtful if commercial greengrocers could maintain very high prices in the face of such competition.) It is clear from the oral evidence that vegetables did play an essential part in the diet of these two towns.

Although there were similarities in the bread-based meals of the day (i.e. breakfast and tea) between Barrow and Lancaster on the one hand, and Preston on the other, there were some noticeable differences in the main meal. As was seen in chapter 3, approximately one-third of Preston's married women worked full-time outside the home. The actual women involved varied very considerably, of course, from decade to decade, but the great majority of Preston's working-class women continued to work full-time in the mill after marriage until circumstances forced or permitted them to give up. It is argued that the domestic habits acquired during these early years of marriage affected their families, not only while they were working, but also to a greater or lesser degree in the years after they had given up full-time work. We have already seen that full-time working women were unfairly accused of lacking cooking skills, although they all learned cooking from their mothers or other female relatives when children. Many cooked admirable meals after they stopped full-time work (for example, Mrs Calvert's mother, who excelled at stuffing cows' hearts). Yet a woman who worked full-time inevitably faced more difficulties than her less harassed contemporaries. Before the first world war, mill hours were from 6 a.m. until 5.30 p.m. with 1½ hours off for meals, leaving little free time or energy to make the broths and casseroles which took a lot of preparation and cooking time. A few very energetic ones prepared hot-pots in the evening (a mixture of potatoes, onions and meat, with a pastry top), which their children took to the public bake-house at breakfast-time and collected ready-cooked at dinnertime. Most mill women, however, were forced by sheer exhaustion to rely on convenience foods: there were thousands (probably hundreds of thousands) of pies sold during this period — meat, meat and potato, and potato pies. There was tripe which required only the addition of salt and vinegar, fish and chips, and various cold cooked meats. This diet was not necessarily unnutritious, but it was monotonous, conspicuously lacked vegetables, and was expensive. Those who did cook tended to rely on the kind of animal protein which could be cooked quickly — there are many references to fried bacon, chops and eggs. Although many women did cook more economic dishes when they ceased work, old habits did not die, and Preston families altogether relied more on quickly cooked or pre-cooked food. The conclusion seems to be that the average family there either spent more on food than did their Barrow and Lancaster counterparts, or ate less.

Certainly the number of shops selling convenience foods in Preston substantially increased at the beginning of the period. In 1892, there was one fish and chip shop to every 1,533 people; by 1907, this had doubled to one to every 785. In the same period the number of confectioners selling pies and cakes increased from one to 853 people, to one to 472 people; while the number of butchers fell from one to 672 people, to one to 813 people.[87] This can be contrasted with Barrow and Lancaster, where fish and chips, for example, were bought only occasionally and then not as a family meal but by adults going home late from a theatre, cinema, or pub. (This is confirmed by ex-owners of fish and chip shops as well as by their customers.)

In all three towns one form of convenience food, the tinned variety, was more conspicuous by its absence than by its consumption, except for tinned condensed milk, which was cheaper when diluted than fresh milk. There are hardly any memories of tinned food except in some more prosperous families, when a tin of fruit or a tin of salmon may have graced the table for festive Sunday tea. Some housewives, however, still had a definite prejudice about tinned food, believing it to be detrimental to health: 'There was a suspicion that anything in a tin was the cause of cancer';[88] 'She wouldn't have any canned stuff. She said that it would poison you.'[89]

Many Preston families speak of only having vegetables on a Sunday, when they had their only 'proper' dinner of the week (that is, meat, two vegetables, and a pudding). The relative absence of vegetables from the Preston diet is partly explained by the lack of time so many women there had to prepare them, and by the comparative absence of allotments and gardens compared to Barrow and Lancaster. However, rather more Preston families in the sample had an allotment than was anticipated when the survey was started. (In fact one-third had garden plots.) But in fact virtually no allotments existed in the congested central area of Preston where the poorest section of the population lived; those who might have benefited most either from having an allotment or having access to a supply of free or cheap fresh vegetables. Rather, the families in the survey who had allotments lived on the outskirts of the town, and although these included some labouring families, the majority were aspiring members of the working class, usually with a good wage, whose need

In the 1920s younger women were beginning to shorten their skirts but aprons remained standard daytime wear. (University Library, University of Lancaster)

for vegetables as a vital supplement to their diet was rather less than the poor's.

It is reasonably clear from the available evidence that many Prestonians were less economically and less nutritiously fed than their counterparts in

Barrow and Lancaster. One can only admire the Preston working women who struggled to balance their budgets and feed their families in the face of overwhelming odds.

Clothing

How well did working-class women manage to clothe their families? It is interesting to note that although changes and developments in household equipment had hardly touched the working-class home in general before the first world war, it was quite common for working-class women to have sewing-machines. Those who had them (with some interesting exceptions in Preston) made a wide variety of garments; the very skilful (like Mrs Sharp in Barrow, who had trained as a tailoress) were able to make their husbands' suits, but more usual were the women who made their own and their children's clothes, often from cheap remnants from the markets, or from cut-down larger, donated garments, or, as in Lancaster and Preston, from material acquired both legally and illegally from the mill. In Lancaster, a material frequently mentioned was 'wiper', a fluffy flannelette-type material which was issued to all workers in the linoleum factory each week for the cleaning down of machinery. Self-respecting workers took the 'wiper' home, and instead used 'proper rags' for wiping down. The wiper was washed and used to make baby clothes and pillow cases; occasionally it was dyed and made up into curtains.

In Preston many women made good, cheap clothes at home, but there was another smaller group who had a curiously ambivalent attitude to home-made clothes, which they felt did not have the status of bought, ready-made clothes. Some women had a sewing-machine, but rarely used it. They did not share the sense of achievement at having made something out of nothing. Curiously though, the machine was kept as a status symbol, alongside the other status symbol, the bought clothing. Mrs Bridges, whose mother worked full-time, and who therefore had little time for sewing, said: 'We hardly ever used it. I think it was only there for the article [i.e. as a status symbol].'[90] Another woman claimed that her mother made her polish the machine, but refused to teach her how to use it.

The Prestonian devotion to conspicuous spending on clothing can best be seen in the annual Whit Monday processions, when tens of thousands of children and adults walked through Preston. Each church chose its own children's clothes. These were often beautiful, but equally often quite impractical. The social and religious solidarity displayed on these occasions is admirable, but the effect on working-class budgets must have been less than happy.

It would be quite untrue, however, to suggest that there was a completely different attitude towards clothing between the towns. In all three, working-

On Biggar Bank. Walney Island. Aug. 17/08.

On Bank Holidays and during August, those who could went to the sea.
Prestonians went to Blackpool for a week, Barrovians and Lancastrians could
visit a nearby beach for the day. Everyone is wearing their 'best' clothes. It was
obviously quite acceptable for respectable women to show their legs.
(Barrow Library)

class women took pride in making cheap clothes; and in all three women found
that some clothing had to be bought. Footwear, especially for growing children,
was a particular nightmare. In Preston and Lancaster clogs were popular as an
economical and very long-lasting purchase, and were handed down in families.
Old shoes could be converted into clogs by the clogger who added the wooden
sole and metal reinforcement (called 'caulkers' locally). Other clothes which
had to be purchased included metal-workers' moleskin trousers which were
too thick to be stitched on an ordinary domestic sewing-machine.

Some women, however, found they simply did not have the skill to do
anything more ambitious than mending, and so had to buy clothes. Often this
meant getting them second-hand, and jumble sales and second-hand clothes
dealers were very popular. Even those who could sew made judicious use of
them. The mother of Mrs Mulholland was a proficient dressmaker and on
occasion took in sewing. The three women in the family took a great pride in
their appearance and augmented their home-made outfits with some interesting
purchases from the second-hand shop:

You got pretty good quality stuff, because the wardrobe dealers used to go round high-class houses and buy their cast-offs which were hardly worn at all. We got some very good clothes from them. We knew the ones that went to the right places. When my sister was a girl, she wore a sable, a little sable collar, and that would be second-hand, but it was really lovely.[91]

Major items of household linen such as blankets had to be bought. The outright buying of these items could well have ruined many a working-class budget, and so families who would never have dreamed of obtaining credit for food, had little hesitation in using the services of the Scotchman or Tallyman (mentioned above). By the inter-war period this method of buying clothing and household linen had become so widespread that it was commented upon in the Board of Trade Survey of Lancashire.[92]

WERE WORKING-CLASS WOMEN SUCCESSFUL HOUSEHOLD MANAGERS?

This is, perhaps, an unanswerable question. First, it is abundantly clear that they had to work within very tightly drawn parameters, not of their own ordering or choosing. The major part of the family wage came from the husband's work; many of the strategies which could be adopted to help balance the budget depended either on the physical environment, and/or the husband's ability to exploit it by various means of living off the land. Women were all too aware of these limits; and this awareness was one reason for their generally low material expectations. It is, however, by the women's own standards and criteria that their success or failure as household managers should initially be estimated. *All* women hoped to be able to feed, clothe and house their families. There are no examples of women failing to do this in the sample: presumably failure would have meant, ultimately, death. It is in the nature of things that fewer such people or their offspring would be expected to be around today. All but the very poorest were concerned with rather more than mere physical survival; they were concerned for the survival of their dignity, which meant avoiding the pawnbroker or, living off credit, and ideally being able to save for certain important goods. As has been seen, not all could avoid getting into debt, but in virtually every family the woman was able to save a little at some point. Ironically, the savings common to all families interviewed were death insurances; it is an interesting reflection on the strength of working-class mores that what little could be saved went not on the well-being of the living, but to ensure the decent burial of the dead. No other form of saving was so widely adopted.

At the turn of the century about a sixth of Barrow's population (and about one-sixth of the sample), belonged to a Friendly Society,[93] ensuring free medical attention for each insured member. There were rather fewer members in Lancaster and Preston. Undoubtedly, poverty was an important reason for not belonging, as a contribution of 1*d*. or 2*d*. a week per head could be a substantial drain on the budget. Other reasons also debarred working-class people from membership. Societies only accepted those who were fit and appeared to be a good insurance risk. Mr Bowker's family, although very poor (his father was a coach-driver, and later a caretaker), belonged to the Oddfellows. When he was small they wanted him to be a member too:

I was the only one who never passed for the Oddfellows. My sister took me by the hand to the doctor, and we had to pass a doctor in those days to go into a Friendly Society, who then for a penny a week provided you with a free doctor. . . . The doctor said, 'Well, what do you want?' The doctors were very severe in those days. 'My mother has sent us to see if you'll put Bert into the Oddfellows.' He said, 'You can take him back and tell your mother she should have drowned him when he was young and I'm not going to do it.'[94]

Many women saved painlessly through buying their food and clothing at the Co-op, and letting the dividend accrue until it made a useful sum which could be withdrawn quarterly. In the days when the dividend could be as high as 2*s*. 6*d*. in the pound, this was a useful amount which could be spent on items of major expenditure like shoes and boots.[95] These were the most common ways of saving; no respondents had a bank account, although a few mention a Post Office Savings account. Those who managed to save a sizeable sum (for example to buy a house) probably kept the cash hidden in the house.

Contemporary observers tended to judge working-class women's abilities as wives, mothers and managers in the light of local infant mortality levels. This was not a standard used by the women themselves. Especially criticised were women who worked outside the home, because it was thought that this was a factor in infant mortality rates. In Preston, undoubtedly, there was both high infant mortality and a high percentage of women in outside employment. The 1902 report of the Preston Medical Officer of Health stated: 'First among these causes [of the high infant mortality rate], is the employment of female labour in mills . . . there is a marked disinclination on the part of many young mothers to stay at home and tend their children, preferring as they do the life at the mill to that of nursing.'[96] (Views like these were widely canvassed and received national prominence in 1906 with the publication of Sir George Newman's *Infant Mortality: A Social Problem*.[97] He argued, with the use of many statistics, that there was a marked correlation between a high percentage of married women in work and a high infant mortality rate. There has been much controversy about this thorny topic ever since; one of the most thorough and detailed surveys of the argument being that by Carol Dyhouse.)[98]

Working-class women themselves did not see their actions as the cause of their babies' deaths. They occasionally (and probably accurately) ascribed a difficult birth to their work in the late stages of pregnancy; they very occasionally felt concern at the way their child was cared for by the baby-minder; they would have preferred to be at home to care for their children; but none displayed any consciousness that their babies' deaths were connected with their full-time work. This attitude is totally understandable in view of the many women they saw around them who also lost babies, who were not, and had not been, working for a long time. Women who had never done any full-time work after marriage lost as many if not more babies than women who worked. The most striking case of a family losing babies was that of Mrs Mulholland whose mother had sixteen children, only three of whom survived childhood. Most women accepted the loss of their babies as a sad, but inevitable part of life; they nursed them devotedly but recognised that there was little they or the doctor could do in many cases. A few were distraught at the loss of a child. Mrs Gregson's mother had sixteen children and raised eleven:

She buried some. She had them too often. . . . I can remember her carrying that little coffin with the baby in. . . . She said that every baby she saw she wanted to snatch. She would have stolen anybody's baby to fill that want. She had all those, but she wouldn't spare one.[99]

Equally, there were quite possibly a few women who welcomed the loss of a baby. Mr Terry, in Preston, was the eldest of seven children, three of whom survived. When asked if his mother was upset when she talked about their deaths he said: 'I don't think so because. . . . it was a question of a loss, yes. In lots of cases a good loss. More so when you had more mouths to feed.'[100] And while the great majority of women were sad when their babies died, if anyone was blamed it was the doctor and/or the midwife; usually though blame was not apportioned, and the deaths were simply accepted.

The association between work and infant mortality remains problematic, especially before the first world war.[101] In Lancashire it is easy to find towns with comparatively low rates of infant mortality, and lower percentages of married women in full-time work, and those with high infant mortality rates and a large percentage of married women in work. But it is also possible to find towns with the opposite characteristics (see table 4.3).

However, a large number of babies died of diarrhoea every year, and it can be argued that babies who were not breast-fed were much more likely to develop infant diarrhoea than those who were. The first annual report in 1903 by the newly appointed Preston Health Visitors included an investigation into the deaths of seventy-eight children who had died of diarrhoea. Of these only

TABLE 4.3: Infant mortality rates and percentages of women
in full-time work in five towns

	Average infant mortality rates, 1901—10[a]	Percentage of married and widowed women in full-time work, 1911
Barrow	119	6.9
Rochdale	113	27.9
Wigan	166	11.8
Burnley	167	40.0
Preston	158	35.0

[a] Infant mortality rate is the number of deaths in the first year of life per 1,000 live births.
The figures refer to registration districts. These are not always exactly the same as the County boroughs for which the employment figures are given.
Source: The Registrar General's Decennial Report, 1911, and the Census of 1911.

six had been entirely breast-fed, fifty-nine had been bottle-fed, and sixteen partly breast-fed.[102] (The arithmetic seems rather confusing.) Again in 1911, Preston Health Visitors reported on 111 babies who had died of diarrhoea, only eight of whom were breast-fed, six partly breast-fed, and ninety-six bottle-fed.[103]

The long tube bottles which were used at that time, with a couple of feet of rubber tubing between bottle and teat, would be difficult to sterilise even today, and must have been a paradise for germs before the first world war. However, it must not be assumed that all babies whose mothers worked full-time were fed with one of these bottles. It was not unknown for babies to be taken by relatives to the mill to be breast-fed by the mother at breakfast and dinnertime; while those who were not breast-fed may both have been spoon-fed with a mixture of bread and milk. This is clear both from oral evidence, and from some documentary evidence.[104] It was not only millworkers who did not always breast-feed their babies. Many other women were unable to do so for a variety of physical reasons (including, most obviously, debility). In the family with the worst record for infant and child deaths, the mother did not manage to breast-feed any of them.[105]

One is left, however, with the question of why so many more babies under the age of one died in Preston than in Barrow and Lancaster? It would be foolish to suggest that none died as a result of their mother working; and an unknown number might have survived if they had been breast-fed. But the complexity of the problem is acute and is perhaps best illustrated by two sets of figures from Preston, which show that in a period when the full-time employment of married women increased, infant mortality decreased. In 1901 30.5 per cent of married and widowed women were in full-time employment, and the corresponding figure in 1911 was 35 per cent. In 1896—1900 the average annual infant mortality rate was 235 per thousand, while in 1906—10 the rate had fallen to 162.[106]

Perhaps the most interesting of all the figures are those relating to a sample of Lancashire towns. The Registrar General's figures for 1901—10 refer to registration districts which were, in fact, larger than the county boroughs; the figures for the 1920s refer to county boroughs. (See tables 4.4 and 4.5.)

TABLE 4.4: Average infant mortality rates in areas of Lancashire, 1901—10

	Infant mortality rate[a]
Textile areas	
Bolton	148
Bury	141
Rochdale	133
Burnley	167
Blackburn	148
Preston	158
(Average)	141
Non-textile areas	
West Derby (incl. Bootle)	145
Prescot (incl. St Helens)	144
Wigan	166
Warrington	140
Barrow	119
Lancaster	125
(Average)	138

[a] Expressed as the number of deaths in the first year of life per 1,000 live births.
Average infant mortality rate for England and Wales 1901—10 = 127.
Source: The Registrar General's *Annual Reports* 1901—10.

It is impossible to argue from these tables that there was a significantly higher infant mortality rate in textile Lancashire than in non-textile Lancashire. The aggregates and averages indicate (as Carol Dyhouse has so ably argued)[107] that there is no clear correlation between high percentages of women in work, as there were in textile areas, and a high infant mortality rate. These tables really present the historian with as many questions as answers. Why, for example, were Barrow, and to some extent Lancaster, the only towns out of the twelve with infant mortality rates near the national average? Why did the other towns have rates in excess of those for England and Wales? Why were there such

TABLE 4.5: Average infant mortality rates*a* in areas of Lancashire, 1921—30

	1921—5	*1926—30*
Textile boroughs		
Preston	107	94
Bolton	91	82
Burnley	113	91
Rochdale	86	78
Bury	85	79
Blackburn	98	83
(Average)	97	84
Non-textile boroughs		
Barrow	78	70
St Helens	103	96
Wigan	110	107
Warrington	84	78
Bootle	91	89
Lancaster	83	74
(Average)|	91	85

a Expressed as the number of deaths in the first year of life per 1,000 live births.
Average infant mortality rate for England and Wales 1921—5 = 76; 1926—30 = 68.
Source: The Registrar General's *Annual Reports* 1921—30.

variations within one county, and within each group of towns? Why was Wigan's rate so much greater than that for Barrow? Why was there usually such a contrast between Burnley and Rochdale? The easiest, and perhaps most simplistic, explanation lies in general levels of prosperity. There does appear to have been a complex, but valid relationship between a low standard of living and high infant mortality rates. It would seem more sensible to attribute high levels of infant mortality to these general economic and social conditions rather than to the mismanagement or neglect of working-class mothers.

5

Families and Neighbours

Working-class women did not live exclusively within the confines of a nuclear family, but were members of neighbourhood groups and extended families. These groups were of great importance in working-class lives, giving social and material support, and providing a strict system for establishing and maintaining social mores. They were operated largely, but not exclusively, by women. Working-class solidarity has usually been discussed in terms of organisations like trade unions, the Cooperative Movement, and the Labour Party. It is rather more meaningful to discuss female solidarity in terms of the extended family and the neighbourhood.

THE EXTENDED FAMILY

It is almost impossible to define precisely who were or who were not regarded as family by working-class people, or perhaps more exactly from whom, and to whom, support and help would either be received or offered. The only workable definition is that deduced from the evidence of the respondents themselves, and it is clear that in some families obligations were felt and acted upon to a very wide network of uncles, aunts, cousins, grandparents, and great-aunts and uncles. In other families meaningful links were maintained with only a very small group outside the immediate co-resident nuclear family. Decisions about who were to be *significant* members of one's family were rarely consciously made; they depended on many factors, most of them of a practical nature. It was, for example, difficult either to offer or receive help from kin who were physically far away.

Both Barrow and Lancaster, in the last decades of the nineteenth century, were towns with large migrant populations. When and if an extended family migrated, *as a group*, migration could strengthen family ties as the group faced a new and sometimes hostile environment together. But if a nuclear family migrated on its own then ties with kin left behind would be broken. One-quarter of the Barrow respondents, one-eighth of those in Lancaster, but only one-sixteenth of those in Preston, do not mention kin. The explanation for these figures would appear to be migration, for all but one of these families with no mention of kin were recent migrants to the area. Migrants who did keep in touch with physically distant kin had contacts at a rather insignificant level: letters and parcels were exchanged, and visits when funds allowed. While these contacts were important, they obviously provided a rather lower level of support than that available from relations living nearby.

However, having a nearby relative did not *always* guarantee help even when urgently needed. Mrs Swann came from a very poor family in Preston; there were eight children, and her mother was an epileptic who spent most of her time in bed:

We were left with little children and an epileptic mother and nobody did a thing for her.
    None of her relations or your father's relations did anything for her?
    They had to go to work themselves. He had a sister lived in Newhall Lane. He also had a sister at Leyland, but she had been left with a big family.[1]

It would seem in this case that the combined problems created by migration (both parents originally came from the West of Ireland), added to the great poverty in which they all found themselves, and made meaningful mutual support virtually impossible. This was observable in another Preston family, also very poor Irish immigrants.[2] But it cannot be overstressed that these cases are very unusual, and in the vast majority of cases kin living within easy (and cheap) travelling distance invariably offered a wide range of help in a wide variety of situations.

Their motives for doing so were very mixed; and it is, of course, very difficult to begin to assess motives at this distance in time. However, some patterns are fairly clear. All the respondents, except one, were brought up with some degree of Christian teaching. As adults, many respondents developed different ideas about Christianity, but there was a wide consensus that it meant at least being kind and helpful to others, especially to family and neighbours. Other respondents do not specifically discuss this duty, for it was simply widely held, unwritten, often unspoken and perhaps all the stronger for being undiscussed. People also loved their relations. There were arguments and quarrels, but an obvious deep affection existed in many families. Relationships with kin were also influenced by feelings of pride; for example, it was important that relations in difficulty were kept out of the workhouse, still a place of dread throughout the period. There was the utmost reluctance to allow any relative to go there, even when keeping them meant considerable self-sacrifice.

Mrs Burns's mother died, aged thirty-two, leaving five young children. Her father was a drunkard, and considered by his mother-in-law to be totally unfit to look after his children:

The neighbours said, 'Rosie, you'll have to put all the children in the workhouse.' M'grandma said, 'Our Margaret Jane's children in the workhouse? Never. Not while I draw breath.' That old woman kept us all that time until she died and she must have been about seventy. Grandfather had to go on working when he might have considered retirement, and grandmother took in washing and lodgers to try to balance the budget.[3]

Mrs Askew said: 'Oh to be sent to the workhouse was dreadful. I think families tended to stick together more. We only had a little bit but we would share it, and I think that happened.'[4] This woman was not simply uttering platitudes in a moral vacuum. Later in her interview she told of her family's long struggle to maintain her grandmother, an alcoholic, who regularly pawned the family's goods to pay for drink. (She not only pawned the respondent's wedding presents while she was away on her honeymoon, but also sold the pawn tickets.)

Lastly, it must be added that the law, from the passing of the Poor Law Act in 1601 until the Public Assistance Act of 1946, placed upon the extended family an obligation to support and care for its members; parents were responsible for their children, adult children for their parents, and grandparents were responsible for grandchildren (but only in Scotland was the reverse true). It was possible to be prosecuted for a failure to maintain: there were about 7,000 prosecutions a year in the 1880s and 1890s, mostly of husbands by wives. It is very important to note, however, that *no* respondent ever mentioned this legal responsibility: some were not aware of its existence; those who were did not see it as in any way relevant to their attitude towards relations, while many families took responsibility for relatives for whom they were not legally responsible. The vast majority of respondents display a mixture of love, duty and pride in their attitudes towards their relatives.

This was not the assumption made by Michael Anderson in his *Family Structure in Nineteenth-Century Lancashire.* There is considerable agreement between his evidence and mine on the great importance of the extended family both socially and economically; but it is difficult to accept his interpretation of the motives for helping kin. He has postulated a theory, starting from the exchange theory of values, which suggests that 'some children were interacting with their parents in a manner which can only be described as one of short-run calculative instrumentality . . . social relationships of any significance only being maintained by considerable sections of the population in situations where both parties were obtaining some fairly immediate advantages from them, in other words where exchanges were reciprocal and almost immediate.'[5] It must be stressed, of course, that Anderson was concerned with Preston at least half a century before oral evidence becomes relevant. It is impossible to say with any certainty either that working-class attitudes and motivation changed fundamentally in fifty years, or that they were never quite as Anderson portrayed them. This thesis is examined more fully later in the chapter, but certainly there is very little evidence in the later period for this 'calculative orientation towards kin', but a great deal of evidence of people helping their relations at considerable cost to themselves in terms of time, energy and money.

Michael Anderson had been particularly concerned with the degree of co-residence among members of an extended family, believing that this revealed the great importance of the kinship group. It is also possible to calculate from the census enumerators' books the extent to which kin lived together in one household. These data are not available to historians studying the period 1890–1940, but respondents were asked if at any time during that period they had either had kin living with them, or if they themselves had lived with relatives. Thirty per cent of the respondents in Barrow and Lancaster had been in this position, while in Preston the very high figure of 45 per cent had lived with kin. Anderson had discovered 23 per cent of Preston's families with co-resident kin in 1851. The figures are not really comparable, but the estimates from the oral evidence illustrate the continuing importance of co-residency. It is also clear from the oral evidence that historians should not concentrate too much on attempts to quantify the number of co-resident families as a way of estimating the importance of the extended family. Even more common than co-resident kin were kin living very near, frequently in the same street, for they were able to offer and receive many important services. These complex relationships will never be traced in the census enumerators' books, as the strongest ties were undoubtedly between women, especially mothers, daughters and adult married sisters, who did not share the same surname, and who are almost impossible to trace through the official records.

However, co-residency was obviously important, and oral evidence reveals a wide range of reasons for it. First, there were orphaned children (orphan meaning here children who had lost one parent before they were fifteen years old). There were many such children; in the sample eleven Lancaster children (23 per cent), seven Barrow children (14 per cent), and fifteen Preston children (23 per cent), had lost a parent before they were fifteen years old. (Anderson found 33 per cent so orphaned in Preston in 1851.) These children were not necessarily cared for by members of the extended family; widows quite often managed to carry on by themselves, especially if their older children were earning. In a few cases they actually prospered. Miss Turner's father died aged thirty-seven when she was nine, her brother five, and her older sisters twelve and fourteen. Her mother was a weaver, as eventually were all the girls. Initially Mrs Turner had a terrible struggle, but as the children started work, and by dint of extreme frugality, the family began to be quite comfortable, affording such luxuries as holidays in the Isle of Man, and eventually, only eight years after her husband's death, Mrs Turner was able to buy a newly-built, semi-detached house with a bathroom and a garden. Her daughter was justly proud of her mother's achievement.[6]

Other women were not able to carry on alone, especially if their children were very small. They were likely to go and live with relatives, usually a widowed or unmarried male relative, to keep house for him in return for financial support. If a man was widowed he was much more likely to seek help from the extended family. Either his children went directly to live with relatives, or a female relation was asked to come and live with the family as a substitute mother. There are a few cases of children losing both parents, and they were inevitably cared for by the extended family; usually, but not always, on the mother's side. This tradition continued right through the period. Mrs Harrison reported on her extended family in the inter-war period. Her family could afford to look after the orphans, but neither expected nor received any financial return:

After I was four she [her own mother] had this operation and she didn't go to work. But what mother did do? She had a brother lived at Blackburn and they had three children and they [her uncle and aunt] died within weeks of each other. Then Mother said she would take the two girls, and the brother went to a relation belonging to his mother at the other side.
Did they bring any money with them, or did she have to pay out for them?
The money they got from the business had to be put in the bank until they were twenty-one.
So she had nothing to help her at all?
No. Father by this time was driving and earning a bit more. It would be between £3 and £4 and it was regular. That was a good wage in those days, in the thirties.[7]

It is difficult to assess how many orphaned children were cared for by the extended family, but both the oral evidence and what little statistical evidence is available would suggest that the vast majority of orphans were cared for either by their surviving parent or by the extended family. There was only one case in the sample of children being sent to the Cottage Homes, the children's branch of the Barrow workhouse. Mr Evans and his sister were orphaned when very young, their father being killed in an accident. Their mother remarried, but later deserted her husband and children. Almost simultaneously the stepfather was sent to prison, and the children to the Cottage Homes. However, after release from prison he withdrew the children, who were subsequently brought up by their step-grandparents (indicating how far the concept of familial duty could extend).[8]

From the 1921 Census results for Barrow it is possible to check how many

children were orphaned (that is, lost one or both parents). Of the total, only
3.4 per cent were cared for in the Cottage Homes. In the absence of privately
run orphanages it must be presumed that the rest were cared for by relations.
There were no examples of orphans being cared for by neighbours.[9]

Some children lived with relations even when both their parents were alive;
some went because there was a shortage of space at home, or because of
parental poverty. Mr Logan's mother's family lived in Lancaster, but his
mother's home was in Salford. His father was a docker and the family were
extremely poor:

I lived there [Lancaster] up to about ten years of age, and I went back to Salford.
My mother had so many youngsters. Her sisters were spinsters and worked in the
mill. We were so poor in those days that mother's sister used to take a couple of
her children. She brought up three of my mother's children from birth.[10]

Other children went to relatives because they chose to:

You said your sister lived with your grannie. Did she live nearby, your grandma?
    Yes. The old grandfather he worked near to as well.
    Why did your sister live with them?
    Well, she wanted to go and live with her grandma, only for a time and then she
would come back home and then go back to her. She stuck to her grandma until
she married.
    I don't think this was unusual because families were very closely knit, weren't
they?
    It would be 'If you hit me again I will go to my grandma's!' was a regular thing
for children. 'I'll go and see my grandad.'[11]

These arrangements were usually casual, unplanned, and appear to have
suited everyone. In a very few cases women were deeply upset by the necessity
of having to give away a child. Mrs Hesketh's mother was very poor, and also
very ill after the birth of Emily, who was taken care of by a group of unmarried
female relatives. At first the mother dreaded the return of the child because
she was still ill, and perpetually poor. Gradually, though, she came to resent
the loss of her daughter, but did not want to upset either the child or the
relations by demanding her return. Mrs Hesketh described the situation:

These cousins, they were four maiden aunts to us and they kept this child and they
grew fond of her. When she used to come past (they lived in a nicer house and
were posher than us) and whenever she [the mother] saw them passing I remember
her saying, 'Oh my God, they are here with the child!' She thought each time that
they were bringing it back and she wasn't really fit. There came a time when she
said that she would like her back and she thought they would break their hearts to

part with her. She always said, 'Don't ever forget, she's my child!' . . . And before she went home, 'Don't you ever forget, you are my little girl. You know that, don't you? And these are your sisters, don't ever forget, Emily, these are your brothers and sisters!' Because she was posher than us. I remember at school they couldn't understand it, one so posh.

And she stayed with these aunties, did she?

She was brought up with them. . . . She [the mother] could never break her heart enough. I have heard her many a time say to neighbours and friends, 'I might have eight but I haven't one to spare. I parted with one and I've regretted it all my life.' That was her opinion.[12]

But a case like this was unusual; it was much more common for working-class children to spend a lot of time living with different relatives, and for both them and their parents to regard this as a happy arrangement.

A different type of co-residence occurred when elderly parents went to live with married children. There were not very many cases of this in the sample, partly because old people preferred, undoubtedly, to continue to live in their own homes and be visited regularly by their children, and partly because there were proportionately far fewer older people in the population than today (see table 5.1). As they tended to have had rather more children than people now, the statistical chances of a respondent remembering a co-resident grandfather or grandmother were reasonably small, but they did exist. As with orphans, it is clear that old people were almost invariably looked after at home, rather than being sent to the workhouse. There was only one case of this in the sample, and it was in Preston. This family also had the problem of a drinking grandmother who pawned the family's possessions.[13]

TABLE 5.1: Percentage of the population aged 65 and over

	Barrow	Lancaster	Preston
1891	1.9	4.1	3.4
1901	2.4	3.8	3.5
1911	3.7	4.8	4.1
1921	4.4	6.4	5.0
1931	6.1	7.8	6.4
(1971	13.7	15.1	14.6)

Source: Census of 1891, vol. III, table 3; Census of 1901, County of Lancaster, table 24; Census of 1911, County of Lancaster, table 16; Census of 1921, County of Lancaster, tables 14 and 14a; Census of 1931, County of Lancaster, tables 14 and 15; Census of 1971, County of Lancaster, Part I, table 8.

The great majority of co-resident grandmothers (or grandfathers) were not, of course, a burden; they were usually able to perform various tasks which both helped the housewife and gave them a feeling of being useful. But in the cases of neither co-resident children nor old people is it possible to see the attitude of 'calculative instrumentality' in operation. The only cases of obvious mutual benefit resulting from co-residence was when adult relatives lived with kin. Unmarried adult brothers and sisters paid rent, and in return had board, lodgings and company.

In Preston it was very common for newly married couples to live with in-laws. If this arrangement continued, child-minding, and later caring for the elderly, could also develop. Mrs Bridges (born in 1916) took it for granted that each generation lived with the previous one. This kind of arrangement was not unusual in Preston:

When my mother married my dad they got this house. His mother, my grandmother, and father were living with them. They died, one just before Christmas and the other about five weeks after. My grandfather had a cancer in his tongue and with the shock of getting to know, it killed her as well.
   Why did your grandparents live with your mum and dad?
   I don't know. I suppose, in them days you used to look after your parents. Not today, as your parents can go where they want. . . .
   So you lived in Springfield Street right from being a little girl?
   Yes. I stayed in the same house for thirty years and my daughter was born there and she is thirty-five now.
   And it was always the same house, as you didn't move next door?
   No.
   So when you got married you were actually living with your mum and dad?
   He said he'd come and live with us. Well it was no use getting another house. When owt happened to m'mum and dad all furniture and everything were mine.[14]

Her own mother also worked and relied on her in-laws for child-minding until they became ill, when she temporarily gave up work to look after them. (The tradition has now been broken, and Mrs Bridges' daughter does not want to live with her or have her mother to live in her house; hence the sad reference to 'today . . . your parents can go where they want.') Sometimes co-residence was temporary in the sense that an old person who was dying was either moved to a relative's house or a relative moved in to care for them until they died.

Finally, there have been frequent references to strong, dominant women from the evidence, and there were several cases of such women keeping at least one adult, unmarried daughter at home to care for them. This was not necessarily an example of co-residence resulting from self-interest on the part of the parent, nor surprisingly was it necessarily resented. Perhaps the most extreme example of this kind appears in the evidence of Mr Sharples of Preston:

My paternal grandmother was a strange old lady. She was a real old battle-axe. She brought up six children, five daughters and one son, who was my father. Her husband died when they were all children. . . . My grandmother forbade her daughters to get married! Apparently she had had such a very bad time herself bringing up a family, and also she had terrible troubles in childbirth, and she decided that her daughters weren't going to suffer as she had done, and she absolutely forbade her daughters to have boyfriends or contemplate getting married. It was all right for my dad, no problem for him! On the whole the maternal *diktat* was observed! One [daughter] kicked over the traces, left home, took a job somewhere in London and got married, and she was the black sheep of the family, and was cut off at that point, and her name may not be mentioned! She was just cut out of the family. . . . One got married in her fifties after the old girl had long been dead. . . . Grandmother died when I was about fourteen and the daughters loved her, they doted on her. She became a matriarchal figure, sitting there in state and everybody fussing around her.[15]

Although co-residence was common, it is clear from both Anderson's statistical material for the earlier period and from the oral history sample that the majority of families did not have co-resident kin. But relatives remained of the greatest importance. In chapter 3 changing attitudes to childbirth were explored. The continuation of traditional relationships must also be emphasised. Many working-class women continued to want their mothers present during labour, and to regard them as the most important member of the medical team. Mrs Wood had her only child in 1930, and despite an apparent difference of opinion on the place of the confinement, she deeply respected her mother's views:

Who looked after you when you had your baby?
My mother. I said that I was going into hospital, but my mother said I couldn't do that as she would come and look after me. Harold [her husband] had arranged his holiday, but he said he didn't need to as my mother was better than anybody. . . . My mother came and was in bed with me. . . . She said, 'We had better have the nurse, Harold.' So he went for the nurse.

Mrs Wood went on to describe her labour in detail, and how the nurse went away, not expecting the baby for some time. Mother's judgement appeared to have been sounder, and in the nurse's absence she delivered the baby. Like many other young mothers, Mrs Wood continued to rely on her mother; she went to the clinic for its cheap food, but not for advice: 'I never got much advice because I got it from my mother.'[16]

It is very rare to hear of an adult daughter rejecting her mother's advice about child-rearing, although there are a very small number of cases of a mother-in-law's advice being rejected. The mother-daughter bond continued to be a very strong kinship tie — not just in Lancashire in the early twentieth century. Young and Willmott, writing of Bethnal Green in the 1950s, commented, 'the local kinship system, as we have said again and again, stresses the tie between mother and daughter.'[17]

The support given to each other by adult sisters was also very noticeable and very valuable, for example, in terms of friendship, gifts and loans, advice and child-minding. In this next account, which relates to the 1930s, the mother's sisters are seen offering material help in the form of children's clothing, and also their company; in some cases relatives were the chief social contacts of working-class women, being friends and companions. The jokes told in this family, as in many others, reinforced the family's basic beliefs and attitudes, in this case to reinforce their class dislike of the tackler, and their deep religious devotion as Catholics:

We were part of a wider circle. My mother was one of four sisters and a brother, and my father was one of half a dozen children. We were closely linked with my mother's people, but my father's people, on the other side of town, we were not so closely linked with. I think my mother took us as a duty, perhaps two or three times a year. But on my mother's side the aunties lived in the same street and the other auntie in the next street and so on, so I was very much part of my mother's wider family in those early years. . . .

What sort of jokes did they tell you?

The gormless tackler who couldn't mend the machinery and couldn't make a cup of tea. The other sort were religious jokes about priests and saints. This puzzled me at first, but I think it was because they felt so secure that they could afford to make jokes about it. They seem very simple jokes now, but somehow I think it was reassuring to them that they were able to joke. Sometimes when the priest came they told jokes to him, somehow to prove to everyone that they were really good Catholics and it was all right to make a joke with the priest. Somehow, that proved something significant. The main jokes were against tacklers and priests, but not really meaning it in the case of priests. . . .

Where did she get your clothes?

I am not certain, but I think it was a combination of local shops, with a lot of contributions from aunties who would, if they saw anything they liked in the local shops, put so much a week and buy it at Christmas or whatever.

Like a clothing club?

Yes. Except it was not called that, you simply had a quiet word and they put it on one side.[18]

In other families children's clothes which had been grown out of were passed on. Sometimes money changed hands, although this seems to have happened exclusively between adult children and their parents (from the latter to the former in times of unemployment, and from the former to the latter in times of old age and hardship). Even orphans, once past babyhood, could be offered significant support by family living away from the house (as Mrs Sullivan described, in chapter 3). Mr Gaskell's mother died leaving six children aged

10—20 years. Their grandmother cared for them by calling in each day, and the rest of the time they managed themselves.[19]

Attitudes towards relations

It would appear that working-class extended families, and most particularly the female members of those families, were acting altruistically, unselfishly, lovingly; the cynic may well ask if this is not a romanticised, idealised view. Although the duty to care for relatives was a paramount one, rarely ignored, it is also true to say that the quality of the care varied from the dreadful to the superb. Mrs Burns's grandmother, who refused to let the children go into the workhouse (above), expected a lot of work from them: 'My grandmother used to say, "Come on mind, you'll be up by six o'clock." She was Irish, m'grandma, and she'd a temper like a billy goat.' This small girl was responsible for preparing a cooked breakfast for her grown-up brothers and grandfather when they returned from the mill at 8 o'clock; doing the family's shopping (which sometimes involved dragging a cart-load of potatoes up a hill for her grandmother to sell to the neighbours), and all the breadmaking. If she was not at school by nine o'clock she was given the strap by her teacher; if she did not get the domestic chores done she was hit by her grandmother.[20] The worst case of exploitation and ill-treatment comes from the 1890s. Mr Riley is recounting his wife's childhood in Lancaster:

I think when I look back she lost her father, mother, brother and sister when she was five, and she was battered from one relative to another, child labour exploited, nothing else. She was here there and everywhere for them. There was three or four of them had public houses . . . she was their, slut you could call her. One used to come, 'The Excise man is on the round' and he used to tell her what to say: 'Don't say anything else.' Of course there was fiddling going on in them days, like there is today.[21]

There was also neglect witnessed later in the period. One Preston doctor working in the poorest part of Preston in the 1930s reported several elderly neglected people living with relations in his practice:

They were very often pushed into a corner where they were neglected. Old people were very much neglected. You can understand as they had so many problems on their hands with children growing up and children being ill, starvation wages. . . . In some cases they were looked up to, they had control of the home, but in others they were not looked after well, they were not washed or kept as clean as they should have been.[22]

While in no way excusing lack of care for the elderly, it should be remembered that it was difficult for many poor people to have high standards of personal hygiene.

So far there has been little evidence to support Anderson's thesis that kin were acting towards each other in a calculative way, expecting reciprocity for services or kindnesses performed. But is it possible to find this attitude in Preston in particular? There was unquestionably an additional and financial dimension in relationships between kin in Preston which was absent in the other two towns, which is especially obvious in families where the wife was a full-time textile worker. The costs of baby-minders and of having meals with relatives were referred to in chapter 4. Mr Thomas's wife went out to work before the first world war, and paid her mother-in-law to look after her two daughters. Mr Thomas remarked: 'She would pay. You wouldn't get my mother to do anything like that unless you gave her something. You always paid people to look after your children.'[23] It is only in Preston that there is evidence of paying for services (except for the previously mentioned wage-earning adult lodgers). The custom is frequently mentioned and little resented: although it is sometimes justified as maintaining the principle that relatives should not be exploited. In the great majority of cases, where these payments took place, they were simply taken for granted and accepted as an integral part of the very closely knit family relationships which existed in Preston.

In virtually all nuclear families in this area before the second world war all wage-earning members were expected to contribute to the family budget, which was almost invariably controlled by the mother. Because the lives of extended families in Preston were rather more interconnected than those in Barrow and Lancaster (mostly because of the practice of kin either living with kin or very close to them), the expectation of sharing income extended beyond the nuclear family to the kinship group. Paying for services was the most obvious way of sharing income, and moreover only appears to have taken place when those providing the service had a smaller income than those paying for it. For example, if a woman worked only part-time, it was unheard of for her to pay her relatives for child-minding (and admittedly the hours of service in such a case were far fewer).

It is clear from this rather brief examination of the extended family that women played the major part in its functioning; with their control of the family budget, their dominance within the immediate family and home, and the close affective ties with their female relations, this was probably inevitable. But men too belonged to, and played a part in, its functioning. Marriage did not cut them off from their kin, who were as likely to become co-resident with them as were their wives' relatives. Men also performed services for relations who lived nearby — minor property repairs, help with the allotment, and so on. They enjoyed many social contacts with their male relatives —

fishing expeditions, walks, visits to pubs and music halls — activities in which women did not usually join them. Finally, because they were much more likely to be in full-time work than women, men were more important in helping relatives to find jobs (although women did play a similarly important function in the textile industry). Most respondents mentioned male members of the family 'speaking' for relatives at their place of work.

Changes in the extended family

Old people are almost unanimous that the extended family is not as strong as it was. They are probably correct. The historian, however, should be careful about dating the decline of the extended family. Many families still function in the manner described in this chapter, and it is difficult to see much evidence of its decline in the study period. However, it is possible to set within that period developments which ultimately, after the second world war, fundamentally affected the kinship group.

Migration continued throughout the period, most markedly in Barrow in the years of the inter-war depression. Between 1921 and 1931, Barrow lost 16.2 per cent of its population in this way.[24] While not inevitably weakening family ties, migration did considerably reduce the range of services kin could provide. In some cases families lost contact with even close relatives. Mrs Matthews spoke sadly, but fatalistically, about her brothers who had dispersed:

They all just scattered and I wouldn't know where they are. They left Barrow in the twenties looking for work. It was a bad time, and there was nothing at all. It just happened that way, and we never got to hear about them at all. There's only me left. I'm the only one who stayed at home.[25]

Five of her husband's brothers also left home for work: 'Three of them stayed [away] and never came back.'[26]

State intervention in the form of payments to those in need made independence both more possible and more imperative. Old age pensions, first paid in 1909, although they were small (initially only 5s. a week), helped to a degree to prolong an independent life for the elderly, as did the pensions for widows and orphans (paid after 1926). The economic depression of the inter-war years made it necessary for the state to make previously unparalleled payments to the unemployed. But the state was faced with an insoluble dilemma. Under the old Poor Law, as has been seen, adult children were responsible for their parents, and there were often responsibilities within the extended family. However, the Poor Law Guardians in the 1920s, and the

Public Assistance Officers in the 1930s, could not square the circle of family needs and family responsibilities. If a man was responsible for the care of his extended family, and if he was unemployed, then he should also have been entitled to claim benefits for them. But because of government economies it became a rule that a man could only claim for his wife and dependent children. The allowances were so small that the unemployed simply could not have supported members of their extended families, and this presented substantial problems for the long-term unemployed. The state was in effect redefining family responsibilities as being confined to the nuclear family. Their policies went further, and drove apart members of co-resident families. There were particular difficulties when both father and adult children were unemployed and living in the same house; their allowances were reduced because of the supposed ability of the others to contribute to the family budget. In Barrow especially, the rigours of the means test forced families apart:

Young people were driven out of their homes . . . if they were at home they were a hindrance to their father getting relief. In the summertime what they did was get a tent down the lanes in Roose or up in Hawcoat out in the fields, and grouped together they could go to the Board of Guardians and get a three bob food ticket each . . . that eased their parents as well. Girls couldn't do that so they were taken into service in houses all over the place.[27]

Young people could and did return home when times improved, but for some the old ties of interdependence were broken forever.

There were also important demographic changes in the inter-war period: the percentage of elderly people in the population began to rise, and the birth rate fell very dramatically, leading after the war to the position of proportionately more old people with fewer kin to care for them. There were also changes in attitude. Throughout the period, in the great majority of working-class homes, family concerns were more important than personal ones, and there are many examples of social advancement, education or self-determination being sacrificed for what were seen to be the more important needs of the family. It is *just* possible (but still quite difficult) to discern some changes in this attitude before 1939, with some individuals' growing self-awareness and determination to put their own interests before those of their extended family.

Finally, although many mourn (perhaps prematurely) the passing of the extended family, few regret the ending of the acute poverty which made its services so essential. Whatever may or may not have happened to the extended family since the second world war — and the work of L. A. Shaw, Young and Wilmott, and M. Kerr would indicate that the extended family was still very much alive and active in metropolitan areas in the 1950s[28] — it remained of the greatest importance as a provider of social services, social contacts, and to a lesser degree financial assistance in working-class life in the period 1890—1940. Relations did their best for relations, often at considerable personal expense, and at the heart of the kinship system were the women. Kerr described areas of Liverpool as matriarchies; Firth and Djamour called their area of study in South London matri-centred or matral in action and in sentiment.[29] It is hoped that the evidence in this chapter, which is representative of a very substantial body of data, is sufficient to show a similarly important role in the kinship group of women in Barrow, Lancaster and Preston.[30]

NEIGHBOURS AND NEIGHBOURHOODS

It is clear that working-class people throughout this period suffered from many stresses and had a multitude of problems: illness, unemployment, drunken relatives, death, migration, poverty. This book has attempted to discover how working-class people, and women in particular, sought and possibly found solutions to these problems. Some contemporary observers, historians and sociologists, while accepting that kin, for whatever motives, could and did help in times of crisis, have tended to suggest that neighbours, unconnected by birth or marriage, would be unlikely to help in such situations. Louis Wirth, for example, argued that 'the close living together and working together of individuals who have no sentimental or emotional ties foster a spirit of competition, of grandisement, and mutual exploitation. . . . frequent close physical contact coupled with great social distance accentuates the reserve of unattached individuals toward one another . . . and gives rise to loneliness.'[31] Wirth was writing of American experience, but some writers, like C. F. G. Masterman at the turn of the century, doubted the capacity of the working class to withstand the stresses and strains to which it was exposed.[32] I would agree wholeheartedly with Standish Meacham, who rejected this description:

The picture is a false one . . . the urban working-class village shared with rural communities of the past, a foundation built of mutual responsibilities and obligations . . . the working class undertook to look after itself, relying when necessary on families and neighbourhoods for physical support and psychological sustenance.[33]

In other words, problems were as likely to be found and solved communally as by isolated individuals.

Whereas not all respondents had extended families, all had neighbours, although it is obvious that not all neighbours, like not all kin, were regarded as being in need of or deserving of help and attention. It is as difficult to define what was meant by 'neighbour', as it is difficult to define who constituted 'kin'. There was an observable fundamental difference in the respondents' perceptions of neighbourhoods on the one hand and of neighbours on the other. All spoke of belonging to an area within the town: in Barrow and Lancaster these were geographically clearly defined, and everyone knew where one neighbourhood began and another ended. Boundaries were rather less clearly defined in Preston, but the respondents all had a feeling of belonging to a specific area, one usually associated with the main road running through it — Ribbleton Lane, Newhall Lane, and so on. It would be tempting to describe these areas or neighbourhoods as Standish Meacham does, as 'urban villages', but it is difficult to find any evidence of them behaving *as a unit*. There was no focal point, no parish council (for example), no machinery through which they could act. Many inhabitants of a certain area belonged to the parish church, but just as many were likely to belong to a Catholic or nonconformist chapel. In some areas (like Vickerstown in Barrow), all the men worked for one company (Vickers). This did give a feeling of unity, but there is again no evidence of the community *functioning* as a whole. Not only did these 'urban villages' lack a structure through which communal action could be channelled, they were far too large for people to feel they 'knew everyone', as is possible in a rural village. What seems to have been of considerably greater importance to working-class people was the street, or possibly the small group of streets, in which they lived. Respondents often claim to have known everyone in their neighbourhood, but this usually turns out to have been no more than three streets. Some only knew those in their own street.

These small geographical areas, however, were of the greatest importance in the lives of working-class families: they offered a system of support, and with it a system of social control. Occasionally, respondents have voiced the idea that neighbours were more supportive than kin, and it is difficult to argue with this view, unless kin also lived close by: 'It didn't need your own relatives to rally round to help in those days, you'd neighbours in your house helping.'[34] Neighbours were the people living within a stone's throw of one's own house, and towards them people, especially women, felt an especial duty to help. As with kin, their motives were complex and mixed, but it is possible to trace through the oral evidence the strong religious motivation of helping those in need. Working-class attitudes included a clear duty to help your neighbours, which surmounted other considerations. It is clear, for example, that the working class as a whole, even at the level of the urban village, was divided, sometimes bitterly, on political and religious lines, but these

Great attention was paid to keeping windows and doorsteps clean. This task was also a way of meeting the neighbours, some of whom can be seen keeping an eye on the street's happenings. (Lancaster Museum)

differences were disregarded in relationships with neighbours. Mrs Calvert's family in Preston, for example, belonged to the Orange Club, and always walked in the Orange procession on Whit Monday. However, any feelings of hostility towards Roman Catholics were suspended when neighbours were concerned:

They were neighbours and that was all. Religion didn't come into it, because there were quite a few Catholics round us and I played with some of the Catholics. It never came into discussion or anything. They were your neighbours and they were your friends and that was all there was to it.[35]

Some of the most striking examples of working-class solidarity, especially between women, can be found in working-class streets. The historian needs once again to look at Michael Anderson's picture of neighbourhood life in the mid-nineteenth century. Certainly he gives a very different view of the importance (or lack of it) of neighbourhood support. Still using as his basic premise the exchange theory of values, he wrote of mid-nineteenth-century Preston: 'Neighbours lacked a firmly enough structured basis of reciprocation in a heterogeneous and mobile society. Kinship by contrast could provide this structural link and could thus form a basis of reciprocation.'[36]

*This group of 'Neighbourly Neighbours' lived on a Lancaster council estate built
in the 1920s. Obviously by 1936 friendly relationships were well established.*
(Lancaster Museum)

Standish Meacham accepts Anderson's description of the limited support
available in working-class neighbourhoods in times of migration and
upheaval.[37] He also recognises that by the turn of the century neighbourhood
relationships were quite different, for not only does oral evidence reveal this,
but so too do many contemporary writers and autobiographers. Borrowing
the term from Robert Roberts (who had himself adopted it from Engels's
description of Manchester as a classic slum), he describes this period as the
'classic' one. He says: 'Sickness, unemployment, poverty, removal; in the
struggle to counter these unsettling conditions of its daily life, the working
class looked to neighbourhoods for stability and connectedness. Neighbourhood meant more than houses and streets. It meant a mutually beneficial
relationship one formed with others, a sort of social symbiosis.'[38]

Meacham believed that working-class society had changed so fundamentally
in half a century because the great waves of migration had stopped and
neighbourhoods had become more settled. This settling was certainly true of
Preston, although it was not true of either Barrow or Lancaster, which
continued to receive waves of migrants. It may well have been that new
migrants, especially when moving into newly built areas (which were very
common in both Barrow and Lancaster), where everyone was a stranger,

made particular efforts to get to know each other and to build new networks quickly, a phenomenon observed by sociologists on new housing estates in post-second world war Britain.

As with the kinship relationship, we can never be sure if working-class neighbourhood relationships changed fundamentally between 1850 and about 1890, or if they were never quite as Anderson and others have described them. Certainly the 'classic' neighbourhood is very evident from all the available oral evidence. Was there *any* evidence of the principle of reciprocity being applied? Neighbours certainly tried to repay good deeds done to them by others; but that is a very different matter from one woman helping another in the expectation of an immediate repayment in kind or cash.

Mutual help and friendship

The range of help provided by neighbours was immense: children were minded; the sick and dying were fed and nursed; clothes were passed on; funeral teas prepared for the mourners; the dead laid out; shopping done for the elderly; and companionship and friendship provided for all ages. Mrs Morrison describes here life in a small, very poor street in central Preston in the 1920s. It is interesting to note the street's attitude towards a slightly deviant member:

We had wonderful neighbours there. They were a wonderful lot of people.

How would they help?

One took the washing in when I was in bed confined, another one took all the children's washing. One would bring tea, and all this sort of thing. I had a lady across the road who had her leg off and was confined to bed, and I would run across and give her a cup of tea when she had nobody to attend to her.

Was there much loaning money?

I can't say anything about that. We used to have one that came across, and one day she asked me if she could borrow my shoes to go to the pictures in. I wanted my shoes to go to work, but she wouldn't work! Another time she came across and asked if I had any bedding to spare. I said that I hadn't. She said that I had had a drawer full the other day. She had happened to be in when I had had my drawer out. I said that that drawer had been for me to go to bed with Annie [for child birth]. I always kept certain things for going to bed. I said that I couldn't part with that. That person would go round to one for an onion and one for a carrot and one for something else and a penny for the gas.

So she lived on the neighbours, really. Was there a lot of genuine running out of things?

Yes. And they would always help one another. I have never known anyone refuse! Mind you, they got to know this person! Well apart from this, she could go to the pictures and we couldn't. It was only 2*d*. or 3*d*. but she could find that when we couldn't! . . .

Do you remember them ever quarrelling in that little street? What would they quarrel about?

Children. Noise. I shouldn't think it would be anything else. They used to use all the words. Because my children would come in and ask what the words meant.

You don't remember them actually fighting, just quarrelling?

Oh, no. I have never seen anybody fight. It would just blow over. It would mostly be about children running up and down and there was a lobby through and there would be no peace. This was mostly what they fell out about.

Did they used to sit on the doorstep?

Of course we did! When it was hot in summer we sat on the doorstep and talked. Look at the fresh air we got!

What did you talk about?

I suppose anything. I don't suppose it would be war as we had had enough about war. It would mostly be about children. This woman used to bring all her children out and comb their hair looking for. . . . Yet, she was a grand person. She would have done anything for anybody. My husband had to go for an interview one day and I was at work and she said she would have the child. When she came home she was covered from head to foot with treacle toffee. She had given her treacle toffee, she would do anything like that.

Did you ever go into each other's houses for a cup of tea?

Yes. Not in everybody's house but one neighbour and I were very friendly. In fact, they thought of putting an archway up so we could go when it rained. She would come in a lot and I would go into her. She would clean up for me while I sewed for her. She couldn't sew and I would make her child a dress or knit. She would come and scrub my floor or something like that or take my washing while I did a job for her.[39]

This degree of intimacy with a neighbour was fairly unusual. Indeed, the degree of intimacy with neighbours varied considerably from individual to individual, and from area to area. Some one just talked to in the street, some called in, some were offered tea. However, it is clear that the majority of working-class women relied on their neighbours (and their kin) for sociability and friendship. There are few examples of women having friends outside their own neighbourhood or their place of work or worship. Contacts with these friends remained casual and unarranged: you bumped into them in the street, or outside the local shops, or at church, or you dropped in when passing. Working-class women very rarely issued a formal invitation unless it was for a very special occasion like a wedding or funeral (and usually even these were restricted to the family). No particular efforts were exerted to 'keep in touch'. It was assumed that informal casual contacts would be frequent, as indeed they usually were. Women talk of friendly, helpful or good neighbours, but they rarely talk simply of friends. The sociability between neighbours was very important. It was the chief method of passing on neighbourhood news and advice; it was the most effective way of exerting neighbourhood control; and it was an important way for women in particular to find comfort and friendship.

The working-class habit of *public* sociability, usually in the form of conversations in the street, was a remnant, an echo, of a social custom which had once been widespread throughout all ranks of society. Philippe Ariès, in his examination of the art of previous centuries, found that until the seventeenth century there was a great lack of interior and family scenes. He believed that this reflected a fundamental fact about social life: 'Life in the past, until the seventeenth century, was lived in public.' He suggests that after that point family life became more important and more privatised, and this was at the expense of sociability.[40]

The concept of privatised, isolated family life was much later in reaching the working class than other strata of society, for financial, social and moral reasons. That the concept had begun to affect some working-class people has already been seen, but vestiges of the old public sociability continued to be a very important part of working-class life throughout the period.

The sick and dying had a very special claim on a neighbour's services. Almost all respondents speak of taking food to newly delivered women and their families, or sick people. When there was a death only a certain few women were called upon to lay out the dead. They were often the same women who delivered babies until the training of midwives became compulsory. Here Mrs Morrison describes what she did in laying out dead people, after she had washed the body:

Did you used to put pennies on their eyes?

Yes, and cotton wool up their nose and back-passage, and a nappy on, and a pair of stockings. There's many a man gone with a pair of silk stockings on when we couldn't find anything else. . . . And a night-shirt or what ever they had. We would generally put them a clean one on . . . and put a book, a prayer book, under their chin to hold it. And if they had any teeth get them back in if you could.[41]

(More usually the chin was bound and this binding and the pennies on the eyes is curiously reminiscent of the pennies on the newly born baby's navel, and the binder on top.)

At the turn of the century most of the processes of birth and death were in the capable hands of women in the family and their neighbourhood helpers. Male doctors rarely attended births, and male undertakers merely took the body in the coffin they had made from the house to the church and/or cemetery. The personal, practical direct help was given by women. Mrs Armstrong commented:

The neighbours were far better than what they are today. They were not as

Neighbours, Lancaster, late 1920s. (Lancaster Museum)

clannish. If the nextdoor neighbour was poorly we would go in and help. We'd do her washing, do her ironing, and we'd take them back and if they wanted any messages going we used to do it. They were always willing to help you. Now today, they're more clannish, they seem as if they want to be on their own.

Do you remember people doing bowls of broth or soup when people were ill?

When they were ill they used to get a sheep's head and a marrow bone and then twopennyworth of pot herbs and make a good pan of soup, and some split peas and barley and take them a good bowl of soup in at night. We perhaps used to take them their dinners. . . . Really they were better friends than what they are. They're good friends today but they're more for themselves. In the olden days it was sisterly love and more motherly love. I used to be knocked up time out of time when anybody died. They used to come and knock at the door at midnight and say, 'Will you come and lay the baby out? Will you come and lay so-and-so out?' I used to go and lay them out.

Do you remember how old you were when you first laid somebody out?

Oh, I'd be about twenty. I would have loved to have been a nurse, but my mother made me go as a cook. One night I had a knock at midnight and I'd three little girls and I got up and an old lady up the street had passed on and they asked me if I'd go and lay her out. I said, 'Just give me time to get dressed.' I got dressed and when the children got up in the morning to go to school they said, 'Who was that man knocking the door again through the night?' 'It was only Grandma Houldsworth had passed away and they asked if I'd go and lay her out.' Mabel turns round and said, 'Why don't you put a blinkin' card in the window "laying-out taken in" not washing taken in, laying-out taken in?' We never used to take anything off them, never bothered. But now, today, everything is altered and the undertaker does all that.

Would people give you a present? Were they grateful for what they did, or just take it for granted?

No, they would ask you and try to offer you summat or buy you summat. They hadn't the money and we used to say no. I never took nothing off them and it used to be our good deed for them. Good neighbours.[42]

Favourite cures were shared by women. There were almost as many cures as there were families and ailments, but there was much consultation about the best cures for such things as coughs, colds, bowel and stomach upsets. Some women always kept a jar of goose grease or their favourite herbs for dispensing to the neighbours.

There was also a significant borrowing service. Whatever was borrowed was paid back, otherwise the system would have broken down; one could say that within the system, reciprocity existed:

. . . a little bit of tea, a little bit of sugar, a shilling, but it usually came back. People were very honest round there. They were very poor but I don't think they would do anything they shouldn't have done. If they borrowed a bit of sugar you got it back again. Often they knocked, 'Can I borrow a cup of sugar? Have you a bit of margarine?' . . . .

I don't think there was much borrowing of money, people hadn't it to lend. There was nobody had a bank balance in those days, not round our area. It was hand-to-mouth, more or less. Each day was spent, each day's money spent.[43]

Only one respondent speaks of *not* repaying a loan: 'Those were the days when you would borrow a cupful of sugar or you would borrow a loaf, but you didn't pay a loaf back as that was bad luck.'[44] Special occasion clothes might also be lent: a black outfit for a funeral; a christening gown for a baby.

Neighbourhood control

Neighbours provided a mutual support society, but like all societies it had its rules and regulations, and it was expected that all members would obey these rules. The rules were unwritten, but understood by all. Those who broke them were punished by self-appointed judges and juries. The system for controlling behaviour was an effective one. Positively, it helped control some of the excesses of drunken behaviour, it maintained standards of cleanliness, and it tended to limit vandalism and petty crime. Negatively, the system interfered with and influenced many aspects of life which would now be regarded as matters of individual choice and decision, and it produced a very conforming and conformist class of people.

The system began with the children. Unlike other clubs, the neighbourhood was one you *had* to belong to; there was little choice. There were many street games, all of which required cooperation within the peer group, and an acceptance of group standards and decisions. There was no room for the solitary, individualistic child either physically in the home or psychologically in the street. One old man remarked: 'There were twenty-one boys, one short for two football teams. Those that didn't play were called cissies.'[45] A child learned early his group's mores, and the wisdom of conforming to them. It was commonly expected that neighbours would tell off, and if necessary hit, someone else's child, especially if they were interfering with or damaging property:

I remember this lady, and she was a widow, and she had two children, and she had this shop, and it was all sweets and these parched [dried] peas. One night there were two lads standing outside. Somebody said, 'What's them two lads doing at Cartmel's window?' There was a hole in the window at the side of the wood and they had made a long hook and they were hooking toffees out.

They used to bolt all the windows and that hole was the bolt hole to bolt them up.

Mrs Cartmel came out and gave them a jolly good skelping and she said, 'You'll not take my toffees again.'

Do you ever remember any of the other neighbours telling children off for doing things wrong?

They didn't tell you off, they would give you a smack. If you had done wrong, you knew you had.

Even the neighbours would wallop you?

Yes. If you had done wrong on their property they always used to do. Sometimes neighbours fell out about their children.[46]

Girls also played street games, but probably learned as much about the street codes from their mothers and their neighbours, for girls were in the home more, and there they overheard a lot of talk about the neighbours, their behaviour, and so on. Gossip, in fact, was the most usual and very effective way of establishing and maintaining street standards. Very many aspects of life were covered. In some streets even the way you donkey-stoned your front was a matter for neighbourhood concern:

Did she do the front doorstep?

Oh yes, the front doorstep and four flags to the right. Usually in terraced houses the two doors were together with the lobby in between, and so you did your step and half the lobby and you did four flags up to the edge of the window and everybody did the same thing. Of course, if anybody deviated they would say, 'Oh look at her, she has done five flags.'

A lot of people didn't do the donkey-stoning?

You would just say about them what you would say if the people opposite you hadn't changed their curtains.

They were a bit dirty?

Not necessarily dirty, but they would expect them to do it. They would comment about it, the other women in the street would talk about the one that wasn't doing it. If you ever got somebody that came up from the South of England, and they didn't know about northern ways, well, of course, they didn't do this sort of thing, then this was it.

You used to stand at the top of the street and look down and the next row of flags from the door was yellow or white all the way down.[47]

Neighbourhood pressure on the individual to be both clean and respectable, and to be conformist, was widespread and has been commented upon in many areas.[48] If you were a baby-minder you had to do the job properly, or you got a bad name (see chapter 4). Getting a bad, or indeed a good, name mattered immensely to most working-class people. They knew that they would be talked about; some also realised that on certain momentous days those decisions were somehow made public:

When I got married all the street come out and they all got confetti. You got your character — she was a nice lass or she wasn't. At a funeral and a wedding you got the character — she was a nice person and would help anybody, or whistle that.[49]

The fear of being talked about undoubtedly acted as a great restraint on sexual relationships between young people (see chapter 2).

Gossip was the most usual, and the most powerful, means of maintaining neighbourhood standards, but there was also physical punishment, or the threat of it. The most commonly mentioned cause of this was a husband's drunken behaviour. Usually another male went to sort out the problem. In reply to the question 'When you were young, what did you think of as a rough family?', Mr Crellin said:

One where the father was a boozer. I have one or two recollections of that. I remember coming back from Blackpool one time, I should be about eighteen and my father had a neighbour on the floor. My father had him by the throat as this neighbour had come home drunk and turned out his wife and kiddies in their nightclothes. My father reprimanded him and he struck at my father and my father retaliated. That was one incident. There was another, with a chap named —— from across the road, he was ill-treating his wife and my father reprimanded him and that led to some trouble. It was booze that was the trouble.[50]

Women also played an important, though less physical, role in the restraint of drunken behaviour. Mr Maguire lived in a poor, rough street in Lancaster, and here the women offered practical help for the distressed wife, and total moral condemnation for the man:

Neighbours would sympathise. Someone would bring her half a loaf. 'What's to do? Has your Bill been knocking you about?' 'Aye, he's been drinking and come home without any money.' 'Here you are Mrs so-and-so, here's half a loaf, you're welcome to it. Maybe I'll be in the same boat myself one day and you might do the same for me.' So they'd bring out half a gill of milk. Somebody else might bring her a bit of butter and somebody else a bit of sugar and they rallied round. That man was thought of less than the dust among his neighbours.[51]

The story told in chapter 2 of the public stoning of the pregnant bride is unique in the sample, but it illustrates the length to which some women would go in their determination to establish and preserve their concept of decent moral behaviour.

Changes in neighbourhoods and neighbours

There were undoubted changes within the neighbourhoods and in the relationships between neighbours in the period. Elizabeth Bott wrote of neighbourhood networks: 'Localised networks are most likely to develop in areas where the inhabitants feel that they are socially similar to one another; such feelings of solidarity appear to be strongest in long-established working-class areas in which there is a dominant industry or a relatively small number of traditional occupations.'[52] Problems appear to have developed in working-class neighbourhoods when the feeling of being the same both socially and economically began to break down. It is noticeable in the oral evidence that the neighbourhoods displaying the most solidarity were the poorest. Mr Maguire said: 'Everybody was the same, so you hadn't a neighbour with £30 when you only had 30s. You hadn't that to upset you, so there was no resentment.'[53]

But some streets did have families who were either financially better-off than their neighbours, or who thought themselves to be socially superior, or indeed who regarded themselves as both economically and socially in a better position than their neighbours. The attitudes and motives of the aspiring families are complex. There were always, at any time, some working-class people who wanted to improve their lot. They were united in their belief that this improvement would not come if they were in any way associated with rough people. There was, therefore, on the part of the aspiring, an increasing and noticeable reluctance to interfere in drunken quarrels for example. There may have been an element of physical cowardice in this reluctance, but it was much more the result of a fear of being tainted by an involvement with such unpleasantness. Consider the evidence of Mr Askew. His father was a prosperous shopkeeper, and they lived in a very desirable terrace. But even these houses could contain rough neighbours:

What were thought of as rough families on the Island?
I think the roughest family was where drink was prevalent and where the men used to go home and abuse the wives. I remember one incident next door to us, we lived in twenty-eight and they lived in number thirty, where there was a big family and he was a real drunkard. He had a girl of eighteen and the mother died and she had a private account and she willed this private account to the daughter. I'll never forget one night the father came home drunk and he thrashed this girl with a belt for her to give up the bank book.
Did she?
Yes she did. She had to. She'd have been killed if she hadn't have done. Next day she went to the solicitors and complained . . . she went to her aunt really and they took her to a solicitor and they recovered it eventually and she left home. It was a terrible night we put in listening to her screaming.
Your father didn't think of calling the police?
I think he did, eventually.[54]

There was also, among the more aspiring, a growing fear of being too open with neighbours in case one became the object of gossip. Understandably, there were aspects of family life which they did not want discussed on the street. Some families did suffer quite acutely from prying neighbours who watched their every movement, and this sometimes led people to develop a passion for 'minding their own business', and 'keeping themselves to themselves'. Linked with this desire for privacy was the bourgeois ideal, already referred to, of the home being a private haven from the stresses and strains of the world. Men in particular wished to come home to peace and tranquillity, and did not like the visits of neighbours. Women whose husbands liked to think of their home, poor as it may have been, as their private inviolate castle, took care to have their neighbours visit during the day, when the husband was out at work. Men were more likely to turn away from social contacts with neighbours: they did not need them so much, for they had their companionship at work or in the pub if they needed it.

The evidence of Mrs Pearce about her neighbours in a little, rough street in Preston is interesting because it reveals various rather ambivalent attitudes. Her husband (an unskilled labourer) displayed some very definite attitudes to his home and to his neighbours, wishing not only to distance himself from the rough, but from the respectable too. His wife was in conflict with him in some ways, needing neighbourhood support and companionship during the day. But she too reveals that she had some concept of keeping one's distance, disapproving of rough rows and excessive borrowing:

Why did he not want you to talk to the neighbours? Why did he worry about you gossiping?

He wanted his own home. He said that when he had worked all day he wanted his home. He didn't like me talking in the day. Although I did talk, I didn't stand around a lot.

The neighbour had to talk on the doorstep, did she?

She couldn't come in when he were in, really, but she would come just before he had come for his tea. He would make rows if he thought I had been talking to her.

We hadn't been in very long and there was such a noise. . . . Anyway, I said I was going to the door with this noise to see what was going on, and he told me to come back. I asked why. He said, 'Sit down!' I said, 'I'm like Cinderella at the fire, I can never get to the door or anything!' So the week after, there was windows smashing and all sorts were going on there. He said, 'Now, Cinderella, are you going out tonight?' I said, 'Not tonight!'

The thing I detested above anything was on Sunday you would see them going from one end of the street to the other with a roasting-tin and getting the meat cooked in their house. Then you would see somebody else through the week going with a dolly-tub and posser [a wooden stick for pounding the wash]. I thought it was horrible, it was like living in one another's houses. I couldn't do with that. My husband would never allow me to have anybody in. They might come for change for the gas, or something like that, but I never had a neighbour in.[55]

Some women shared Mr Pearce's reluctance to be too friendly with neighbours. It should be stressed, however, that this social isolation did not imply a distancing from neighbourhood duties in the case of emergencies. Only quite prosperous bourgeois families, like that of Mr Askew, could be so detached from their neighbours. Mrs Winder's mother would help her neighbours, but she was wary of over-familiarity, perhaps aware that families who started off face-to-face all too often ended up back-to-back!

Were there many neighbours popping in and out?

Well, my mother never encouraged neighbours in and out, and we were never allowed to go into neighbours' houses. I mean, this is a thing perhaps we were different. Even the old lady that I was talking about that m'mother got to vote, lived across, the two yards were across and the passage but we never went in and out . . . I can remember when I got working going in to see the old man when he was poorly. But we weren't allowed to go in and out of neighbours.

Your mother didn't either?

She didn't. Oh no, she didn't either. I know m'sister went to this family that lived on the side street. They were a family of girls and they all worked. I think there were three daughters and the mother, and they all worked in the mill. She went to the pictures with them but I've seen at times mother has clamped down, 'Now you're stopping going.' Perhaps some little thing has come back from somewhere else that she has said there and they've told somebody else.

So your mother was worried about possible gossip?

She didn't like gossip and she didn't like this running in and out.[56]

This evidence is echoed by Robert Roberts, who wrote of Salford, 'Some sociologists have been apt to write fondly of the cosy gregariousness of the old slum-dwellers. This picture has I think been overdrawn, close propinquity together with cultural poverty led as much to enmity as it did to friendship.'[57]

Certainly there were quarrels, and apart from those caused by drink, which usually caused trouble within the family, the most common cause between neighbours was children. Children's street games usually annoyed someone and, rather more rarely, they caused damage to someone's property. They made a lot of noise; they could spoil rows of clean washing hanging in the back street. As already noted, one of the most frequent forms of social control was the chastisement of children by any adult who caught them committing an offence. It is clear, however, that this practice was a contentious one throughout the period. On one hand, the vast majority of working-class adults believed that children required at least verbal chastisement if they did wrong, but they became very ambivalent about the subject when their own children were concerned, either feeling that they had been punished too severely or that they had been innocent in the first place. It must be emphasised that it was not just aspiring families who had these attitudes.

Mr Lawson spent a large part of his childhood, at the turn of the century, in one of the roughest areas of Preston (rougher than any area of Barrow or Lancaster), which was so unruly that the police would either not go there, or if they did went in twos, since they were very likely to be attacked by the inhabitants. This meant that the area had to be largely self-policing. The following incident took place at the beginning of the century, and illustrates how even a very rough family took the gravest exception to the assault on their child. He was innocent, and he was gravely injured; and their objection resulted in the summoning of the usually despised police force, and is symptomatic of an attitude which grew throughout the period. Eventually adults became very reluctant to chastise other people's children. As a result, children became bolder, and probably more of a nuisance, and one dominant aspect of neighbourhood control of behaviour collapsed.

Another time, this nearly was a tragedy, next door to us there was a chap named Garth and he was a holy terror. We used to go and tie three or four doors, fasten the door-knobs to the lamp-post. We would tie the string and get to the bottom of the street and then we would start pulling this string and the door-knob would be, bang, bang! As soon as ever they opened the door the lights went out in the street. My eldest brother happened to be working and he just happened to be passing and old Garth, he walked with a big knob-stick, with big ebony knobs, he just came out as my brother was passing and he thought it was him. He hit him at the back of the head and it split all his head open. He got six months in jail for it. It made a right mess of my brother.

The police wouldn't come. When the police did come they took my brother in the ambulance to the hospital. They wanted to know what had happened, and they took old Garth's evidence, but the police knew what old Garth was like as they had had trouble a few times with him.

Why were the police frightened to go down Ribbleton Lane on their own?

They would get murdered. Ribbleton Lane was known for hooligans. Newhall Lane wasn't so bad, but Ribbleton Lane was always noted for hooligans.

What sort of things did they do to the police?

Lay them out. Three or four chaps would come out of a pub and see the policeman and they would take him. Ribbleton Lane was noted for attacks on police.[58]

There can be little doubt that increasing affluence also helped to weaken old neighbourhood ties. Mr Logan, discussing the inter-war period, remarked: 'Help? There was a lot of it, but it was gradually dying out. It died away somehow as you got richer.'[59] One reason for this is perhaps obvious: increased affluence meant less borrowing from neighbours; less nursing, as someone could be paid to do it. More money meant that less help was asked for. In general, working-class families, where the father was in work, were better-off in financial terms in the inter-war period, and for some it became

A Barrow street scene in the 1920s, with a total absence of traffic and a rather more surprising absence of adults. (Barrow Library)

both easier and more imperative to become involved in a game of matching status object with status object — radios, holidays, new clothes, furniture and furnishings, and house improvements all became status symbols. Envy, the enemy of solidarity, became more open.

Not everyone, of course, improved their lot. The unemployed had a particularly difficult time, and their plight aroused mixed feelings in their neighbours. In some was the old, strongly felt urge to help in whatever way was possible. Others regarded the unemployed with suspicion; deeply ingrained concepts of the work ethic made it impossible for them to regard the unemployed as anything but idle layabouts, content to cheat the authorities and take more public money than they were entitled to. There are a few dreadful stories of neighbours reporting unemployed families for breaches of the rules of the Poor Law Guardians or the Public Assistance Board. Old standards of solidarity broke down.

Mrs Dawson might have suffered because she had moved to a new social environment — a village near Barrow. Her husband was an unemployed ex-soldier who had had a complete nervous breakdown. She tried to help out by cleaning for some neighbours, for which she got 2s. for a half-day:

The first job was your front, your step and the hall. I went the second Friday and do you know I'd just got the buckets in m'hand and the Manager of the Bureau [the dole office] come. He said, 'Now then there's been a letter sent to me, it's anonymous . . .' I said, 'They can't say anything, but I haven't received anything . . . not a ha'penny . . . I was just going to help with this.'. . . He said, 'Well, I'll have to report it.' Anyway m'husband got a letter. He was on the dole and he had to come to Barrow to a tribunal. That was why I come off the dole, to do what I liked. They stopped his dole money for nearly six weeks, and I'd to keep him six weeks.[60]

She was the breadwinner for many years, and when her husband finally recovered and found a job she continued to work.

Mrs Wilkinson did not have the problem of living in a strange neighbourhood; she lived where she had lived since childhood, but she too had problems with her neighbours when her husband was unemployed. He had been told by a friend that if he had a small, part-time job before becoming unemployed then he would be entitled to carry on with it after being made redundant. So he began sweeping chimneys before the expected dismissal came. The family needed the extra money because their only child was very delicate and needed special food:

She needed it, she was so delicate, so when he came on the dole he'd do a few chimneys which helped out. People did report him because this young fellow told him, 'I've had another report about you again.'

It must have caused a lot of bad feeling?

Well, no. But it makes you feel a bit small to think folk are checking on you like that.

Did it make you a bit less open with the neighbours?

I'd to be very careful what I said. . . . They'd stand and watch what you bought in a shop and that is why I never shopped round here. . . . They were very spiteful, very ready to report anything.[61]

The oral evidence for this breakdown in solidarity is most common in Barrow where the economic slump was the most sudden, the most traumatic, and the most long-lasting. The sudden dislocations in so many people's lives, with subsequent loss of family and kin through migration, and of income, coupled with a constant feeling of insecurity, seemed in some cases to break long-established customs and neighbourhood links.

But it would be wrong to end this chapter on a negative note. The old neighbourliness *did* generally survive very strongly, even in Barrow. It remained particularly strong where whole neighbourhoods remained poor: Mr Maguire, speaking of the 1920s in a very poor area of Lancaster, said: 'Everybody was out to help each other, nobody had nothing at all, all they had was kindness.'[62] And speaking of a slightly later period, in another very poor area of Lancaster, Mrs Metcalfe said:

There was nothing too good for anyone to do or to give, to say. Any accidents, they'd be there to see what they could do with the child, if it was a child, or if it was the husband who'd had an accident, and the husband couldn't work, and the wife had to find a bit of a job, the neighbours would all help and bake, wash and do anything. We had a neighbour called Mrs B. and I tell you when my stepmother had these varicose veins, although she had a family of six of her own, she was in every morning to see to stepmother and she showed me what to do. What I couldn't do she did. It was no trouble to her to help at all. It was never any trouble to them, everyone did the same. Your trouble was their trouble, and your happiness was their happiness.[63]

Nor did these patterns die after the second world war. It is clear from various post-war researches carried out in other areas, that the old classic neighbourhood survived, whether in Liverpool or in London. Madeline Kerr, writing of Liverpool's Ship Street, said: 'The extent of neighbourliness especially in times of adversity, cannot be overstressed.'[64] It was apparent to this researcher that, in all three towns studied, examples of the old neighbourhood network of relationship can still be found. They are not universal, but where they exist they are valued and still of considerable significance.

Conclusion

There has been evidence of both change and continuity in the lives of working-class women between 1890 and 1914. The most striking change was the reduction of family size, as a woman having children in the inter-war period was virtually certain to have fewer children than her mother had at the turn of the century. This demographic change was strikingly illustrated in the lives of individual women in Barrow. For example, the three women whose mothers had the largest number of children (21, 16 and 15 respectively) had themselves 2, 1 and 2 children. This change in family size was a result of both changing attitudes and changing economic circumstances. There is evidence that people, especially women, in the inter-war period were coming to see a large number of children as a hazard to women's health and a probable impairment to standards of living. It is clear that many (but by no means all) adult women in the inter-war period had physically easier lives than had their mothers. Less time and energy was spent in child-bearing and child-rearing, and there was less housework to do. Many households, while still without almost all modern domestic appliances (e.g. vacuum cleaners), were easier to run: there were more gas cookers, baths and inside toilets. There were some subtle changes too in women's relationships with their husbands. Some evidence can be found of more sharing in child rearing and domestic work, and certainly leisure activities were more often shared, with the relative decline in popularity of the pub and the rapid rise of the cinema. Important decisions, especially those concerning family size, appear to have been shared between husband and wife.[1]

These changes, however, were in their early stages, and really had their impact after 1940. Increased educational opportunities with free secondary schooling for all, and improved standards of living resulted in the late 1940s in many working-class families sending their children to grammar schools and later to university for the first time. Thus, for many, the old working-class social patterns were broken.

In the period before 1940, despite the changes in family size and standards of living outlined in this book, one is left with a sense of continuity in the lives of working-class women, centred on their homes, families and neighbourhoods. It is difficult to trace in the oral evidence any expansion of their horizons as a result of the lessening of their workload between the wars. Indeed, their sphere probably became *more* domestic; there was less economic need in many families for women to go out to work even part-time, and consequently more opportunity for them to indulge their ambition of staying at home.[2] There was a noticeable increase in the time devoted to knitting, embroidery, crotcheting and sewing. On the other hand, many women still lived lives of incessant toil which would have been familiar to their mothers. Ironically, yet obviously, it was the poorest and those with the largest families who most often had the double burden of housework and a wage-earning job outside the home. It must be remembered too that these women were likely to live in substandard houses which required much physical labour if the family were to be only moderately clean and comfortable.

Whether women had more leisure than their mothers or worked just as hard, and despite the beginnings of change in marriage patterns, the dominant role of the woman in the home is still apparent: bringing up the children, organising the household and controlling the finances. Charles Madge, writing in 1943, found that as many as 50 per cent of Lancashire men gave up their wages intact to their wives, and concluded that 'women are the dominant personalities of Lancashire.' In the early 1950s, Ferdynand Zweig interpreted this custom as revealing a 'matriarchal strain' in Lancashire.[3]

It has not been the purpose of this book to argue the case either for a patriarchal or matriarchal model of working-class society, but simply to present and interpret working-class views of women's lives. The evidence would suggest that neither model is adequate if a comprehensive analysis of women's lives is to be attempted. The oral evidence is complex; it reveals a mass of individual differences, and yet has shown a large section of society following and upholding a clearly understood, if infrequently discussed, set of mores. These produced women who were disciplined, inhibited, conforming and who placed perceived familial and social needs before those of the individual. Women did not seek self-fulfilment at the expense of the family because they saw little distinction between their own good and that of their families. There was a very low level of self-awareness. Women's considerable powers were all exercised, firmly, in the perceived interests of their families — that is how they saw their 'place'.

Appendices

1 POPULATION OF THE THREE TOWNS, 1891—1931

	Barrow	Lancaster	Preston
1891			
Total	51712	31038	107573
Males	27273	15431	49305
Females	24439	15607	58268
1901			
Total	57586	40329	112989
Males	31494	19746	51686
Females	26092	20583	61303
1911			
Total	63770	41410	117088
Males	33374	20204	53915
Females	30396	21206	63173
1921			
Total	74244	40212	117406
Males	37950	19004	53993
Females	36294	21208	63413
1931			
Total	66202	43383	119001
Males	34034	20540	55214
Females	32168	22843	63787

Source: Census of Population 1891, 1901, 1911, 1921, 1931.

2   WOMEN'S OCCUPATIONS, 1891–1931

	Percentage of the total female workforce				
	1891	*1901*	*1911*	*1921*	*1931*
In domestic service					
Barrow	40	35	34	36	43
Lancaster	n/a	29	25	25	30
Preston	13	12	9	10	13
Textile workers					
Barrow	21	12	10	4	0.2
Lancaster	n/a	29	29	23	24
Preston	71	68	69	64	54
Dressmakers, tailoresses, milliners					
Barrow	14	18	15	8	4
Lancaster	n/a	12	11	6	3
Preston	6	6	6	5	5
Shop assistants, dealers, etc.					
Barrow	6	10	14	18	20
Lancaster	n/a	7	14	14	13
Preston	5	6	8	6	12
Clerical workers					
Barrow	0.2	1	0.8	10	9
Lancaster	n/a	n/a	0.4	6	5
Preston	0.1	0.2	0.5	8	3
Teachers					
Barrow	6	7	6	7	6
Lancaster	n/a	4	4	4	3
Preston	2	2	2	2	2
Nurses					
Barrow	0.6	2	2	2	3
Lancaster	n/a	n/a	1	7	8
Preston	0.4	0.4	0.6	1	1

Source: Census of 1891, vol. III, table 7; Census of 1901, County of Lancaster, tables 35 and 35a; Census of 1911, County of Lancaster, tables 23 and 25; Census of 1921, County of Lancaster, table 16; Census of 1931, County of Lancaster, tables 16 and 17.

3 PERCENTAGES OF WOMEN AT WORK, 1891–1931

	Barrow	Lancaster	Preston
1891: aged 10+	32.4	n/a	61.43
1901: aged 10+	20.9	30.5	52.36
1911: aged 10+	20.9	22.2	54.3
1921: aged 12+	22.3	30.2	51.86
1931: aged 14+	23.8	32.7	52.73

Source: Census of 1891, vol. III, table 7; Census of 1901, County of Lancaster, tables 35 and 35a; Census of 1911, County of Lancaster, tables 23 and 25; Census of 1921, County of Lancaster, table 16; Census of 1931, County of Lancaster, tables 16 and 17.

4 WAGE INDICES FOR 1905

	Building labourers	Engineering labourers
Barrow	98	82
Preston	84	75

Towns with more than 30% of married women in full-time work

Blackburn, Burnley, Preston	85.6	77

Towns with less than 20% of married women in full-time work

Barrow, Bolton, Liverpool, Manchester, Oldham, Warrington, Wigan	91.4	80.2

Mean for Lancashire and Cheshire	88	79

London = 100
Source: Board of Trade Inquiry into Working-Class Rents, Housing, and Retail Prices in the Principal Industrial Towns (1908).

5 RESPONDENTS' BIOGRAPHIES

When interviewed, each respondent was promised anonymity and therefore the transcripts of his/her interview are kept with a code letter. These have been retained in the notes so that readers wishing to look at individual transcripts can do so. They are held in the University of Lancaster Library and the Centre for North-West Regional Studies. Respondents have been given pseudonyms in the text to prevent confusion.

The biographical details are for the respondents quoted in the text only. It had been hoped to include details of all respondents, but unfortunately shortage of space prevented this. In each entry, details of one respondent's parents and their family precede the full stop; the respondent's own details follow the full stop.

Barrow

Mrs A1B, b. 1872. Father a blacksmith from Scotland; ten children. A domestic servant later a cook; married, four children; Presbyterian, Gospel Hall.

Mrs A2B, b. 1904. Father a boilermaker's holder-up from Liverpool, mother from Ireland; mother went out cleaning and took in washing after marriage, father frequently ill; four children. A domestic servant, later shopwork; married, one child; Anglican, Labour.

Mr A2B, b. 1904. Father a pawnbroker from Hull; mother from Barrow, no paid work before or after marriage; four children (one died). A joiner; married Mrs A2B; Anglican, Labour.

Mrs A3B, b. 1893. Father a labourer from Staffs.; mother ran a shop before marriage in Staffs.; after marriage took in washing and went out cleaning; nine children (two died). A domestic servant cook and housekeeper; married, six children (three died); Anglican, Conservative.

Mr B1B, b. 1897. Father a coachman from Surrey, mother a domestic servant from Furness; later joint caretakers; thirteen children (two died). A baker; married, two children; Gospel Hall, Congregationalist, Labour.

Mrs C2B, b. 1887. Father a moulder, mother no wage-earning job, from Ireland; eight children. A shop assistant; married, three children; Roman Catholic, no political affiliation.

Mrs D1B, b. 1899. Father a sailor labourer from Ireland, mother a farm servant before marriage from Preston; nine children (one died). A domestic servant, later munitions worker, cleaner; married, one child; Salvation Army.

Mrs D2B, b. 1896. Father a shipwright; mother's occupation not known; twenty-one children (twelve died). A shop assistant; married, two children.

Mr F2B, b. 1900. Father a postman from Barrow (ex-tailor), mother a domestic servant (at 10 Downing Street for the Gladstones) from Cheshire, three children. A railway clerk; unmarried; Anglican, Labour.

Mrs G1B, b. 1888 in Scotland. Father a fitter and turner, mother no paid job before or after marriage; sixteen children (five died). Ran a domestic register before marriage; married, two children; Anglican (ex-Presbyterian), socialist.

Mrs H1B, b. 1893. Father a labourer from Southport, mother a domestic servant before marriage; four children. A servant, later munitions worker, shopwork; married, one child; Anglican, Labour.

Mrs H2B, b. 1885. Father a labourer from Whitehaven, mother a domestic servant from Ireland; after marriage took in lodgers and sewing; four children. A dressmaker; married, no children; Methodist.

Mrs H3B, b. 1887. Father a clerk from Bishop Auckland, mother a teacher before marriage; shopwork after marriage, from Barrow; six children. A clerk, later untrained teacher; married, no children; family Anglican, Conservative, but Mrs H. later atheist, Communist.

Mrs L2B, b. 1900. Father a labourer, mother a barmaid and briefly munitions worker; six children. A confectioner, later a barmaid; married, two children.

Mrs M1B, b. 1898. Father a boilermaker, mother a domestic servant before marriage, no job after; both from Staffs.; five children (one died). Married Mr M1B, one child; Methodist, Conservative family, later Labour.

Mr M1B, b. 1892. Father railway labourer from Isle of Man, mother domestic servant from Furness, twelve children (two died). A grocer in the Coop; married Mrs M1B; Methodist, Liberal then Labour.

Mrs M3B, b. 1886. Father a shipwright, mother a cook before marriage, after ran a parlour shop; both from Ireland; ten children (five died). A pupil-teacher; married, no children; family, Anglican, Unionists; Mrs M. Anglican, socialist.

Mrs M6B, b. 1896. Father a labourer from Scotland, mother a dressmaker before and after marriage, from Lake District; sixteen children (thirteen died). A professional drummer; married Mr M6B, one child; atheist, socialist.

Mr M6B, b. 1892. No details of parents. Tyneside. Came to Barrow in 1913 to work as shipwright; married Mrs M6B; atheist, socialist.

Mr M8B, b. 1901. Father retail and wholesale business, mother no paid occupation, both from Barrow; two children. A rent collector/clerk; married, one child; Liberal.

Mrs M10P, b. 1908. Father a brass finisher from Cumberland, mother dressmaker before marriage from Ireland; four children. A secretary; married, one child; Anglican, Conservative.

Mr P1B, b. 1900. Father a labourer from Warwicks., mother jute works labourer before marriage, auction-room dealer after, six children. A fitter and turner; married, three children; Anglican, socialist.

Mrs R1B, b. 1889. Father a captain of coastal vessel from Ellesmere Port, mother labourer in jute works before marriage, from Birmingham; six children. A jute works labourer; married, two children; family Methodist, Liberal; Mrs R. atheist, socialist, later Communist.

Mrs S2B, b. 1895. Father a labourer, mother took in sewing and went out nursing, both from Barrow; ten children. A tailoress; married, four children; mother Wesleyan, Labour; father Anglican, socialist; children various views.

Mrs W1B, b. 1900. Father a moulder, mother worked at box factory before marriage, no job after, both from Manchester; ten children (two died). A servant, later a shop assistant; married, one child; Anglican, no political views.

Mrs W2B, b. 1889. Father a shipwright from Wales, mother a servant before marriage, fish and chip shop after, from Barrow; fifteen children (five died). A jute works labourer; married, one child; family Liberal, Salvation Army, but Mrs W Labour.

Mrs W3B, b. 1884. Father a miner from Cornwall, mother from Barrow; six children. A domestic servant; married, two children; family Methodist.

Lancaster

Mrs A1L, b. 1908. Father a labourer from Bradford, mother a weaver before and after marriage, from West Yorkshire; two children. A weaver; married, no children.

Mr A2L, b. 1905. Father an electric cable jointer from Batley, mother a domestic servant from Blackpool; four children (two died). A heating and ventilating engineer; married Mrs A2L, one child; family Congregationalist, Liberal.

Mrs A2L, b. 1907. Father a gardener, mother a mill worker before marriage, both from Lancaster; two children. A confectioner; married Mr A2L; family Methodist.

Mrs B1L, b. 1888. Father a labourer, mother a weaver before and after marriage; both from Lancaster; five children. A weaver before and after marriage; four children; Roman Catholic.

Mr C4L, b. 1914. Father a gardener, mother a weaver before and after marriage, both from Lancaster; one child. A clerk; married, one child; Anglican.

Mr G1L, b. 1904. Father a labourer from Colne, mother a domestic servant before marriage, took in washing and went out cleaning after, from Thirsk; five children. A labourer, then professional soldier; married, one child; Methodist, Liberal then Labour.

Mr H1L, b. 1904. Father a bricklayer, mother seamstress before marriage, both from Ireland; two children. A bricklayer; married, no children; Anglican.

Mrs H2L, b. 1889. Father a labourer, mother a weaver before marriage, lodgers after, both from West Cumberland; eleven children (three died). A weaver, then domestic servant; married, three children; Roman Catholic.

Mr H3L, b. 1904. Father a blacksmith, later general handyman (after an accident), mother weaver before and periodically after marriage, both from Lancaster; four children. A stripper and grinder; married Mrs H3L, three children; Roman Catholic, Liberal.

Mrs H3L, b. 1903. Father a matting weaver, mother a domestic servant before marriage, child-minding, washing and sewing after, both from Suffolk; ten children (three died). A shopworker, domestic servant, mill worker; married Mr H3L; Wesleyan, Labour.

Miss H4L, b. 1883. Father a colour mixer in mill, from Lancaster, mother a weaver before and after marriage, from Manchester; one child. A weaver; Anglican.

Mr K1L, b. 1907. Father a baker, mother a weaver and periodically cook and munitions worker before marriage, took in lodgers after, both from Lancaster; four children. A baker; married, two children; Anglican.

Mr L1L, b. 1896. Father a docker from Salford, mother from Lancaster; nine children (four died). Childhood with relatives in Lancaster; soldier then labourer; married, two children; Roman Catholic, socialist.

Mr M3L, b. 1906. Father a joiner from nearby rural village, mother a domestic servant before marriage from Morecambe; three children. A joiner; married Mrs M3L, two children; Anglican, Conservative later socialist.

Mrs M3L, b. 1917. Father a fitter, also a labourer, mother died (also stepmother), both from Lancaster; eight children. A domestic servant; Anglican, socialist.

Mrs M5L, b. 1914. Father a street trader from Lancaster, mother a washerwoman from Cornwall; six children. A weaver; married, no children; Methodist, Labour.

Mrs M1L, b. 1899. Father a painter and decorator, mother a slubber (twisting wool for spinning) before marriage, took in washing and cleaning after, both from Lancaster; nine children. A slubber; married, eight children; Methodist.

Mr P1L, b. 1894. Father a clerk from Kendal, mother no paid work before or after marriage, from Shrops.; three children. An engineer; married Mrs P1L; one child; socialist.

Mrs P1L, b. 1898. Father a foreman in linoleum works, mother no paid occupation before or after marriage, both from Lancaster; five children (one died). A weaver, then a clerk; married Mr P1L; Anglican, Conservative.

Mr P2L, b. 1899. Father a labourer from Nelson, mother a confectioner before marriage, from Whitehaven; nine children. A labourer; married, two children; Anglican, Labour.

Mr R3L, b. 1890. Father a wood carver and turner from Leeds, mother a nurse before marriage, from nearby village; two children. A cabinet maker; married, six children; Anglican, Labour.

Mrs S1L, b. 1898. Father a tinsmith from Kendal, mother a weaver before marriage, from Heysham. A shop assistant; married, three children; grandparents (brought Mrs S up) Liberal, but Mrs S Labour, Methodist.

Mrs S4L, b. 1896. Father a gravedigger from nearby village, mother a washerwoman from Lancaster; nine children. A weaver; married, one child; Anglican.

Mr T1L, b. 1888. Father electric wirer, mother a farm hand before marriage, a washerwoman after; seven children (one died). A painter; married, two children; Anglican, Conservative.

Mr V1L, b. 1908. Father a nurse in a lunatic asylum, from Leyland, mother a domestic servant before marriage, from Preston; four children (one died). A joiner; married, two children.

Mrs W2L, b. 1910. Father a grocer, later a clerk, mother a domestic servant before marriage, took in sewing after, both from Penrith; three children. A shop assistant; married, three children; Congregationalist, Conservative.

Preston

Mrs A2P, b. 1910. Father a domestic servant, later a caretaker, mother a domestic servant, both from East Anglia; ten children (eight died). A winder, dressmaker, bookkeeper's clerk; married, four children (two died). Methodist.

Miss A3P, b. 1899. Father a weaver, mother a weaver then child-minder and washerwoman, both from Preston; three children (one died). A weaver; Anglican.

Mrs B1P, b. 1900. Father a moulder from Wigan, mother from Preston, died young; father had three marriages so Mrs B had three half-sisters, three brothers and sisters, and thirteen stepbrothers and sisters (of the nineteen children nine died). A weaver before and after marriage; four children; Anglican.

Mrs B2P, b. 1916. Father a labourer, mother a winder before and after marriage, both from Preston; two children (one died). A weaver; married, two children (one died). Methodist.

Mr B4P, b. 1896 in Adlington. Father a beatler (a beatler worked a machine which hammered the cloth to make it very smooth) in bleach works, mother a poultry dresser; ten children. A bleacher; married, no children; Anglican, Conservative. (Wife contributed to interview.)

Mrs B5P, b. 1898. Father a docker, mother took in washing, both from Preston; eight children. A weaver and labourer in shoe polish factory, cleaner; married, two children; Anglican.

Mr B9P, b. 1927. Father a waiter, mother a weaver, both from Preston; two children. A college lecturer; married; Roman Catholic.

Mr C1P, b. 1884. Father railway worker from Isle of Man, mother a weaver before marriage, from Leyland; six children (two died). A weaver, married, no children; family Methodist, Liberal; Mr C atheist, socialist.

Mrs C2P, b. 1899. Father a waistcoat-maker from Preston, mother a tailor's machinist before marriage, took in sewing after, from a nearby village; three children. A weaver, married, two children; Anglican.

Mrs C3P, b. 1897. Mother a weaver from Preston; one child (illegitimate). A shop assistant, later commercial traveller; married, one child (died); Anglican.

Mrs C5P, b. 1919. Father a carter, mother a winder before and after marriage, then washerwoman, both from Preston; six children (one died). A weaver before and after marriage, later a cleaner; married, three children.

Mrs D1P, b. 1908. Father a labourer, mother a weaver, later a washerwoman, both from Preston; one child. A shop assistant; as a widow, a factory worker; married, one child; Anglican.

Mr D2P, b. 1910. Father a professional soldier later commissionaire, from London, mother a domestic servant before marriage, took in sewing and cleaned after, from East Anglia; nine children (two died). A cabinet maker, clerk of works; married, three children; family Anglican, Conservative; Mr D socialist.

Mrs D3P, b. 1905 in Wigan. Father a miner from Wigan, stepfather paper deliverer and knocker-up, from Preston, mother a tailoress before marriage, later munitions worker and took in lodgers, from Wigan; two children. A carder, after marriage kept pubs with husband; six children; Anglican.

Mr F1P, b. 1906 in West Cumberland. Father a miner from Cumberland, in Preston a poultry dresser, mother a cook before marriage, washerwoman after, from Northumberland; five children. An electrician; married, seven children (six adopted); Roman Catholic, Labour.

Mr G1P, b. 1903. Father a slasher's labourer, later preparation manager in mill, mother a weaver before and after marriage, both from Preston; eight children (two died). A weaver; married, five children (one died); Anglican, Labour.

Mr G3P, b. 1913. Father an engineer, mother a weaver before marriage, child-minder after, both from Preston; four children (one died). Mill worker, winding overlooker; married, two children; Anglican. (Wife contributed to interview.)

Mrs H1P, b. 1911 in Darwen. Father a publican, mother helped in pub, both from Lancs.; fifteen children (five died). A weaver; married, three children; Roman Catholic.

Mrs H2P, b. 1898. Father a mule spinner, mother a weaver before and after marriage, both from Preston; three children. A weaver; married, one child; Anglican, Labour.

Mrs H4P, b. 1903. Father a fitter, mother a weaver before and periodically after marriage, both from Preston; ten children (two died). A weaver, then domestic servant; married, two children; Anglican, Labour.

Mrs H7P, b. 1916. Parents and Mrs H. from an industrial village on outskirts of Preston. Father a railing maker, later engine driver, mother carder before and after marriage; six children (three died). A weaver; married, no children; Roman Catholic, Labour.

Mrs H8P, b. 1903. Father a clogger, mother a winder, child-minder after marriage, both from Preston; twelve children (four died). A weaver, cleaner after marriage; married, one child; Anglican, Conservative.

Mrs J1P, b. 1911. Father a shuttle-maker from London, after marriage helped in wife's family post office, mother from Preston; four children. Worked in family post office; married, two children.

Dr K1P. Doctor in Preston. Practised 1928—78.

Mr L1P, b. 1894. Father a carter, unemployed and casual work after injury, mother's work unknown, both from Preston; twelve children (one died). A weaver, then soldier and loom sweeper; married, two children; Anglican, Labour.

Mrs M1P, b. 1913. Father a fitter and turner from N.E. Lancs., mother a weaver before marriage, child-minder after, from Preston; six children (one died). An intermediate tenter; married, two children (one died); Roman Catholic, socialist.

Mrs M3P, b. 1898. Father a checker in Preston docks, mother a dressmaker before marriage, cleaner after, both from York; seven children (four died). A lamp-worker, cleaner after marriage; five children; Methodist.

Mrs M6P, b. 1904. Father a docker, mother a weaver before and after marriage; five children (one died). A weaver, married, no children; Roman Catholic.

Mrs O1P, b. 1902. Father a weaver, mother a dressmaker before and after marriage, both from Preston; eleven children (two died). A weaver, then a piano teacher; married, four children; Roman Catholic.

Mrs P1P, b. 1899. Father a blacksmith, mother a doffer (unskilled mill-worker) before marriage, a hawker after; five children (one died). A weaver before and after marriage, also a cleaner; married, six children (two died); Roman Catholic.

Mrs P2P, b. 1907. Father sketching-master in mill, mother a weaver before marriage, kept a shop after, both from Preston; six children (two died). A weaver before marriage, kept a pie shop after; married, one child; Baptist.

Mr S1P, b. 1900. Father a carter from Preston, mother a domestic servant before marriage, cleaner after, from Cumberland; four children. A weaver, soldier, labourer; married, no children; Methodist.

Mrs S3P, b. 1892. Father a carder, mother a weaver, both from Ireland; ten children (two died). A ring spinner; married, no children; Roman Catholic.

Mr S4P, b. 1915. Father a pattern-maker, mother a machinist, later a teacher before marriage, both from Preston; two children (one died). A teacher; married, three children; Roman Catholic, Labour.

Mrs S5P, b. 1898. Father a blacksmith from Lancaster, mother a ring spinner, before and after marriage, from Preston; ten children (two died). A weaver; married, no children; Methodist, father Labour, mother Conservative.

Mrs S7P, b. 1914. Father a cloth-looker, mother weaver before and after marriage, both from Preston; two children. A tailoress; married, one child; Anglican.

Mr T1P, b. 1897. Father professional soldier, later a docker, from Somerset, mother a winder before marriage, ran a small shop after; seventeen children (four died). A weaver, soldier, labourer; married, two children; Anglican.

Mr T2P, b. 1903. Father a slasher's labourer, soldier, labourer, mother a weaver before and after marriage, both from Preston; seven children (four died). A mill-worker, munitions-worker, railway worker, engine driver; married, one child; family Anglican, Liberal; Mr T. atheist, Labour.

Mr T3P, b. 1886. Father a labourer, mother doffer before marriage, washer-woman after, both from Preston; seven children (three died). A spinner, shuttlemaker, insurance collector; married, three children (one died); Anglican.

Miss T4P, b. 1912. Father a mill labourer, mother a weaver before and after marriage, both from Preston; five children (one died). A weaver; Anglican, Labour.

Mrs T5P, b. 1905. Father a tackler (skilled mill worker), mother a weaver; ten children (one died). A weaver; married, two children. Anglican, Labour.

Mrs W1P, b. 1899. Father a stoker, mother a weaver before marriage (died young), both from Preston; nine children (one died). A weaver, then ring spinner before and after marriage; two children; Roman Catholic.

Mrs W4P, b. 1900. Father a bricklayer, mother barmaid before marriage, after widowed ran a shop and took in lodgers, both from Preston; ten children (two died). A weaver before and after marriage; one child; Anglican.

Notes

INTRODUCTION

1 Michelle Perrot, 'De la nourrice à l'employée travaux des femmes dans la France du XIXe siècle', *Le Mouvement Social*, vol. 105 (1978); Louise Tilly and Joan Scott, *Women, Work and Family* (1978); L. Tilly and J. Scott, 'Women's work and the family in nineteenth-century Europe', *Comparative Studies in Society and History,* vol. 17 (1975); L. Tilly, J. Scott and M. Cohen. 'Women's work and European fertility patterns', *Journal of Interdisciplinary History,* vol. VI (1976).

2 Olive Banks, *Faces of Feminism* (1981), p. 3.

3 This book is based on two projects. The first investigated working-class social and family life in Barrow and Lancaster 1890—1930; this was supported by a Nuffield Small Grant in the period 1972—74, and an SSRC grant from 1974 to 1976. The second was a similar project in Preston for the period 1890—1940, and was funded by the SSRC from 1978 to 1981. They were carried out under the aegis of the Centre for North-West Regional Studies at the University of Lancaster.

4 See Jill Liddington and Jill Norris, *One Hand Tied Behind Us: The Rise of the Women's Suffrage Movement* (1978). This is an account of working-class women's involvement in the movement in north-east Lancashire, an involvement which was not shared by women from central and north Lancashire. An examination of possible reasons for this difference is given in Mike Savage's 'Labour Control in Weaving 1890—1940' (unpublished research paper, Sociology Department, University of Lancaster).

5 Banks, *Faces of Feminism*, p. 5.

6 'Most feminists . . . have been eager to recognise [women's history] but they have on occasion been guilty of either a simple-minded search for heroines or a narrow and uncritical use of the "male oppression model" in explaining women's roles.' M. Hartmann and L. Banner (eds), *Clio's Consciousness Raised* (1974), p. vii.

7 The study of traditional attitudes and behaviour has been urged by Mary Hartmann: 'While investigating the agents of change we also need more study of the persistence of traditional attitudes and institutions that

particularly touched women. . . . It is worth knowing to what extent older habits and roles as opposed to new ones actively reinforced women's power.' Ibid., p. xii.

8   Elizabeth Roberts, 'The working-class family in Barrow and Lancaster 1890—1930' (unpublished PhD thesis, University of Lancaster, 1978) includes a fuller analysis of and rationale for the use of oral evidence. See also Paul Thompson, *The Voice of the Past: Oral History* (1978) for a full analysis of oral history.

9   M. Drake and P. Hammerton, *Exercises in Historical Sociology* (1974), and R. Bendix and S. M. Lipset (eds), *Class, Status and Power* (1967); both contain useful analytical surveys of their work.

10   M. Weber, 'Class, status, and party', in Bendix and Lipset, *Class, Status and Power,* p. 22.

11   E. P. Thompson, *The Making of the English Working Class* (1963), pp. 10—11; F. K. Donnelly, 'Ideology and early English working-class history: Edward Thompson and his critics', *Social History,* vol. 2 (1976), p. 221. Both historians develop the relativist concept of class, and criticise those who define 'working class' in terms of occupation.

12   Patrick Joyce has explored reasons for the 'more accommodative, quiescent popular attitudes seen after the mid-century' in textile Lancashire. His interpretation of deference is slightly different from mine, as he links it more closely to class conflict: 'Deference was an aspect of the class relationship of employers and work people with sufficient power at the time greatly to erode the consciousness of conflict but never to displace it, to change the form in which conflict was perceived but not to obliterate its perception.' *Work, Society and Politics: The Culture of the Factory in Later Victorian England* (1980), p. xvi.

13   Standish Meacham, *A Life Apart: The English Working Class 1890—1914* (1977), p. 16.

14   Robert Moore, *Pitmen, Preachers and Politics: The Effects of Methodism in a Durham Mining Community* (1974), p. 25.

15   *Making of the English Working Class,* pp. 392—3.

16   Mr T1P was a respondent from a rough family (see appendix 5), whose mother 'always went to church', though his father did not. The children were sent to Sunday School and as Mr T. got older he played football for the local church team. He abandoned church-going as a married man but did not repudiate Christian teaching. The family always said a prayer before meals when he was at home.

17   A clear example of a family who achieved this was that of Mr M7B. See Michael Winstanley, *The Shopkeepers' World, 1830—1914* (1983), for a national and very thorough examination of this topic.

18   See Roberts, 'Working-class family'.

19   Census of 1911, County of Lancaster, table 23. The Census does not, of course, mention Vickers, but in Barrow it can safely be assumed that those enumerated under General Engineering and Ships and Boats, worked for this company.

20   Ibid., table 13.
21   Ibid., table 24.

CHAPTER 1.   GROWING UP

1   Philippe Ariès, *L'Enfant et la vie familiale sous l'ancien régime* (1960); published in England as *Centuries of Childhood* (1962).
2   Mrs D3P, p. 31.
3   See Tamara K. Hareven, 'The history of the family as an interdisciplinary field', in T. K. Rabb and R. I. Rotberg (eds), *The Family in History* (1971); Tamara K. Hareven (ed.), *Family and Kin in Urban Communities 1700—1930* (1977); Robert H. Bremner, John Barnard, Tamara K. Hareven and Robert M. Mennel (eds), *Children and Youth in America: A Documentary History,* 3 vols. (1970—4).
4   But see F. Musgrove, 'The family as an educational institution, 1760—1860' (unpublished PhD thesis, University of Nottingham, 1958).
5   Helen Bosanquet, *The Family* (1906), p. 50.
6   Alexander Paterson, *Across the Bridge* (1911), p. 16.
7   Mrs H8P, p. 20.
8   Paul Thompson, *The Edwardians* (1975), p. 60.
9   Mrs W2B, p. 19.
10   Mrs H7P, p. 23.
11   Mrs P1L, pp. 39—40.
12   Mr T1L, p. 32.
13   Mrs H2B, p. 137.
14   Mrs P1L, p. 40.
15   Stephen Humphries, 'Steal to Survive: The Social Crime of Working-Class Children, 1890—1940', *Oral History*, vol. 9, no. 1 (1981); and *Hooligans or Rebels?: An Oral History of Working-class Childhood and Youth, 1889—1939* (1981).
16   Mrs H7P, p. 37.
17   Mrs S2B, pp. 45—6.
18   Mrs W1P, p. 12.
19   Mrs S2B, pp. 49—50.
20   Mr D2P, p. 34 (manuscript).
21   Robert Roberts, *The Classic Slum* (Pelican, 1973), p. 44.
22   Mr M1B, p. 40.
23   Mrs C5P, p. 30.
24   Mrs W1B, p. 77.
25   Mrs S4L, p. 68.
26   Mrs B2P, p. 3.
27   Mrs C5P, p. 49.
28   For an examination of some medical views on menstruation, see Carol Dyhouse, *Girls Growing Up in Late Victorian and Edwardian England* (1981), ch. 4. It was thought that during puberty the growing girl needed

to conserve all her energies in order to establish a regular menstrual cycle. If energy was diverted into intellectual pursuits, it was feared that permanent damage could be done to her reproductive system.

29 Mrs R1B, p. 5.
30 Mrs D1P, pp. 60—1.
31 Mrs H4P, p. 16.
32 Mrs D1P, p. 32.
33 Mr T2P, p. 26.
34 Mrs S4L, p. 35.
35 Mrs S3L, p. 27.
36 Mrs P1L, p. 9.
37 See Cynthia Hay, 'The pangs of the past', *Oral History*, vol. 9, no. 1 (1981), for an examination of the problem of respondents recalling painful memories.
38 Mrs A3B, p. 3.
39 Mrs J1P, p. 9.
40 Mrs S2B, pp. 2—3.
41 Mr B1B, p. 31.
42 See I. Pinchbeck and M. Hewitt, *Children in English Society,* vol. 2 (1973), p. 368.
43 Mrs P2P, pp. 7, 15, 25.
44 *The Family*, p. 305.
45 Mrs M1P, p. 14.
46 Mrs P2P, p. 10.
47 See Patricia Branca, *Silent Sisterhood: Middle-Class Women in the Victorian Home* (1977), p. 146. For a development of working-class attitudes to motherhood, see ch. 4.
48 Mrs P3B was born in 1873 and came from Wales to Barrow as a small child. Her reasons for not attending school was described as ill-health. It is likely that no particularly strenuous efforts were made by the authorities to get her into school, as Barrow's very rapid expansion had led to a serious shortage of school places. In 1873 the local press estimated that there were 5000 children of school age in Barrow, but only half of them attended school. It urged the newly formed Board of Education to build more schools (*Barrow Herald*, 18 January 1873).
49 Mrs M1P, p. 31.
50 Mrs B1L, p. 31.
51 Mrs H2L, p. 9.
52 *Hooligans or Rebels?*, ch. 1.
53 Mrs N1L, p. 66.
54 *Barrow News,* 21 January 1893, 28 January 1893.
55 *The Classic Slum*, p. 138.
56 Mrs N1L, p. 66.
57 Mrs H4P, pp. 44—5.
58 1958, p. 75.
59 The *New Code of Regulations for Education* issued by the Lords of the

Committee of the Privy Council of Education (Cd. 1458, vol. LIX, p. 1).

60 Carol Dyhouse, 'Good wives and little mothers: social anxieties and schoolgirls' curriculum 1890–1920', *Oxford Review of Education,* vol. 3, no. 1 (1977). See also Dyhouse, *Girls Growing Up,* ch. 3.

61 Miss T4P, pp. 35–6.

62 Mrs C5P, p. 12.

63 *Barrow News,* 21 January 1893.

64 Mrs H2B, p. 69.

65 Mrs S2B, p. 54.

66 Mrs S2B, p. 61.

67 Interdepartmental Committee on Physical Deterioration, vol. III, *P.P.* 1904 XXXII, pp. 153–4.

68 Board of Education, *Special Reports on Educational Subjects, School Training for the Home Duties of Women;* (Part I), *The Teaching of Domestic Science in the United States of America (P.P.* 1905 XXVI, p. 783ff); (Part II), *Belgium, Sweden, Norway, Denmark, Switzerland and France (P.P.* 1906 XXVIII, p. 437ff); (Part III), *The Domestic Training of Girls in Germany and Austria (P.P.* 1908 XXVIII, p. 1ff).

69 Peter Stearns, 'Working-class women in Britain 1890–1914', in M. Vicinus (ed.), *Suffer and Be Still* (1972), p. 103.

70 Mrs G1B, p. 7.

71 Census of 1921, County of Lancaster, table 18.

72 B. S. Rowntree, *Poverty: A Study of Town Life* (1901), p. 60. Rowntree estimated that 37.5 per cent of all 5–15-year-olds in York were living in poverty.

73 Harold Silver, 'Ideology and the factory child: attitudes to half-time education', in P. McCann (ed.), *Popular Education and Socialisation in the Nineteenth-Century* (1979).

74 *Preston Guardian,* 4 June 1910.

75 *Preston Guardian,* 7 August 1909.

76 Mrs A3B, p. 21.

77 Mrs H2B, p. 140; Miss H4L, p. 1.

78 Mrs H7P, pp. 40, 33.

CHAPTER 2.   YOUTH, WORK AND LEISURE

1 Mrs D2B, Mrs H3B, Mrs H1B, Mrs R1B, Mrs S2B and Mrs P3B.

2 Mrs M1B and Mrs F1B.

3 1974, p. 131.

4 Mrs H2L, p. 4.

5 Mrs M6B, pp. 4, 5.

6 Mrs S2B, pp. 18, 20.

7 Mrs H3B, p. 19.

8 Meacham, *A Life Apart,* p. 156.

9 Mrs H8P, Mrs D3P and Mr L1P.

10 Mrs D3P, p. 33.
11 Mrs D1B, pp. 44, 45.
12 Mrs T5P, in transcript D3P, p. 13.
13 Mrs C3P, pp. 8, 10, 24.
14 Mrs P1P, pp. 34, 66.
15 N. Smelser, *Social Change in the Industrial Revolution: An Application of Theory to the Lancashire Cotton Industry, 1770—1840* (1959), p. 190.
16 Gillis, *Youth and History,* pp. 56, 66.
17 Harold J. Perkin, *The Origins of Modern English Society, 1780—1880* (1969), pp. 178, 177.
18 Joyce, *Work, Society and Politics*, p. 90.
19 Philip Gooderson, 'The social history of Lancaster 1780—1914 (unpublished PhD thesis, University of Lancaster (1975), p. 571).
20 See Nigel Todd, 'A history of labour in Lancaster and Barrow c. 1890—1920' (unpublished MLitt thesis, University of Lancaster (1976) passim), for a well-documented study of the contrasting labour movements in Barrow and Lancaster.
21 Luisa Paserini developed this idea in a paper given at the International Oral History Conference at Essex in 1979. An extended version, but without references to the family, was published later: Luisa Paserini, 'Work, ideology and consensus under Italian Fascism', *History Workshop*, vol. 8 (1979).
22 Mrs S4L, p. 39.
23 His 'spy' book can be studied in the Lancashire Record Office, Preston.
24 Mrs B1L, p. 9.
25 Mrs H1P, p. 8.
26 Mrs H1P, p. 9.
27 Mrs R1B, p. 7.
28 J. D. Marshall, *Furness and the Industrial Revolution* (reprinted 1981), p. 387.
29 *Barrow Herald,* 19 July 1884.
30 *Women's Work and Wages* (1906), p. 72.
31 *A Life Apart,* p. 182.
32 Mrs P1P, p. 5.
33 Luisa Paserini, 'Work, ideology and consensus', passim.
34 Mrs P1O, p. 85.
35 Mrs B1P, p. 62.
36 See, for example: N. B. Dearle, *Industrial Training* (1914); Arnold T. Freeman, *Boy Life and Labour* (1914); Reginald Bray, *Boy Labour and Apprenticeship* (1911); Sidney and Beatrice Webb, *Industrial Democracy,* 2 vols (1897).
37 See Gillis, *Youth and History*, on boy labour.
38 Meacham, *A Life Apart*, p. 181.
39 Mr and Mrs P1L, pp. 69, 101.
40 Mr F2B, p. 4.
41 Mrs W2L, p. 89.
42 Mrs H2L moved from the mill to domestic work in a hospital.

43 C. V. Butler, *Social Conditions in Oxford* (1912), pp. 77, 32.
44 Mrs W3B, pp. 1, 2, 46.
45 S. Caunce, 'East Riding Hiring Fairs', *Oral History,* vol. 3, no. 2 (1975); J. D. Marshall and J. K. Walton, *The Lake Counties* (1981), pp. 68—9 and passim.
46 Mrs A3B, p. 15.
47 Mrs A3B, pp. 15—16.
48 Mrs W1B, pp. 17, 81.
49 Readers may wish to refer, as a comparative study, to *Amoskeog* by Tamara Hareven and Ranolph Langenbach (1979). This is an in-depth study, based on oral evidence and a large photographic collection, of the history of an American cotton mill and textile community in Manchester, New Hampshire.
50 Miss A3P, pp. 2—3.
51 Mrs B1P, pp. 11—12, 54.
52 Mrs C5P, p. 46.
53 Mrs W2L, pp. 22, 224, 225, 226, 228.
54 Mrs H2B, p. 65.
55 Mrs L2B, p. 9.
56 Mrs A2L, in W2L, pp. 70, 220.
57 Mrs H2B, pp. 3, 4, 63, 64, 65.
58 Mrs S7P, pp. 2, 3, 4.
59 Miss H4L, pp. 17—18.
60 Mrs W2L, p. 235.
61 Mrs M10B, pp. 61, 62.
62 Mrs M6B, pp. 57, 110.
63 Mrs H7P, p. 25.
64 See Meacham, *A Life Apart*, pp. 192—3; C. E. B. Russell, *Manchester Boys* (1905), pp. 115—16; Humphries, *Hooligans or Rebels?*, p. 139.
65 Gillis, *Youth and History*, p. 62.
66 Mr F1P, p. 12.
67 Mrs B2P, p. 3.
68 Mrs W2B, p. 23.
69 Mrs A2B, p. 106.
70 Derek Thompson, 'Courtship and marriage in Preston between the wars', *Oral History,* vol. 3, no. 2, p. 41.
71 Mr S4P, p. 14.
72 Mrs D1P, p. 33.
73 Mr P4B, Mr M1L, Mrs S5L, Mr E1B, Mrs H3L and Mr R2L.
74 Mrs H2P, Mr H6P, Mr S1P and Mrs M1P.
75 Mr B9P, Mr E1P and Mr F2P.
76 Mrs S5P and Mrs D1P.
77 Some respondents have mentioned the custom prevalent in certain country areas of a girl getting pregnant before marriage to prove her fertility. No repondent believed that this was a custom which it was 'proper' to follow.
78 Mr K1L, p. 35.

79 Mr P1L, p. 44.
80 Mrs M3L, p. 17.
81 Marshall and Walton, *The Lake Counties*, pp. 81—2, 148.
82 This incident was recounted in a conversation and not recorded. It sounds an almost incredible remark to have been made, but the lady was a truly remarkable woman, and was later a socialist and, when she felt necessary, a flouter of social conventions.
83 Mrs W1B, pp. 80, 78, 79.
84 Mrs R1B, p. 7.
85 Mrs B1L, p. 24a.
86 Mr T1P, pp. 5, 9, 13.
87 Mrs C3P, pp. 1, 3, 4, 7, 25.
88 Thompson, 'Courtship and marriage', p. 40.
89 Mrs D1P, p. 16.
90 In 1980, while the interviews were taking place, there was a discussion on Radio Blackburn of the legend of the Preston Banister Doll in which a Victorian father chained up his daughter, and publicly flogged her to death. One respondent was distressed because the radio version differed from that passed down in her own family. Mrs H4P, p. 16.
91 Mrs D3P, p. 18.
92 Mrs T5P, in Mr D3P, pp. 16 and 30.
93 Mrs H7P, p. 25.
94 Registrar General's Annual Reports 1890—1940; Local Medical Officers of Health Annual Reports; B. Mitchell and P. Deane, *Abstract of British Historical Statistics* (1962); B. Mitchell and H. Jones, *Second Abstract of British Historical Statistics* (1971).
95 Mrs A3B, p. 15.

CHAPTER 3.   MARRIAGE

1 These figures are calculated from the Census of 1891, vol. 3, table 6; and Census of 1931, County of Lancaster, table 14.
2 Diana Gittins, 'Women's work and family size between the wars', *Oral History*, vol. 5, no. 2 (1977) (this relationship between age at marriage and occupation is further discussed in her *Fair Sex: Family Size and Structure, 1900—1939* (1982), ch. 3); Stearns, 'Working-class women in Britain 1890—1914', p. 112.
3 These figures were calculated according to a formula given and used by J. Hajnal, 'Age at marriage and proportions marrying', *Population Studies* (1953), vol. 7, pp. 111—36.
4 Mrs W1P, pp. 19—20.
5 Mrs S7P, p. 14.
6 Mr B1B, p. 9.
7 Mr B9P, p. 9.
8 Mrs D1P, p. 31.

9   Mrs M3P, p. 53.

10 Mrs D2B.

11 R. M. Titmuss, 'The position of women', *Essays on the Welfare State* (1976), pp. 91—2.

12 The fertility rates for the period 1911—20 in Barrow are undoubtedly too high. This period saw a huge influx of munition workers and their families into the town. They arrived after the 1911 Census, and left before that of 1921. Consequently their numbers cannot be estimated in the intercensal calculations. During the war, however, the Medical Officer of Health estimated the population to be over 90,500. The 1921 Census gave it as 74,244. It would seem reasonable to suggest that there were in fact more married women than calculated on the basis of the Census returns, and that therefore the fertility rates were in fact considerably lower.

13 Gittins, *Fair Sex*. This is a much more detailed study of this interesting and difficult subject than her earlier work, and is obviously essential reading for anyone looking at the question of family limitation.

14 Mrs H8P, p. 36.

15 Mrs W1B, p. 80.

16 Mrs G1P, p. 19.

17 Mrs M1P, p. 39.

18 Mrs H3L, p. 72.

19 Jean-Louis Flandrin, *Families in Former Times* (1979), has a very thorough study and analysis of French family size, fertility rates, and the attitude of the Church to the sharp decline in the French birth rate. See especially ch. IV, 'Reproduction and sexual life'.

20 Mr S4P, pp. 28—9.

21 Mrs P1P, p. 98.

22 Mrs M3P, p. 12.

23 Mrs B1P, p. 44.

24 Mrs P1P, p. 12.

25 Mrs D1P, p. 54.

26 J. A. Banks, *Victorian Values, Secularism and the Size of Families* (1981), p. 7.

27 *Fair Sex*, p. 181.

28 H. J. Habakkuk, *Population Growth and Economic Development since 1750* (1971), p. 57.

29 Ibid., pp. 57, 60—3.

30 Diana Gittins, 'Married life and birth control between the wars', *Oral History*, vol. 3, no. 2 (1975), pp. 58—61; and 'Women's work and family size' p. 85.

31 Mr R3L, p. 57.

32 Mrs S2B, p. 29.

33 Mrs B5P, pp. 22, 43.

34 Mrs W1P, p. 16.

35 Mrs P2P, p. 22.

36 Gittins, *Fair Sex,* ch. 5.

37 Mrs P2P, p. 22.
38 Branca, *Silent Sisterhood* (1977), pp. 144—5; Alex Inkeles, 'The modernisation of men', in Myron Weiner, *Modernisation: The Dynamics of Growth* (1966).
39 Habakkuk, *Population Growth,* p. 57.
40 Mrs W4P, p. 18.
41 Mrs G1B, p. 12.
42 Mrs H8P, p. 27.
43 Titmuss, *Essays on the Welfare State,* pp. 88—94.
44 See, *inter alia*, Jane Lewis, *The Politics of Motherhood* (1980), ch. 7.
45 Ibid., pp. 211, 212.
46 M. Spring Rice, *Working-Class Wives* (1939), p. 44; also Lewis, *Politics of Motherhood,* ch. 7.
47 Mrs D3P, p. 30.
48 Medical Officer of Health for Preston, Annual Report, 1902.
49 *Barrow Herald,* 7 September 1895.
50 Mrs M6B, p. 53.
51 J. A. and O. Banks, *Feminism and Family Planning* (1964).
52 Gittins, 'Married life and birth control', pp. 53—64.
53 Flandrin, *Families in Former Times,* pp. 221—3 for a survey of the practice of coitus interruptus in France from the Middle Ages onwards. He argues that it was the most usual method of birth control in France and by the end of the eighteenth century was being practised by all classes (despite the condemnation of the practice by the Church). For the later and more relevant period, Diana Gittins, *Fair Sex*, wrote 'Up until the nineteenth century and for some sectors well into the twentieth century the most common forms of birth control were coitus interruptus and abortion/abortifacents.' My reasons for not regarding the latter as a common form of birth control are given later in this chapter. Gittins, when writing of the records of the Family Planning Association for Manchester and Salford Mothers' Clinic, shows that during the inter-war period, coitus interruptus was the most common form of birth control practised by men from all social classes (ibid., p. 169).
54 Mrs W4P, p. 19.
55 Mrs M3P, p. 12.
56 Mrs P1P, pp. 71, 28.
57 Mrs W2L, p. 14.
58 Mrs W1B, p. 88.
59 This woman was not interviewed, but contributed to part of Mrs H7P's interview.
60 J. A. Banks suggested that they would in fact have been too expensive in the late Victorian period: 'It does not seem very likely that many working-class couples even among the aristocrats of labour . . . would have spent much money on any of these contraceptive devices — they would have had to rely on long courtship marked by sexual restraint, and abstinence, even

once married, mutual masturbation and coitus interruptus' (*Feminism and Family Planning*, p. 109).

61   Mr D2P, p. 50.
62   Branca, *Silent Sisterhood*, p. 133.
63   Ibid., p. 135.
64   In 1896, rubber condoms cost between 2*s*. and 10*s*. a dozen (J. Peel, 'The manufacture and retailing of contraceptives in England', *Population Studies* (1962), vol. 18, p. 116). Patricia Knight, 'Women and abortion in Victorian and Edwardian England', *History Workshop* (1977), vol. 4, p. 59, quotes 6*d*.—3*s*. a dozen for sheaths before 1914.
65   Ibid., p. 57.
66   Mary Chamberlain, *Old Wives' Tales* (1981), p. 119.
67   E. Lewis Faning, *Report of an Inquiry into Family Limitation and its Influence on Human Fertility during the past 50 years*, Papers of the Royal Commission on Population (1949), vol. 1, table 115, p. 166.
68   Mrs M3P, pp. 12—13.
69   Mrs D1P, p. 53.
70   Mrs H8P, p. 36.
71   Mrs H4P, p. 31.
72   Mrs D3P, p. 30.
73   Knight, 'Women and abortion', p. 57.
74   Parts of this section first appeared in Elizabeth Roberts, 'Working wives and their families', in T. Barker and M. Drake (eds), *Population and Society in Britain, 1850—1980* (1982).
75   Quoted by Angus McLaren, 'Women's work and regulation of family size', *History Workshop* (1977), no. 4, p. 70.
76   J. W. Innes, *Class Fertility Trends in England and Wales, 1876—1934* (1938).
77   Gittins, 'Married life and birth control' (1975), p. 97.
78   *Census of England and Wales 1911*, vol. XIII, *Fertility of Marriage*, Part II, pp. cxiii, cxvii.
79   Ibid., p. cxiv.
80   Ibid., p. cxiv.
81   Mr G1P and Mrs B1L.
82   Royal Commission on Population, *Family Limitation* (1949), vol. I, Cmd 7695, ch. VIII, table 14. It is very difficult to differentiate between the voluntarily and involuntarily infertile. The report stated that of those married between 1900 and 1944, 12 per cent were actually childless and denied using any birth control. The reasons for arriving at the 8.2 per cent infertility figure for those married before 1925 are developed fully in chapter VII of the report.
83   Mrs B4P, p. 28.
84   Mrs S5P, pp. 12—13.
85   Mr G3P, p. 28.
86   Mrs M6P, in Mrs D3P, p. 31.
87   Mrs C5P, p. 30.

88 Lewis, *Politics of Motherhood*, pp. 35—8, 122—4.
89 Medical Officers of Health for Preston, Annual Reports, 1911—40 inclusive.
90 Medical Officer of Health for Preston, Annual Report, 1937.
91 Medical Officer of Health for Preston, Annual Report, 1940.
92 Mrs A2P, p. 19.
93 Medical Officer of Health for Preston, Annual Report, 1930.
94 Mrs L1P's mother, for example.
95 J. D. Marshall and M. E. McClintock (eds), *The History of the Lancashire County Council* (1977), pp. 90—1.
96 Mrs H2L, p. 39.
97 Mrs D2B, p. 3.
98 The Midwives Act of 1902 stated that all new midwives had to undergo a period of training. Midwives already practising but untrained could continue to practise providing they registered with the local health authority. A Central Midwives Board (CMB) was set up to keep the list of certified midwives and to oversee midwifery practice.
99 Medical Officer of Health for Lancaster, Annual Report, 1917.
100 Marshall and McClintock, *History of the Lancashire County Council*, pp. 90—1.
101 Elsewhere in her evidence Mrs H2L quotes the midwife as charging 7*s.* 6*d.* Jane Lewis quotes the average midwife's fee for the pre-first world war period as 10*s.* (*Politics of Motherhood*, p. 141).
102 p. 113.
103 Mrs H8P, p. 27.
104 *Silent Sisterhood*, p. 1.
105 Mrs W1B, p. 76.
106 Mrs P1P, p. 18.
107 Medical Officer of Health for Preston, Annual Report, 1939.
108 Mrs B1P, pp. 44, 46.
109 K. Marx and F. Engels, *Selected Works*, vol. 2 (Foreign Language Publishing House, Moscow, 1951), p. 205.
110 Mr L1P.
111 Mrs H3L, p. 20.
112 Mrs W2L, p. 93.
113 Bosanquet, *The Family*, p. 199.
114 Tilly and Scott, *Women, Work and Family*; Michelle Perrot, 'De la nourrice à l'employée', *Le Mouvement Social*, 105 (1978), p. 4; Paterson, *Across the Bridge*, p. 32.
115 Mrs A2L, in Mrs W2L, p. 130.
116 Mr P1B, p. 52.
117 Mr M1B, p. 30.
118 Mr S1P, p. 4.
119 *The Family*, p. 199.
120 Mr L1L, p. 24.
121 Mrs C2P, p. 15.
122 Mrs H2B, p. 30.

123   Mr S4P, p. 23.
124   Mrs W1B, pp. 84—5.
125   Mrs D1P, p. 49.
126   Mr M1B, p. 33.
127   Mr M1L, p. 78.
128   Mrs H7P, p. 17.
129   Mrs W1B, p. 28.
130   Mr M3L, p. 8.
131   Mrs S2B, p. 16.
132   Mrs H2B, p. 103.
133   Elizabeth Bott, *Family and Social Network* (1971), p. 60.
134   Mrs W2L
135   *The Family*, p. 277 and passim.
136   Mr G1P, p. 48.
137   Mrs W1P, p. 8.
138   It is not easy to generalise about what happened to the role-relationships in marriage when married women gave up full-time work. Much depended on how long the wife had worked, and how established therefore were their habits of sharing the housework. Other factors were the personalities of husband and wife, and the nature and extent (if any) of the wife's part-time work. Certainly in the sample, examples can be found both of role separation and of continuing role sharing after the giving up of the woman's full-time job.
139   Gittins, 'Women's work and family size', p. 97.
140   In their devotion to such items as gold jewellery, these men were untypical of the great majority of working-class men. From discussion of this particular model of marriage with a group of local divorce lawyers it is clear that this type of working-class man is still instantly recognisable, and frequently encountered in their offices. This provides a neat example of both continuity and change in social history. The male type continues, but their wives no longer tolerate their behaviour, and seek remedies in the divorce court.
141   Mrs H4P, pp. 3, 10, 14, 19.
142   Mrs O1P, pp. 11, 12, 13.
143   *Lancaster Guardian*, 22 February 1890.
144

Convictions for drunkenness per 1,000
population (five-year averages)

	Barrow	Lancaster	Preston
1906—10	6.72	1.62	3.48
1911—15	6.28	1.22	1.86
1916—20	2.86	0.94	1.29
1921—25	1.16	0.92	0.7
1926—30	1.26	0.68	0.48

Source: Licensing Acts, 1906—30 inclusive

145 Report of the Committee on Bad Time-Keeping, *P.P.* (1914—16) LV, 220, p. 24; Defence of the Realm Act, 19 May 1915, and 10 June 1915.
146 Report of the War Cabinet for 1918, *P.P.* (1919) XXX, Cmd 325, p. 293.
147 Mrs C3P, p. 31.
148 Mrs P1P, p. 93.
149 *Barrow Herald*, 23 February 1898.
150 Evidence to the National Council on Public Morals: the Cinema (1917), pp. 5—6, quoted in A. Marwick, *The Deluge: British Society and the First World War* (1965), pp. 140—4.
151 Mr H1L, p. 48.

CHAPTER 4.   WOMEN AS HOUSEWIVES AND MANAGERS

1 Mrs M1P, pp. 9—12.
2
Number of persons per inhabited dwelling

	1901	1911	1921	1931
Barrow	5.60	6.70	5.00	4.50
Lancaster	5.40	5.40	4.80	4.50
Preston	4.67	4.54	4.29	3.89

Source: Census of 1901, County of Lancaster, table 9; Census of 1911, tables 27, 27c; Census of 1921, table IX; Census of 1931, County of Lancaster, table 11.

Percentages of total population living
more than two to a room

	1911	1921	1931
Barrow	8.7	11.0	6.9
Lancaster	3.5	4.1	4.5
Preston	5.6	7.4	4.5

Source: Census of 1911, tables 27, 27a; Census of 1921, County of Lancaster, table IX; Census of 1931, County of Lancaster, table 11.

3 Mr M3L, pp. 2—3.
4 Mrs A1B, p. 8.
5 Mrs W1B, p. 2.
6 Mr L1L, p. 17.
7 Mr M1L, p. 2.
8 Mrs A1L, p. 2.
9 Mr H3L, p. 55.
10 Mr V1L, p. 4.
11 Mrs M1B, p. 2.

12   Mrs S4L, p. 37.
13   Mr M1L, p. 83.
14   Mrs B1L, p. 35.
15   Mrs N1L, p. 52.
16   Medical Officer of Health for Lancaster, *Annual Report*, 1900.
17   Medical Officer of Health for Preston, *Annual Report*, 1910.
18   Mr C1P, p. 3.
19   Mrs H3L, p. 54.
20   Mrs P1P, pp. 74—5.
21   Mrs H3L, p. 114.
22   A much more detailed examination of housing provision, and the complex interaction of national and local government action and working-class standards and aspirations, appears in Elizabeth Roberts, 'Working-class housing in Barrow and Lancaster, 1880—1930', *Trans. Hist. Soc. Lancs. and Ches.*, vol. 127 (1978).
23   Elizabeth Roberts, 'Working-class standards of living in three Lancashire towns, 1890—1914', *International Review of Social History,* vol. XXVII (1982), and 'Working-class standards of living in Barrow and Lancaster, 1890—1914', *Economic History Review* 2nd ser., vol. XXX, no. 2. (1977).
24   Rowntree, *Poverty: A Study of Town Life*, p. 296.
25   A. L. Bowley and M. H. Hogg, *Has Poverty Diminished?* (1925), p. 37.
26   B. Seebohm Rowntree, *Poverty and Progress* (1941), pp. 28—9.
27   Ministry of Labour, *21st Abstract of Labour Statistics of the U.K.* (1919—33), Cmd 4625, p. 104.
28   *Manchester Guardian,* 7 August 1923 (for figures for 1922 and 1923); M. P. Fogarty, *Prospects of the Industrial Areas of Great Britain* (1945), p. 33 (for figures for 1929, 1931, 1932, and 1937).
29   *Report of the Royal Commission on Unemployment Insurance* (1932), p. 20; Rex Pope, 'Unemployment in North-East Lancashire 1920—38' (unpublished MLitt thesis, University of Lancaster, 1974).
30   John Benson, *The Penny Capitalists: A Study of Nineteenth-Century Working-Class Entrepreneurs* (1983). This includes examples from the oral history archives for Barrow, Lancaster and Preston, and is a very thorough study of this long-neglected area.
31   Carol Dyhouse, 'The role of women from self-sacrifice to self-awareness', in Laurence Lerner (ed.), *The Victorians* (1978), p. 175.
32   Mrs S1L, p. 5.
33   'Women's work and European fertility patterns', p. 462.
34   Tilly and Scott, *Women, Work and Family*, p. 195.
35   Mrs M3P, p. 19.
36   Mrs M6B, p. 5.
37   Mr P1B, p. 53.
38   Mrs S4L, pp. 15, 9, 51.
39   Mrs B1L, pp. 11—12.
40   Miss T4P (b. 1912), 3s. per child (1916); Mr T3P (b. 1886), 10s. per child, for his own children. There are many other examples.

41 Mrs B2P, p. 16.
42 Mrs M5L, p. 18.
43 *Cost of Living of the Working Classes: Board of Trade Inquiry into Working Class Rents: Housing and Retail Prices in the Principal Industrial Towns* (1908), Cmd 3864.
44 Mr T2P, pp. 23—4.
45 Mrs H7P, p. 15.
46 Mr T2P, p. 18.
47 Medical Officer of Health for Preston, *Annual Report*, 1930.
48 Mrs P1P.
49 Mrs H2P, pp. 1—2.
50 Mr G1P, p. 47.
51 E. H. Hunt, *British Labour History, 1815—1914* (1981), p. 103.
52 Preston Weavers, Winders, and Warpers Association, 'Cases and Complaints Book', 'Minute Book', 'Wages Calculation Book', all in the Lancashire Record Office, Preston.
53 Pilgrim Trust, *Men Without Work* (1938), pp. 85, 235.
54 Mrs P2P, p. 4.
55 Mr M1L, p. 49.
56 Mr G1P, p. 69.
57 Mr M8B, p. 16.
58 Mrs W2L, p. 17.
59 Mr G1L, p. 10.
60 Mrs N1L, p. 35.
61 Mr G3P, p. 23.
62 Working-class attitudes to charity are explored in Elizabeth Roberts, 'The recipients' view of welfare', in H. Perkin (ed.), *The Roots of Welfare* (forthcoming).
63 Rowntree, *Poverty: A Study of Town Life*, p. 105.
64 Inter-Departmental Committee on Physical Deterioration, *P.P.* (1904), Cd. 2175 XXX, p. 11; XXXII, p. 224.
65 D. J. Oddy, 'Working-class diets in late nineteenth-century Britain', *Economic History Review*, 2nd ser., vol. XXIII (1970), p. 314.
66 Eunice Schofield, 'Food and cooking of the working class about 1900', *Trans. Hist. Soc. Lancs. and Ches.,* vol. 123 (1971), pp. 106, 152.
67 *Wives and Mothers in Victorian Industry*, pp. 75, 78—80.
68 *The Classic Slum* (1973 edn), pp. 109—10.
69 D. E. Allen, *British Tastes: An Enquiry into the Likes and Dislikes of the Regional Consumer* (1965); D. E. Allen, 'Regional variations in food habits', in D. J. Oddy and D. S. Miller (eds), *The Making of the Modern British Diet* (1976), pp. 135—47.
70 Oddy, 'Working-class diets', p. 314.
71 Mrs S2B, p. 4.
72 Mr M1B, p. 3.
73 Mrs H2L, p. 28.
74 Rowntree, *Poverty: A Study of Town Life*, p. 105; Schools' Medical

Officer of Health's Report, in *Borough Accounts of Barrow-in-Furness* (1912).

75   Mrs W1B, p. 37.
76   Mrs S2B, pp. 66—7.
77   Mrs S4L, p. 63.
78   Mrs C5P, p. 9.
79   Mrs A3B, p. 8.
80   Mr A2L (in Mrs W2L), p. 62.
81   Rowntree, *Poverty: A Study of Town Life,* ch. VIII; Oddy, 'Working-class diets', p. 318.
82   Mr P2L, p. 4.
83   Mr M1B, p. 3.
84   Mr H1L, p. 37.
85   Mrs W1B, p. 4.
86   Mrs S2B, p. 3.
87   *Barratt's Directory of Preston and District* (Preston, 1892 and 1907).
88   Mr F2B, p. 4.
89   Mrs H1B, p. 2.
90   Mrs B2P, pp. 26—7.
91   Mrs M6B, pp. 8—9.
92   Board of Trade, *An Industrial Survey of Lancashire* (1931), p. 185.
93   The figures are taken from membership figures given periodically in the Barrow press. They relate to those societies which helped with medical treatment and sick pay. They do not relate to firms providing death insurance. Membership of these schemes was very much higher.
94   Mr B1B, p. 15.
95   This was not the highest dividend paid in 1900. 20 per cent of cooperative societies paid dividends of 1s.-2s. in the pound; 35 per cent paid dividends of 2s.-3s.; 32 per cent paid 3s.-4s.; and 6 per cent 4s.-5s. (A. Bonner, *British Cooperation* (1961), pp. 101—2).
96   Medical Officer of Health for Preston, *Annual Report* (1902).
97   George Newman, *Infant Mortality: A Social Problem* (1906).
98   'Working-class mothers and infant mortality in England, 1895—1914', *Journal of Social History,* vol. 12, no. 2 (1978).
99   Mrs G1B, p. 19.
100 Mr T2P, p. 37.
101 Medical Officer of Health for Preston, *Annual Reports* (1892, 1902).
102 Medical Officer of Health for Preston, *Annual Report* (1903).
103 Medical Officer of Health for Preston, *Annual Report* (1911).
104 *Health Visitors' Report for Coventry* (1906). 20 per cent of non-breast-fed babies were spoon-fed. I am indebted to Marjorie Lodge for these figures. See also Nella Last, *Nella Last's War* (1981), p. 32. She records her family tradition of spoon-feeding babies rather than bottle-feeding.
105 Mrs M6B.
106 Censuses of 1901 and 1911, and the Medical Officer of Health for Preston, *Annual Reports.*

107   'Working-class mothers'.

CHAPTER 5.   FAMILIES AND NEIGHBOURS

1   Mrs S3L, pp. 5—6.
2   Mrs S2P, passim.
3   Mrs B1L, p. 3.
4   Mrs A2B, p. 62.
5   Michael Anderson, *Family Structure in Nineteenth-Century Lancashire* (1971), p. 178. His book was based on evidence from Preston, and Anderson remains the only historian of note to have published a substantive book on the town. I must record my gratitude to him for his help with my Preston project.
6   Miss T4P.
7   Mrs H7P, p. 13.
8   Mr E1P, passim.
9   Census of 1921, County of Lancaster, tables 12 and 24.
10   Mr L1L, p. 1.
11   Mr T3P, pp. 11—12.
12   Mrs H4P, p. 4.
13   Mrs M1P, p. 64.
14   Mrs B2P, p. 17.
15   Mr S4P, p. 17.
16   Mrs W4P, pp. 20—1.
17   M. Young and P. Wilmott, *Family and Kinship in East London* (1957), pp. 187—8.
18   Mr B9P, pp. 5—6.
19   Mr G1P, p. 7.
20   Mrs B1L, pp. 2, 7, 8, 9.
21   Mr R3L, pp. 58—9.
22   Dr D1P, p. 10.
23   Mr T3P, p. 63.
24   Census of 1931, County of Lancaster, Table 2.
25   Mrs M1B, p. 21.
26   Mr M1B, p. 21.
27   Mr M6B, p. 27.
28   L. A. Shaw, 'Impressions of life in a London suburb', *Sociological Review* (new series), vol. 2, no. 2 (1954), p. 183; Wilmott and Young, *Family and Kinship,* passim; M. Kerr, *The People of Ship Street* (1958), chs. IV and VI.
29   R. Firth (ed.), 'Two studies of kinship in London', *L. S. E. Monographs on Social Anthropology,* no. 15 (1956).
30   This part of the chapter is a development of a paper presented to an International Oral History Conference at Aix-en-Provence, September 1982, and published in *Oral History* (forthcoming).

31 Quoted in Meacham, *A Life Apart*, p. 58.
32 C. F. G. Masterman (ed.), 'Realities at home', *The Heart of the Empire* (1902), p. 8.
33 Meacham, *A Life Apart*, p. 59.
34 Mr M1L, p. 22.
35 Mrs C5P, p. 39.
36 Anderson, *Family Structure*, p. 171.
37 Meacham, *A Life Apart*, p. 40.
38 Ibid., p. 45.
39 Mrs M3P, pp. 20—1.
40 Ariès, *Centuries of Childhood*, pp. 405, 407.
41 Mrs M3P, pp. 5—6.
42 Mrs A3B, p. 23.
43 Mrs A2B, p. 60.
44 Mrs H8P, pp. 39—40.
45 Mr C4L, p. 15.
46 Mrs H8P, p. 9.
47 Mr G3P, p. 23.
48 E.g. Meacham, *A Life Apart*, p. 31.
49 Mrs B2P, p. 10.
50 Mr C1P, pp. 98—9.
51 Mr M1L, p. 43.
52 Bott, *Family and Social Network*, p. 103.
53 Mr M1L, p. 27.
54 Mr A2B, p. 75.
55 Mrs P1P, pp. 92, 25, 62.
56 Mrs W2L, p. 47.
57 Roberts, *The Classic Slum*, p. 47.
58 Mr L1P, p. 17.
59 Mr L1L, p. 13.
60 Mrs D1B, pp. 24—5.
61 Mrs W1B, pp. 87—8.
62 Mr M1L, p. 38.
63 Mrs M3L, p. 44.
64 Kerr, *The People of Ship Street*, pp. 102—3.

CONCLUSION

1 Gittins, *Fair Sex*, p. 182.
2 Ibid., p. 181.
3 C. Madge, *War Time Patterns of Saving and Spending* (1943) p. 53; F. Zweig, *Women's Life and Labour* (1952), p. 49.

Select Bibliography

D. E. Allen, *British Tastes: An Enquiry into the Likes and Dislikes of the Regional Consumer* (London, 1965)

D. E. Allen, 'Regional variations in food habits', in D. J. Oddy and D. S. Miller (eds), *The Making of the Modern British Diet* (London, 1976)

M. Anderson, *Family Structure in Nineteenth-Century Lancashire* (London, 1971)

M. Anderson (ed.), *Sociology of the Family* (Harmondsworth, 1971)

P. Ariès, *Centuries of Childhood: A Social History of Family Life* (London, 1962; Harmondsworth, 1973)

J. A. Banks, *Victorian Values, Secularism and the Size of Families* (London, 1981)

J. A. and O. Banks, *Feminism and Family Planning in Victorian England* (Liverpool, 1964)

O. Banks, *Faces of Feminism: A Study of Feminism as a Social Movement* (London, 1981)

R. Bendix and S. M. Lipset (eds), *Class, Status and Power* (London, 1967)

J. Benson, *The Penny Capitalists: A Study of Nineteenth-Century Working-Class Entrepreneurs* (Dublin, 1983)

C. Booth, *Life and Labour of the People,* 2 vols (London, 1889)

H. Bosanquet, *The Family* (London, 1906)

E. Bott, *Family and Social Network* (London, 1971)

A. L. Bowley and M. H. Hogg, *Has Poverty Diminished?* (London, 1925)

P. Branca, *Silent Sisterhood: Middle-Class Women in the Victorian Home* (London, 1977)

P. Branca, *Women in Modern Europe since 1750* (London, 1978)

R. Bray, *The Town Child* (London, 1911)

R. Bray, *Boy Labour and Apprenticeship* (London, 1911)

R. H. Bremner, J. Barnard, T. K. Hareven and R. M. Mennel (eds), *Children and Youth in America: A Documentary History,* 3 vols (Harvard, 1970—4)

J. Burnett, *Plenty and Want* (Harmondsworth, 1966)

J. Burnett, *Useful Toil* (London, 1974)

C. V. Butler, *Social Conditions in Oxford* (London, 1912)

E. Cadbury, *Women's Work and Wages: A Phase of Life in an Industrial City* (London, 1906)

D. Caradog Jones (ed.), *The Social Survey of Merseyside* (Liverpool, 1934)

M. Chamberlain, *Old Wives' Tales* (London, 1981)

M. Chamberlain and R. Richardson, 'Life and death', *Oral History,* vol. 11, no. 1 (1983)

M. Cruickshank, *Children and Industry: Child Health and Welfare in North-West Textile Towns during the 19th Century* (Manchester, 1981)

A. E. Dingle, 'Drink and the working-class standard of living in Britain', *Economic History Review,* 2nd ser., vol. XXV, no. 4 (1972)

M. Drake and P. Hammerton, *Exercises in Historical Sociology* (Milton Keynes, 1974)

C. Dyhouse, 'Good wives and little mothers: social anxieties and schoolgirls' curriculum 1890—1920', *Oxford Review of Education*, vol. 3, no. 1 (1977)

C. Dyhouse, 'Working-class mothers and infant mortality in England, 1895—1914', *Journal of Social History,* vol. 12, no. 2 (1978)

C. Dyhouse, 'The role of women from self-sacrifice to self-awareness', in L. Lerner (ed.), *The Victorians* (London, 1978)

C. Dyhouse, *Girls Growing Up in Late Victorian and Edwardian England* (London, 1981)

J. L. Flandrin, *Families in Former Times* (London, 1979)

M. P. Fogarty, *Prospects of the Industrial Areas of Great Britain* (London, 1945)

A. T. Freeman, *Boy Life and Labour* (London, 1914)

E. Gauldie, *Cruel Habitations: A History of Working-Class Housing, 1780—1918* (London, 1914)

J. Gillis, *Youth and History: Tradition and Change in European Age Relations, 1770—Present* (New York, 1974)

D. Gittins, 'Married life and birth control between the wars', *Oral History,* vol. 3, no. 2 (1975)

D. Gittins, 'Women's work and family size between the wars', *Oral History,* vol. 5, no. 2 (1977)

D. Gittins, *Fair Sex: Family Size and Structure, 1900—1939* (London, 1982)

H. J. Habakkuk, *Population Growth and Economic Development since 1750* (Leicester, 1971)

J. Hajnal, 'Age at marriage and proportions marrying', *Population Studies*, vol. 7 (1953)

T. K. Hareven, 'The history of the family as an interdisciplinary field', in T. K. Rabb and R. I. Rotberg (eds), *The Family in History* (New York, 1971)

T. K. Hareven (ed.), *Family and Kin in Urban Communities 1700—1930* (1977)

T. K. Hareven and R. Langenbach, *Amoskeog: Life and Work in an American Factory City in New England* (London, 1979)

M. Hartmann and L. Banner (eds), *Clio's Consciousness Raised* (London, 1974)

M. Hewitt, *Wives and Mothers in Victorian Industry* (London, 1958)

P. Hollis, *Women in Public: The Women's Movement 1850—1900* (London, 1979)

S. Humphries, 'Steal to survive: the social crime of working-class children, 1890—1940', *Oral History*, vol. 9, no. 1 (1981)

S. Humphries, *Hooligans or Rebels?; An Oral History of Working-Class Childhood and Youth, 1889—1939* (Oxford, 1981)

E. H. Hunt, *British Labour History, 1815—1914* (London, 1981)

J. Hurt, *Elementary Schooling and the Working Classes, 1860—1918* (London, 1979)

J. W. Innes, *Class Fertility Trends in England and Wales, 1876—1934* (Princeton, 1938)

P. Joyce, *Work, Society and Politics: The Culture of the Factory in Later Victorian England* (Brighton, 1980)

M. Kerr, *The People of Ship Street* (London, 1958)

P. Knight, 'Women and abortion in Victorian and Edwardian England', *History Workshop*, vol. 4 (1977)

N. Last, *Nella Last's War* (Bristol, 1981)

J. Lewis, *The Politics of Motherhood: Child and Maternal Welfare in England, 1900—39* (London, 1980)

J. Liddington and J. Norris, *One Hand Tied Behind Us: The Rise of the Women's Suffrage Movement* (London, 1978)

E. Llewelyn Davies (ed.), *Maternity: Letters from Working Women* (London, 1915; reprinted London, 1978)

G. A. Lowndnes, *The Silent Social Revolution* (London, 1937)

P. McCann (ed.), *Popular Education and Socialisation in the Nineteenth Century* (London, 1979)

A. McLaren, 'Women's work and regulation of family size', *History Workshop*, vol. 4 (1977)

C. Madge, *War Time Patterns of Saving and Spending* (Cambridge, 1943)

J. D. Marshall, *Furness and the Industrial Revolution* (Barrow-in-Furness, 1958; reprinted Beckermet, 1981)

J. D. Marshall and M. E. McClintock (eds), *The History of the Lancashire County Council* (London, 1977)

J. D. Marshall and J. K. Walton, *The Lake Counties from 1830 to the Mid-Twentieth Century* (Manchester, 1981)

A. Marwick, *The Deluge: British Society and the First World War* (London, 1965)

S. Meacham, *A Life Apart: The English Working Class 1890—1914* (London, 1977)

B. Mitchell and P. Deane, *Abstract of British Historical Statistics* (Cambridge, 1962)

B. Mitchell and H. Jones, *Second Abstract of British Historical Statistics* (London, 1971)

R. Moore, *Pitmen, Preachers and Politics: The Effects of Methodism in a Durham Mining Community* (London, 1974)

F. Musgrove, *Youth and the Social Order* (London, 1964)

G. Newman, *Infant Mortality: A Social Problem* (London, 1906)

D. J. Oddy, 'Working-class diets in late nineteenth-century Britain', *Economic History Review*, 2nd ser., vol. XXIII (1970)

D. J. Oddy and D. S. Miller (eds), *The Making of the Modern British Diet* (London, 1976)

A. Paterson, *Across the Bridge* (London, 1911)

J. Peel, 'The manufacture and retailing of contraceptives in England', *Population Studies,* vol. 18 (1962)

M. Pember Reeves, *Round About a Pound a Week* (London, 1913; reprinted London, 1979)

H. J. Perkin, *The Origins of Modern English Society, 1780—1880* (London, 1969)

Pilgrim Trust, *Men Without Work* (Cambridge, 1938)

I. Pinchbeck, *Women Workers in the Industrial Revolution* (London, 1930)

I. Pinchbeck and M. Hewitt, *Children in English Society,* vol. 2 (London, 1973)

E. Richards, 'Women in the British economy since 1700', *History* (1974)

E. Roberts, 'Learning and living: socialisation outside school', *Oral History,* vol. 3, no. 2 (1975)

E. Roberts, *Working-Class Barrow and Lancaster, 1890—1930* (Lancaster, 1976)

E. Roberts, 'Working-class women in the North-West', *Oral History,* vol. 5, no. 2 (1977)

E. Roberts, 'Working-class standards of living in Barrow and Lancaster, 1890—1914', *Economic History Review*, 2nd ser., vol. XXX, no. 2 (1977)

E. Roberts, 'The working-class family in Barrow and Lancaster, 1890—1930' (unpublished PhD thesis, University of Lancaster, 1978)

E. Roberts, 'Working-class housing in Barrow and Lancaster, 1880—1930', *Trans. Hist. Soc. Lancs. and Ches.,* vol. 127 (1978)

E. Roberts, 'Oral history and the local historian', *The Local Historian,* vol. 13 (1979)

E. Roberts, 'Oral history investigation of disease and its management by the Lancashire working class 1890—1939', *Health, Diseases and Medicine in Lancashire, 1750—1950,* Occasional Publication U.M.I.S.T. (1980)

E. Roberts, 'Working-class standards of living in three Lancashire towns 1890—1914', *International Review of Social History,* vol. XXVII, part 1 (1982)

E. Roberts, 'Working wives and their families', in T. Barker and M. Drake (eds), *Population and Society in Britain, 1850—1980* (London, 1982)

E. Roberts, 'The recipients' view of welfare', in H. Perkin (ed.), *The Roots of Welfare* (forthcoming).

R. Roberts, *The Classic Slum* (Harmondsworth, 1973)

M. Rose, *The English Poor Law, 1780—1930* (Newton Abbot, 1971)

E. Ross, 'Survival networks: women's neighbourhood sharing in London before World War One', *History Workshop*, vol. 15 (1983)

C. Rosser and C. Harris, *The Family and Social Change: The Study of Family and Kinship in a South Wales Town* (London, 1965)

B. Seebohm Rowntree, *Poverty: A Study of Town Life* (London, 1901)

B. Seebohm Rowntree, *Poverty and Progress: A Second Social Survey of York* (London, 1941)

D. Rubinstein, *School Attendance in London 1870–1904* (Hull, 1969)

C. E. B. Russell, *Manchester Boys: Sketches of Manchester Lads at Work and Play* (Manchester, 1905)

E. Schofield, 'Food and cooking of the working class about 1900', *Trans. Hist. Soc. Lancs. and Ches.*, vol. 123 (1971)

E. Shorter, *The Making of the Modern Family* (London, 1976)

N. Smelser, *Social Change in the Industrial Revolution: An Application of Theory to the Lancashire Cotton Industry, 1770–1840* (Chicago, 1959)

F. B. Smith, *The People's Health 1830–1910* (London, 1979)

M. Spring Rice, *Working-Class Wives* (Harmondsworth, 1939)

P. Stearns, 'Working-class women in Britain 1890–1914', in M. Vicinus (ed.), *Suffer and Be Still* (Indiana, 1972)

J. Stevenson, *Social Conditions in Britain between the Wars* (Harmondsworth, 1977)

L. Stone, *The Family, Sex and Marriage in England 1500–1800* (London, 1977)

J. N. Tarn, *Working-Class Housing in Nineteenth-Century Britain* (London, 1971)

D. Thompson, 'Courtship and marriage in Preston between the wars', *Oral History*, vol. 3, no. 2 (1975)

E. P. Thompson, *The Making of the English Working Class* (London, 1963)

P. Thompson, *The Edwardians: The Remodelling of British Society* (London, 1975)

P. Thompson, *The Voice of the Past: Oral History* (Oxford, 1978)

T. Thompson, *Edwardian Childhoods* (London, 1981)

L. Tilly and J. Scott, 'Women's work and the family in nineteenth-century Europe', *Comparative Studies in Society and History*, vol. 17 (1975)

L. Tilly and J. Scott, *Women, Work and the Family* (New York, 1978)

L. Tilly, J. Scott and M. Cohen, 'Women's work and European fertility patterns', *Journal of Interdisciplinary History*, vol. VI (1976)

R. Titmuss, *Essays on the Welfare State*, 3rd edn (London, 1976)

M. Vicinus (ed.), *Suffer and Be Still* (Indiana, 1972)

J. Walvin, *A Child's World: A Social History of English Childhood, 1800–1914* (Harmondsworth, 1982)

S. and B. Webb, *Industrial Democracy*, 2 vols (London, 1897)

M. Winstanley, *The Shopkeepers' World, 1830–1914* (Manchester, 1983)

E. A. Wrigley, *Population and History* (London, 1969)

M. Young and P. Wilmott, *Family and Kinship in East London* (London, 1957; Harmondsworth, 1962)

F. Zweig, *Women's Life and Labour* (London, 1952)

Index